Sea Serpents and Lake Monsters
of the British Isles

SEA SERPENTS
and
LAKE MONSTERS
of the
BRITISH ISLES

PAUL HARRISON

ROBERT HALE · LONDON

© Paul Harrison 2001
First published in Great Britain 2001

ISBN 0 7090 6923 5 (hardback)
ISBN 0 7090 7082 9 (paperback)

Robert Hale Limited
Clerkenwell House
Clerkenwell Green
London EC1R 0HT

A catalogue record for this book is available from the British Library

2 4 6 8 10 9 7 5 3 1

Set in Garamond by
Derek Doyle & Associates, Liverpool.
Printed by
St Edmundsbury Press Limited, Bury St Edmunds
and bound by
Woolnough Bookbinding Limited, Irthlingborough

A larger body of evidence from eye-witnesses might be got together in proof of ghosts than of the sea serpent.

Sir Richard Owen, 1882

Contents

Acknowledgements

No book of this sort has ever been produced exclusively about the United Kingdom and Ireland. This work has taken many years to research and compile – a task that could never have been achieved without the kind assistance of other individuals, organizations and official bodies. Principal among these is John Carter for the countless hours he spent alongside me, poring through dusty newspaper and magazine archives. My thanks also go to Errol Fuller for his support and personal encouragement, which helped me complete the task, Mike Dash and Paul Sieveking at *Fortean Times* for their assistance with archival information, the staff of the Maritime Museum Library, Greenwich, for their marvellous intuition and enthusiasm in helping locate many elusive official records, the staff of the British Newspaper Library, Colindale, the staff of the Public Records Office, Kew, Carol Gokce, BSc, MSc, and the library staff of the Natural History Museum, Kensington, and the archives of the Loch Ness Monster Research Society. I am also grateful to Adam Fogarty, a fine actor and keen researcher who helped in locating rare newspaper articles, Jon Downes, Anne Marie Jamieson, Otto Black, John Locksley, L.P. Herrington, Nigel Howse, Miss A.M. Jenkins, Sheila Smith, Helen Hadley, Robert Cornes, Daev Walsh and his excellent Blathersite, Lars Thomas, Gordon Rutter, Anne Adsten of the Storsjoodjuret development resource, the *Blackpool Evening Gazette*, the *Eastern Daily Press*, the *Fortean Times*, Kim

ACKNOWLEDGEMENTS

Cooper, Librarian, Cornish Studies Library, Redruth, Tom Matchett, Secretary of the British Conger Club and Tony White, of Animal X, who is a fellow researcher into the mysterious, including anomalous lake monster sightings. My apologies to anyone I may have omitted from this list.

Introduction

Sea serpent and lake monster sightings from around the British Isles are very real. Ask anyone who believes they have seen one of these creatures; they are not figments of an over-worked imagination, nor are they optical illusions. The perception of the general public of this phenomenon can only be described as sceptical, yet the media avidly report anything and everything relating to such mysteries, and the public flock to places like Loch Ness in their millions in the hope of catching a glimpse of the creature affectionately known worldwide as 'Nessie', which has become a tourist industry in its own right. In the United Kingdom and Ireland few people actually admit to visiting Loch Ness or similar haunts with a view to seeing a monster because of the public ridicule of anyone who actively seeks out or expresses a belief in such creatures. To proclaim a belief in them is, in effect, socially unacceptable and those who do so are regarded as either eccentric or just plain mad. Subjectivity of this kind reveals why so many witnesses refuse, or are at the very least reluctant, to report sightings or incidents.

The earliest reports of sea serpents and lake monsters provoked amusement and curiosity from a society influenced by a reluctance to accept that there existed creatures and powers beyond their control – a view that is still evident in the twenty-first century. Despite this, there can be no doubt-ing that terrifying encounters with sea and lake monsters from around the globe have, for countless centuries, captivated our imagination. We need look no further than the Bible, which makes reference to the 'great leviathan' which some will tell us, adds credibility to the existence of such creatures. Researchers and analysts of the Bible text have arrived at a simple conclusion for the leviathan: it was a whale or a crocodile, depending on whom we choose to believe. Undoubtedly, sea-faring folk did witness giant creatures in the seas and oceans of the world and many were hitherto unknown species. For example, those who encountered the whale for the first time could be forgiven for misinterpreting it as a nemesis of evil, surfacing from the deep to wreak carnage and devastation upon civilization as we know it.

The human race has a deep-rooted desire for knowledge, not only for educational reasons, but also for a 'feel-good factor', to lessen our insecurity. Knowledge is ultimately accompanied by power, power to control everything around us. The average human being is reluctant to accept that dark and sinister mysteries exist within our domain. The presence of sea and lake monster on the same planet is seen as a threat to our very existence, it opposes the sense of rationality with which we have been indoctrinated during our lives, and arouses a subconscious feeling of insecurity. In order to strengthen our belief and power, 'experts' are called upon to dismiss such speculation.

We have no power or control over the world's oceans and seas, or over anything which may reside within their dark impenetrable gloom. Water covers almost three-quarters of the earth's surface, taking up a total area of around 360,000,000 sq km. Around 20,000 different species of fish have been identified in the world's rivers and oceans, and there will be countless new discoveries of marine life in the future, as we explore ocean floors and delve deeper into murky depths of the world's waters. Despite this fact mainstream science will not officially accept a belief in sea serpents or lake monsters until evidence of such a creature can be produced, a criterion they have worked to for many centuries.

Science though, is not always correct, and is often based on probability as opposed to hard physical evidence. The discovery of a living coelacanth in 1938 off the coast of South Africa, measuring over 5 ft in length and weighing 127 lb, left science dumbfounded. The coelacanth, science had proclaimed, died out over 70 million years ago. It was plain ridiculous for anyone to claim that such a creature could still exist into the twentieth century and beyond. Today, the coelacanth species continues to exist, somehow surviving the passage of time and thereby defying all scientific logic.

The argument is well documented: 'If one species of fish could manage to survive this period of time, then why not other unknown sea creatures?' There is no reason why this could not be so, other than the fact that no physical specimen which could suitably be classed as a sea serpent or lake monster has yet been discovered, so science has no requirement to develop research in this field further. This leaves researchers and believers with the task of providing suitable evidence, which will then be subject to scientific analysis.

The weight of eye-witness testimony indicates that there exists at least one species of large, hitherto undiscovered, creature in the seas and oceans of the world. Orthodox science, though, will not accept anecdotal evidence or eye-witness testimony as proof of any such creature's existence. I think we would all agree that this is a sensible and reasonable approach, but science applies double standards: there are cases of sea creatures which have not only been accepted by science, based solely upon eye-witness testimony, but have been provided with an official Latin name. Constantin Samuel Rafinesque-Schmaltz, a French-American naturalist, in the early nineteenth century gave an account of a curious whale with two dorsal fins, which was seen by a fellow naturalist, Antonino Mongitore. The sighting was confirmed in 1819 by fellow naturalists J.F.C. Quoy and J.C. Gaimard, who saw a whole school of these creatures off the coast of New South Wales, Australia. No single specimen of this creature has been examined by science, yet it was accepted as a living species and possesses the Latin name, *Delphinus rhinoceros*. A further species of unknown whale was seen off the Shetlands by whale authority Robert Sibbald. This species has since been named *Physeter tursio*. Again, not a single specimen has been examined. This somewhat hypocritical approach of science, which refuses to acknowledge large marine creatures which have been categorized as sea serpents by witnesses who have seen them, is ignorant and perhaps foolish.

The mere mention of the terms 'sea serpent' and 'lake monster' causes some scientists to adopt an attitude of complete and absolute denial. As one zoologist told me, 'It is impractical to contemplate that such creatures exist.' The reason? 'We have no confirmed knowledge of the existence of such creatures, other than the sketchy and grossly exaggerated reports of those who travel the oceans of the world or wander around a Scottish loch looking for a plesiosaur. That is hardly conclusive evidence. We require a specimen, either a complete carcass or a tissue sample to examine and ultimately categorize.' Unfortunately, dracontology (the study of sea serpents and lake monsters) is not an accepted science, nor is cryptozoology (the study of hidden animals, i.e. of still unknown animal forms about which only testimonial or circumstantial evidence is available).

The question remains, is it possible that sea serpents and lake monsters exist? The simple fact is that a wealth of evidence is available which indicates that some form of large unidentified creature is presently living in our waters and has done so for many centuries. Historical records dating back many centuries, when frequent long-distance communication was virtually impossible indicates that descriptions of these creatures recalled by eye-witnesses (mainly sea-faring folk) in one area closely resembled reports from the opposite side of the globe. In days gone by it was reasonable to believe that the creature observed was one and the same beast. Analysis of press reports from previous centuries indicates that sightings in one ocean or sea, irrespective of distance, were classed by those who recorded such information as being of the same solitary creature, as opposed to one of many from a respective species. The general belief at that time was that these creatures were blessed with the power to cover massive areas in a short period of time. Size and length estimates often verged on the incredible. Irresponsible and sensational journalism encouraged outrageous eyewitness accounts. Some creatures were recorded as being upwards of 500 ft in length, so it is little wonder that such tales have moved in the modern age into the realms of absolute fantasy.

Do we blame the eye-witness or over-zealous journalism for this? The basic ethos of newspaper journalism has not changed; it's all about profit – to sell as many copies as is possible – and the more sensational the story, the greater the public interest and the greater the sales. It would therefore seem more reasonable to assume that journalists would instigate public excitement by over-exaggeration of the mariner's tale, since presumably, these people would not return from sea intent on making up such incidents.

There must be an element of truth in each reported incident. Captains of ships whose crew had encountered a sea serpent were often asked to swear an oath as to the validity of the incident. It was also viewed by ship owners as 'inappropriate' to employ a crew who encountered such creatures. After all, many vessels were conveying valuable goods and a trustworthy and honest crew were required to safeguard the cargo. Those who reported encounters with sea serpents often lost their jobs as a result of such tales, as owners believed them to be jinxed or cursed. This forced all talk of the sea serpent into the private as opposed to the public realm, as crews preferred anonymity to unemployment.

With sea serpents being classed as evil, the public perceived the creature as a terrible ferocious beast which could devour entire ships and crews, despite the fact that tales of physical attacks on ships were few and far between. More obvious are the basic sightings of a large, unidentifiable creature curious of its surroundings. The majority of reports indicate that when curious crews sighted such a creature they would approach it, as opposed to it approaching them. The creature, upon seeing the closing vessel, would generally submerge or flee often at a tremendous pace, almost as if panicked or in fear of its curious neighbour. These are not the actions of a fearsome beast, but of a shy and timid creature leading its own secluded life, yet still mankind viewed the sea serpent as a real danger, and very often efforts were made to destroy the beast, even though it posed no physical threat – yet another example of mankind's insecurity leading to brutal violence when presented with a living mass which offered no physical challenge.

On British shores, the public was perhaps lulled into a false sense of security. The mariners' tales more often than not referred to incidents in oceans and seas far removed from us. It was a popular misconception that sea serpents were something from oriental waters or warmer climates. But the British Isles are but a number of small islands surrounded by some uncompromising waters – the North Sea, the Atlantic Ocean, the English Channel, the Irish Sea – and there is no invisible security net protecting our coastline from a visit by a sea serpent. Likewise, many of our lakes, lochs or loughs, are fed from sea inlets.

Today, reports of sea or lake monsters are most uncommon. This may well be due to the fact that we use mechanical means of travelling through water, making a noise and so indicating our presence to shy sea creatures. In general we live in a noisier society, and increased numbers of visitors to particular sites creates more disturbance, which, as had already been proved, tends to frighten these creatures. This factor provides a response to the modern argument that such beasts should be seen more frequently, especially at Loch Ness, where thousands of tourists scour the water surface from all angles in the hope of catching a glimpse of the elusive Nessie.

Having assessed the ethics of newspaper journalism, what of the moral issues for the witness? Do these people simply make up their stories to gain some form of fame, by getting their names in the newspaper? From personal experience, it is most unlikely that witnesses to such events have conjured such tales from nowhere, not least because of the newspaper coverage. Media coverage brings with it nothing but cynicism, and generally casts aspersions on the character of the witness. Can we honestly believe that some people seek short-lived fame by admitting to seeing a water monster in the flesh? Sadly, on some occasions this does occur, especially in areas where these creatures have frequently been reported, such as at Loch Ness, where the tourist has travelled a considerable distance to visit the area and there may be a subconscious desire to see something, anything, which they can regard as a sighting. Analysis of this data by those of us who study such information, tends to indicate a misinterpretation, or, on occasions, a deliberate hoax, the latter being far easier to recognize with modern techniques. The fact that analysis generally occurs after the 'sighting' has been broadcast in the media (some witnesses being so keen to cash in on sightings that they sell their story or 'evidence' to the printed media before allowing analysis to take place) leaves the cryptozoologist with a damage-limitation exercise, not only in providing evidence which indicates inaccurate misrepresentation, but also in showing genuine evidence. It is a double-edged sword, which in either situation inflicts damage upon the credibility of the subject, providing the sceptic with greater ammunition to deny the existence of such creatures.

Despite the weight of public opinion, sightings continue to occur. Some can often be put down to a natural phenomenon, such as a boat wake or a wave formation or even a known species of marine creature. Yet, every so often (on average about one in twenty sightings at Loch Ness) what can only be described as a genuine anomaly does occur, where a living creature of unknown descent has been seen. When these are reported, society at once reflects scientific opinion and refuses to accept them as authentic representations; obstacle after obstacle is created in order to dismiss the matter as an impossibility. This problem is not specific to the area of sea and lake monsters, but to every field of cryptozoology. We are told that the burden of proof for such creatures' existence lies with the cryptozoologist or the researcher, yet when evidence is made available, it is immediately dismissed as hoax or misinterpretation through lack of knowledge.

There have, of course, been hoaxes, particularly at Loch Ness, or with the bigfoot/yeti/sasquatch phenomenon, but that is not the fault of the cryptozoologists; it is a sociological problem perhaps created by a desire to make money from a doctored photograph or piece of video footage. Ultimately, the burden of proof rests upon those who actively seek out hitherto unknown creatures, and genuine efforts are made to provide real evidence in the hope that society may form their own opinion upon the matter. While the public in general find it difficult to discuss any belief in the possible existence of a leviathan or sea or lake monster, we can but record events in the individual fields of dracontology. This is a necessity, and one day our intuition and beliefs may be proved correct.

Research into mysterious sea serpent reports and lake monster sightings from around the world is anything but a modern phenomenon. Since mankind first took to the sea, reports of strange creatures have come flooding back. While mainstream science today refuses to accept such conclusions, many eminent authorities have undertaken research into the subject, some because they had personal encounters with such creatures which they could not explain or justify, others because they believed that they could exist. The number of eye-witness reports indicated that such beasts did exist and, therefore warranted serious discussion as opposed to damning subjectivity.

So far as United Kingdom and Ireland sea and lake monster records are concerned, the original inspiration behind the compilation of such reports was the editor of *The Zoologist* magazine, Mr Edward Newman. In 1847, Newman wrote in his magazine:

It has been the fashion for so many years to deride all records of this very celebrated monster, that it is not without hesitation I venture to quote the following paragraphs in his defence.

Naturalists, or rather those who choose thus to designate themselves, set up as an authority above that of fact and observations, the gist of their enquiries is whether such things ought to be, and whether such things ought not to be; now fact-naturalists take a different road to knowledge, they enquire whether such things are, and whether such things are not ... The only question therefore for the fact-naturalists to decide, is simply, whether all of the records now collected, can refer to whales, fishes, or any other marine animals with which we are at present acquainted.

As the frequency of reports in the press increased, the phenomenon aroused the interest of many eminent authorities. In 1892, Dr Antoon Cornelius Oudemans of Batavia, a biologist and authority on mites and ticks, and Director of the Royal Zoological and Botanical Gardens at the Hague, published a book *The Great Sea Serpent*. This provided details of 187 sighting reports not only from British waters but from around the world. It was the first serious attempt in modern times to analyse the subject. Dr Oudemans was of the opinion that one species of animal was responsible for sightings, possibly a form of long-necked seal which he termed *Megophias* (big snake) a name first given to the New England sea serpent by Rafinesque. The emergence of the Loch Ness monster in the media in 1933 caused him to presume that the mystery of the sea serpent was close to being solved, and that his beliefs would be proved right. He died in 1943, leaving a legacy of data which has been the foundation of modern day research. The publication of Oudemans's work, which was by some deemed as outrageous, provoked a great deal of correspondence in *The Times*. This included a statement from Prof. Thomas Henry Huxley, a British biologist who, from 1846 to 1850, was assistant surgeon on board HMS *Rattlesnake*, surveying the passage between the Barrier Reef and the Australian coast. He collected marine animals, studied them and later made them the subject of scientific papers for the Royal and Linnean Societies. Huxley went on to become Professor of Natural History at the Royal School of Mines and dismissed the possibility of evolution until 1859, when Charles Darwin published *The Origin of Species*; he then became a principal advocate of Darwinism. Well respected, Huxley was asked to sit on a number of royal commissions, and was a great influence in the provision of biology and science education in schools. Unbeknown to most researchers, Huxley was also a firm believer in the existence of sea serpents.

In a letter to *The Times* in 1893, he gave this opinion: 'There is not an a priori reason that I know of why snake-bodied reptiles, from fifty feet long and upwards, should not disport themselves in our seas as they did in those of the cretaceous epoch which, geologically speaking, is a mere yesterday.' The Cretaceous Period, he mentions, lasted from 144 million years ago to about 655 million years ago. It was at the end of the Cretaceous Period that dinosaurs became extinct and mammals and plants began to evolve into different forms.

In 1930, the author and ex-naval officer Rupert Thomas Gould produced *The Case for the Sea Serpent*. Gould, like Oudemans before him, carried out practical research into individual cases of sea serpent sightings. He too believed that a descendant of the plesiosaurus provided the solution to the question of sea serpent identity. He also studied and produced a book on the Loch Ness monster. His well-reasoned and thorough research at the loch itself provided a marvellous insight into the mystery; he admitted to being something of a sceptic prior to his arrival, but a firm believer upon his departure, mainly through witness testimony. Gould's further research at Loch Ness forced him to alter his conclusions as to the identity of the sea serpent and lake monster: 'That they are a vastly-enlarged, long-necked, marine form of the newt is the hypothesis which, however improbable it may appear, I should personally be inclined to favour.'

The work of Dr Antoon Cornelius Oudemans was to become a major source for Dr Bernard Heuvelmans, a zoologist who had progressed to the study of 'unknown animals'. His research and subsequent book upon this subject, *On the Track of Unknown Animals*, published in 1955, is based solely upon land animals. The book aroused immense public interest and with subsequent reprints, it has sold in excess of a million copies, ensuring that Heuvelmans became an international authority on such matters. In 1959, he termed the study of such creatures as 'cryptozoology': 'the scientific study of hidden animals, i.e., of still unknown animal forms about which only testimonial and circumstantial evidence is available, or material evidence considered insufficient by some'.

In 1968 he produced *In the Wake of the Sea Serpent*, a full-length study of sea serpent sightings from around the world. This has been, many feel inaccurately, regarded as the bible of sea serpent literature. Heuvelmans groups the animals into nine different categories: the super otter, which may or not be related to otters; the many-humped, an animal of great length, 60–100 ft, showing a series of long humps, with a shoulder fin and a bilobate tail; the many-finned, about 60 ft long, with lateral fins, moving in undulations; the merhorse, a large creature with a horse-like head, large eyes and a mane (up to 60 ft long); the long-necked, a large creature with a fat body, believed to be amphibious; the super eels (several species), around 50 ft long; the marine saurian, a large crocodile-like beast; the father of all turtles, a large creature with the head of a turtle, which may well be related to the marine saurian; the yellow belly, another large beast shaped like a tadpole, found mainly in tropical waters.

In the Wake of the Sea Serpent, and Heuvelmans's categorization of the types of sea serpent, has come under much criticism in recent years, particularly as much of his data was incomplete, and even worse, inaccurate. The book's mistakes have subsequently been replicated by virtually every other writer on this subject, all of whom who have relied heavily upon the accuracy of Heuvelmans's research. It seems that Heuvelmans had preconceptions as to what his requirements for a sea serpent were, and any data outside his own personal remit was either ignored or adapted to suit. Understandably, in a work of such a size (645 pages) errors are likely to occur, but this can hardly account for the magnitude of some of those found. Nevertheless, as President of the International Society of Cryptozoology, Heuvelmans has been described quite rightly as the 'father of cryptozoology'.

Since the publication of *In the Wake of the Sea Serpent*, theories abound as to the possible identity of sea serpents and lake monsters, with each researcher voicing his own opinion. At present, despite the efforts of Heuvelmans, Oudemans, Gould et al, we are no nearer a universal solution to the question of identity. It would be easier and perhaps more sensible to attempt to place these creatures in a known zoological species rather than creating new categories. Since we know so little about them, we should not make the mistake of type-casting them as fearsome beasts, simply because of their size, nor should we simply place them all in folder marked 'plesiosaur sightings'.

Having had my own encounter with the creature of Loch Ness in March 1999, I am certain that it was not an accepted species currently known to science. It was not the typical plesiosaur image, by which I mean the description promoted in recent times of a swan-like head and neck and a bulky body. The reality is that no one can genuinely confirm the physical appearance of a plesiosaur when it is moving through the water, so it is impossible to confirm any such likeness, and anyone doing so is providing a reckless personal opinion. Moreover, we do not know whether the plesiosaur held its head and neck above the surface, or cruised through the water with just the top of its head or snout in view, much in the way of a crocodile. Whatever the argument in favour of the plesiosaur theory, we cannot with any certainty say a great deal about how the creature responded in its natural habitat.

During my thirteen years of research on this subject, I have spoken to, and discussed case histories with many scientists and scholars. I have heard just about every opinion as to why sea serpents and lake monsters cannot exist. It is claimed by some, that sightings are inventions of the mind or mass hallucination. Other views are that they are the result of ignorance of natural phenomena, pure imagination, optical illusion, attention seeking, indoctrination of inaccurate data into a weak mind, the way of the water, or a conspiracy involving an attack on mainstream science, or an easy way to improve tourism and ultimately the local economy!

These somewhat contentious opinions are a good deal more difficult to explain and accept than the possibility that sightings might be genuine. And, when I have provided data in the form of ey-witness testimony from those who possess accredited skills and academic qualifications in marine matters, I generally receive one answer from the sceptics: 'It must have been a genuine mistake.' From this we can see that unqualified witness testimony is classed as absurd, whereas qualified witness testimony is also ignored, but is classed as a genuine mistake.

There are, in reality, no real experts in the field of sea serpents and lake monsters, as no one can categorically state precisely what they may be, nor, it seems, can they agree on a possible identity. All researchers rely upon historical or anecdotal information; current searches produce very little in the way of real evidence, other than further sighting reports and opinions, most of which continue to cloud the issue further.

To my mind, if we are to make any progress on the subject of identity we must first identify the likely categories or known species. If these can be dismissed, then we are left with the unknown, or perhaps the unlikely – in essence a new or hitherto unknown species, perhaps a hybrid, or even a subspecies of something which existed millions of years ago. Strange as it may sound, the creatures that surround us today are, like us, living descendants of creatures from many millions of years ago. Therefore, it is wrong to dismiss this option. It is unfortunate that some of these creatures bear the sensationalist tag 'monster', as this term makes them socially and scientifically unacceptable from the outset, and devalues the rational thinking and dedicated research attached to their study. However, deep in our subconscious we may well find that we need 'monsters', if only to shock us into the realization that such creatures may well exist, as they most certainly did many millions of years ago when they were scientifically termed dinosaurs or prehistoric reptiles.

Included here are a few ideas about the identity of these creatures, which will hopefully inspire thoughtful debate. It is imperative that we study all areas of the subject before jumping to any irrational conclusions. I have therefore included known zoological species and creatures which have been seen and have lived in British waters, although I am aware that other explanations for sightings can be found, such as standing wave formations, boat wakes, or floating debris.

No one can provide a definitive solution to the mystery, but I do believe that sea serpents and lake monsters are of different species. It may well be that the lake monster has evolved from the sea serpent; they do after all reside in what can only be described as their own very private habitat and may be hybrids of a commonly accepted species. One fact remains certain with all of these creatures: to sustain life there has to be a complete species evolving as each new generation is born. It is foolish to suggest that a solitary creature could survive in a stretch of water without procreation. Those who support such a theory (and there are many) quite simply cannot be correct, unless of course we adopt the somewhat irrational approach that these creatures are of the paranormal or supernatural world. But we are already faced with a difficult task in proving that these creatures exist, without moving into the realms of the supernatural, which is a completely different subject.

The oarfish, or ribbonfish (*Regalecus glesn*) is one of the largest deep-sea marine fish. It has a long ribbon-like, extremely flat-sided body and in some European countries is also called the strapfish. Of the 250–300 (according to some sources up to 400) rays in its dorsal fins, the first ten to fifteen are much longer than the others. They are joined together at the tip by a flat membrane and crown the head like a crest, so that the fish is sometimes known as the 'king of the herrings'. It has small pectoral fins and the ventral fins below them are each formed of a single, long, thread-like ray with a wide, fleshy tip. There is no caudal or anal fin and the anal orifice generally lies below the eightieth ray of the dorsal fin. The fish is toothless. It has a silvery body, marked with irregular short cross-stripes and spots along its sides. There are between four and six longitudinal stripes studded with numerous small tubercles. The fins are dark red. The fish is said to live at depths of 1,000–2,000 ft, but is sometimes carried close to the surface, and it is here that occasional individuals are caught. Others are washed up on beaches by storms. Because of the lifestyle that this fish adopts, little is known about its biology. Small specimens are sometimes found in the stomachs of tunnyfish.

The oarfish would hardly make a reasonable sea serpent; it has a fragile body and is virtually transparent. It is also totally harmless. But ichthyologist J R Norman of the British Museum wrote in his work *A History of Fishes*:

The sea serpents of Aristotle, Pliny and other classical authors seem to have been nothing more than giant eels. The monster described as having the head of a horse with a flaming red mane is the Oar-fish or Ribbon-fish, a species which probably grows to more than fifty feet in length, and may sometimes be seen swimming with undulating movements at the surface of the sea.

The oarfish is fragile and can barely support its own weight; its body easily breaks up when the slightest force is placed upon it. Being virtually transparent, it would not easily be seen from any distance as most sea serpents are. Its dimensions also fail to match those of most of the sightings. It does not have a reasonable girth; it can measure up to 36 ft in length, but its body is approximately 1 ft deep. It can therefore be dismissed as candidate for the sea serpent almost immediately.

The dealfish (*Trachypterus arcticus*) is a relative of the oarfish which lives in the northern parts of the Atlantic Ocean at depths of 1,600–3,200 ft. It can grow to a length of 10 ft and is not dissimilar in appearance to the oarfish, although its dorsal fin, which runs the length of its body, is bright orange and it does not have the elongated spines at its crown. It has dorsal fin spines, which are more semicircular, peaking in height at mid-body. It is also rather thicker in girth than the oarfish. It has rarely been caught alive, but is sometimes found washed up on the North Sea coastline. From this it can be seen that, like the oarfish, it does not correspond with sighting records.

The common sturgeon (Acipenseridae) is one of the few survivors of the ancient group of 'ganoid' fishes. There are sixteen *acipenser* species living in Eurasia and North America, distinguished from each other by the shape of the mouth and the number and shape of the bony plates in the skin. The common sturgeon has a peculiar head, with a characteristic elongated snout and barbells closer to its toothless mouth than to the tip of the snout. It has from nine to thirteen scutes or bony plates on its back, between twenty-four and forty-four on its sides and nine to eleven on its belly. The first ray of its pectoral fin is thicker than the rest. It has a greyish-green or greyish-brown back, a white belly, dingy white scutes and brown-pinkish fins. The tail is asymmetrical and shark-like. It is one of the biggest sturgeons, growing relatively fast and measuring about 5 ft when ten years old.

It originally lived in coastal waters all around Europe and

the east coast of North America, and each year it migrated up the major rivers to spawn, but today only isolated specimens are caught in western European waters, although specimens have been captured in British waters as far inland as Shrewsbury and Nottingham. The males reach maturity when they are seven to nine years old, the females between eight and fourteen. When spawning, the females are extremely prolific, the number of eggs averaging around 3 million in an adult. The fry feed on benthis invertebrates; adult sturgeons feed mainly on fish, but also take molluscs, bristleworms and crabs. In the sea, they probably frequent water over a sandy or clayey bed. Its population today is so small that its economic importance is minimal. A slow-moving fish, it roots about in the mud for small creatures that it feels for with its barbels and sucks up into its mouth. Despite being sluggish, it is extremely powerful. In Britain, if a sturgeon is caught, it belongs to the Crown because it was designated many years ago as a Royal fish.

The sturgeon has been suggested as a candidate for the Loch Ness monster; it was proposed by H.C. Williamson, DSc, FRSE in *The Fishing News*, 1934, in which he claims that the Russian sturgeon can attain a length of 30 ft. He further postulates that if two such fish were in the loch and were chasing each other close to the surface, their action could produce a hump-like image. I can only say that the creature I saw in Loch Ness was a single animal and was not like a sturgeon, nor do the majority of recorded sightings resemble such a creature; it does not possess an elongated neck and a serpentine appearance. The theory that its snout, if raised out of the water, could create a neck-like appearance is far from conclusive, especially as it would be so small as to be unrecognizable from any distance.

It may well be that a more reasonable solution may be found in the eel family; many sightings refer to the creature's 'eel-like' appearance. Eels are very much an unknown quantity to science, possessing many habits which have yet to be understood. The European (silver) eel (*Anguilla anguilla*) is found in freshwater in Europe, Asia and North Africa and in the Atlantic and the Sargasso Sea. It is the commonest snake-like fish found in British waters. It has a lower jaw which is longer than the upper and a pectoral fin and a narrow dorsal fin which is united to the caudal and anal fins, the three forming a parallel fringe all round the posterior half. It has a small round eye, which grows as the fish matures. It has scales which are not clearly visible but are embedded in the skin, which is usually silver or yellow in colour. In March and April, adult eels spawn in the deep water of the Atlantic Ocean, including the Sargasso Sea, and then die. The tiny larvae that hatch from the eggs rise to the surface where they feed off plankton. They are then carried across the Atlantic by the Gulf Stream and other currents moving towards the coastlines of Europe, a distance of over 3,000 miles. On arrival in coastal waters, they temporarily stop feeding and change into elvers – miniature versions of adult eels. In British waters, this movement occurs in winter and early spring. By the second winter in freshwater, they have trebled in length, feeding on small snails and insect larvae.

Eels are nocturnal creatures, hunting for food at night and hiding in mud, vegetation, or under stones during the day. Those living in colder northern areas spend the winter hidden in the mud. As they grow in freshwater, they change colour, and become yellow eels, with a soft body. During the next stage they turn silver, the body hardens and the eyes grow bigger. The male species develops into a silver eel about two years earlier than the female. Once developed, which maybe several years later, migratory eels leave the freshwater habitat and return to the sea to breed. Even those kept in habitat become restless when the breeding eels return to the sea. Migrating silver eels do not feed; they have plenty of stored fat – almost a quarter of their weight – and captive silver eels can live for years without food. They travel down streams and estuaries and across land on dark wet nights, when their skin and narrow gill slits prevent them from drying out. They can reach their destination any time from six to eighteen months after beginning their journey from freshwater. Very little is known about how eels navigate thousands of miles across the oceans – perhaps it is the increase in water temperature and saltiness of the water – but they head towards the Sargasso Sea, where the entire breeding exercise continues.

The Moray eel (*Muraena helena*) is found in Mediterranean and warm Atlantic seas, occasionally reaching as far north as the Bay of Biscay. It has no pectoral fin and the gill opening is small and round (unlike that of the common eel which has a slit). This is surrounded by a black coloration spot. The jaws of the Moray eel extend back beyond the eye and it has long sharp teeth. It has a dorsal fin running the length of its body. It is generally a dark purplish-brown, mottled or marbled with yellow or whitish spots. The pattern is irregular at the front, but becomes more regular at the back. It can be highly aggressive and a bite may cause a septic wound. Its blood is poisonous. There are tales from the Middle Ages of victims poisoned by fresh Moray eel blood in the north of the English Channel. There are only a handful of recorded captures of this species eel in British waters.

The conger eel (*Conger conger*) is found in the Mediterranean, the Atlantic, the English Channel, the North Sea and occasionally, the Baltic. It is particularly common off rocky coastal areas (especially the west coast of the British Isles). It has an elongate body and large mouth which extends back to the centre of the eye, filled with rows of strong triangular teeth, knit very closely together. The upper jaw extends beyond the lower, and it has no scales. The gills extend low onto the belly. Elliptical eye. They are usually grey, but can vary from a pale grey or brownish to an almost black upper body. They are generally lighter below. According to British records, which are set under restricted conditions and guidelines, the conger can grow to a size exceeding 4 ms. In 1975, a 133 lb 4 oz specimen was caught off Berry Head, Devon, by rod and line. Official records are often regarded as the ultimate authority, but in truth they do not always reflect reality. Most records are set under competitive conditions, with expert testimony standing as verification. Experienced eel fishermen, who work the water daily, know of much larger specimens that are regularly fished from the sea, or accidentally trapped in fishermen's nets. There are many reports of eels (particularly the conger) being landed which weigh in excess of 200 lb.

Conger eels are usually bottom-dwellers and scour the ocean floor, often taking fish from nets and lobster pots. They are known to eat dogfish, rockling, flatfishes and pollack, and are also keen on cephalopods such as cuttlefish and octopus, as well as crabs. As maturity approaches, they cease feeding, their skeletons begin to decalcify and certain organs begin to regress. They migrate to somewhere between Gibraltar and the Azores, where the sea drops to a depth of over 3,000 m. Large conger eels can have a girth bigger than a man's thigh. If seen swimming or surfacing (which so far as we know, they rarely do, although such instances have been recorded), a large eel would undoubtedly present the appearance of a sea serpent, and would concur with many descriptions of sightings.

A monstrous conger eel was caught off Dalkey, a small town just south of Dublin on 28 August 1915.

An exciting scene was witnessed at Dalkey a few evenings ago when a conger eel of huge dimensions was captured by that well-known angler, Mr Flanagan, accompanied by Mr Ned Carroll, Mr Mick Flanagan and Mr Pat McBride, set out for an evening fishing, and it is superfluous to remark that the denizens of the finny deep had a rough time of it at the hands, or rather hooks, of this distinguished quartet. Several fine specimens of the square nosed gurnet fell to the hook of Mr McBride, while Mr Mick Flanagan landed some splendid mackerel and also several good specimens of rock bream. Mr Carroll was relentlessly pursued by hard luck throughout the evening, as his line got entangled in the boat, which he nearly upset by pulling it in. He subsequently, after a hard struggle, landed a seagull, which was bathing in the vicinity, but with the exception of a whiting weighing two ounces, he met with no success from a piscatorial point of view. It was nearing nightfall when Mr Flanagan felt a severe tug at his line, and was almost pulled out of the boat. He held on, however, with grim tenacity, and presently a huge conger eel reared its crested head above the billows. The monster fish took a hasty survey of the occupants of the boat and speedily returned to the depths again. Then, a titanic struggle commenced – a tug of war between the four anglers and the eel, which Mr McBride said to the writer, 'Strongly resembled a sea serpent'. Matters were going badly with the fishermen, their boat being dragged hither and thither by the frantic eel, whose sinuous movements aroused the unstinted admiration of the large crowd which had assembled on the beach. At length, however, Mr Carroll, with commendable promptitude, seized a pair of tongs, which were fortunately in the boat, and grasping the fish in a grip of iron, hauled it, or as much of it as would fit, into the boat.

In the meantime, one of the oars was lost, but Mr Mick Flanagan rose to the occasion, and using the tongs as an oar, successfully rowed ashore. The eel, which measured nineteen feet and two and a half inches, was drawn up on the beach, and hearty congratulations were showered upon the gallant quartet, who seemed none the worse for their exciting and somewhat agitating experience.

A Queer Tale by Ram Molloy.

The authenticity of this encounter cannot, due to the passage of time, be verified. In dimension, this eel far exceeds any official records, but that does not necessarily mean that an eel of this size could not exist. The numerous witnesses to the incident themselves individually stated that, when first hooked, the eel looked like a sea serpent. From physical appearance, it can be deduced that such a specimen could relate to many sea serpent sightings.

Eels have the capacity to survive out of water much longer than most fish and are known to travel across land through wet grass. They are able to do this by closing their small gills and keeping them supplied with water held in their large gill cavity. These can be seen as swellings on either side of the head when the eel is out of water. They are scavengers, and will take all kinds of live food including young fish and birds. They are particularly damaging to the spawn of salmon and trout, which are laid in gravel. They usually reside on the bottom, and overwinter hidden in the mud. The oldest fish on record (only because it was held in captivity in Sweden) is a European (silver) eel, which died in 1948, aged eighty-eight.

In appearance, the eel seems to be the most suitable candidate for sightings of both the sea serpent and the lake monster. However, its method of swimming differs from the undulating humping motion so often recorded by witnesses; it swims with a wriggling snake-like motion. The violent commotion in the water, which is often recorded during sea serpent and lake monster sightings, may well be attributed to the water disturbance caused by a large eel's wriggling motion, as opposed to any form of flippers. It goes without saying that many eye-witness reports contain descriptive passages of the unknown creature being 'eel-like'. Later, when the sighting is discussed with the media, the testimony may be misinterpreted or expanded upon, creating a 'serpent' or a 'monster'.

Sightings of several humps surfacing and moving through the sea in an undulating manner have been recorded from shore. Sceptics are quick to assert that this phenomenon is merely the actions of the common porpoise (*Phocoena phocoena*) which belongs to the family of Phocoenidae. They are small beakless whales, with sixty to seventy spatular teeth, and live in coastal waters throughout the northern hemisphere, often ascending estuaries of large rivers. The porpoise is the smallest British whale, the only one of its genus found in British waters, where it makes regular appearances on most coastlines. It has a distinctive round head and short triangular dorsal fin at the mid-point of its back. The upper body is black and the underside white. It rarely grows longer than 7 ft in length and averages about 150 lb in weight. Highly vocal, the common porpoises live in small groups of up to fifteen individuals, but migrate season-ally in very large schools. They have acute hearing and echo-locating ability.

Females have only one calf each year, after an eleven-month pregnancy, born after July. They are rarely seen, however, which suggests that they are born well away from coastal areas. The breeding locality is not known. Calves are suckled for approximately eight months. While the calf feeds, the mother lies on her side on the surface so that it can easily breathe. Maturity is reached in three to four years and life expectancy is about ten to fifteen years. It has a voracious appetite – an adult consumes somewhere in the region of fifty herring-sized fish per day. Porpoises are quite difficult to observe; although they often swim in large schools, their arched backs and dorsal fins are generally all that can be seen. From a distance, when in schools, they give the impression of a hump-backed sea monster, undulating as it moves through the water as they dive and resurface as a group.

Porpoises are not very common around the British coast-line, but they are seen along the cost of Wales, Devon and Cornwall, the east and west coast of Scotland, east Yorkshire and Lincolnshire, and off Kent, where of course, many of the sightings recorded in this work emanate from. In theory, it is easy to see how a school of diving porpoise could be viewed as a many-humped creature swimming through the sea. However, in practice witness testimony fails to corroborate this notion. The continual diving and surfacing motion may well provide a hump-like appearance, but there is no periscope-like extended head and neck, a point which most sceptics and naturalists fail to resolve. Without doubt, the leaping porpoise provides a partial solution to some sightings viewed on the horizon, but it is not an explanation for the majority of sightings.

The narwhal (*Monodon monoceros*) lives in the high Arctic Ocean, but is occasionally seen in British waters. The male narwhal can grow up to 20 ft in length and has a peculiar spiral tusk. This feature is actually its upper left incisor. The tooth comes out of a hole in its upper lip, and may grow as long as 9 ft. Its purpose is unknown, but it may be a sexual characteristic to warn off other males and impress the female. The female often has a short tusk.

Adult narwhals are a mottled brown colour, whereas the young are a dark blue, fading to grey. They feed on squid, crabs, shrimps and fish. They form social units of about six to ten and may often gather in large herds when migrating. As they often lie close to the surface, the males' elongated teeth do protrude from the water, which could possibly explain at least some of the sightings in northern waters, although the tooth is straight and javelin-like. For those unaware of the narwhal's curious appearance, it would indeed be a strange creature to encounter for the first time, and might be classed as a monster from the deep.

Another popular contender for the sea serpent or lake monster is the seal. The common seal (*Phoca vitulina*) is less abundant than the grey seal, with an estimated 20,000 living around our coastline. Considered as a pest to the fishing industry, the common seal can be viewed as a scavenger, very often taking fish from fishing nets. They have a tendency to remain in one area for long periods, and are normally found in the North Atlantic and North Pacific temperate or sub-Arctic coastal waters, but are also wide spread along the western coast of Scotland, the Hebrides, Orkney and Shetland, the Moray Firth, the Tay, the Firth of Forth, the Tees, the Humber and the Wash. They are also common on the eastern and north-eastern coasts of Ireland, but rare on the west. Until a virus epidemic broke out in 1988, common seals were hunted for their skins in Shetland, Orkney, the west coast of Scotland and the Wash.

Common seals can live for twenty to thirty years, and have no natural predators in British waters. Seal pups are generally born on a sandbank and can dive and swim from birth, suckling on land or in water for a month or more. When adult, they can grow to a length of around 6 ft, with the male growing larger than the female. They have large heads with short bodies and flippers, and are generally grey in colour, with dark skin blotches, but this can vary. They feed through the day on fish, squid and crustaceans, and often travel up rivers and lakes in search of food. They have been known to make dives lasting around thirty minutes, but it is more usually around five minutes; they spend much of their time close to the surface.

Seals are mostly silent, but they do make a distinct wheezing and sighing sound as they bask on the surface. Another of the seals' unusual habits is to make surface slapping sounds with their fore-flippers accompanied by a cracking sound which attracts the attention of the colony; this is a regular form of communication between them. As they jump clear of the water in a 'porpoising' fashion, it is easy to see why they could be mistaken for a sea serpent from a distance; this action creates a distinct hump-like shape which could be interpreted as a much larger creature surfacing. They also roll together in the surface water, and several seals doing this together would provide a multi-humped impression.

The grey seal (*Halichoerus grypus*) is Britain's largest carnivorous mammal, and is most commonly found on the rocky coasts of Scandinavia, Britain, Iceland, the Faroe Islands, Labrador, the Gulf of St Lawrence and Newfoundland. The largest of the seal family (apart from the elephant seal), a male grey seal can weigh up to 600 lb, can grow up to about 8 ft in length and can live to between thirty-five and forty years. The male grey seal is identified by his massive shoulders, which are covered with thick skin in folds and wrinkles. It also has an elongated snout, a rounded forehead and a wide, heavy muzzle. The male is more than twice the size of the female. Grey seals tend to remain mostly in coastal waters, feeding on fish and some crustaceans, squid and octopus.

Seals possess a sophisticated mechanism which allows them to dive deeply for food and stay underwater for long periods of time. Blood circulation can be adapted, and during a dive the heart rate can drop from about 120 to four beats per minute without any corresponding drop in blood pressure. This is achieved by restricting the blood supply to the muscles of the heart and to the brain, thus reserving the seals' blood oxygen for only the vital organs.

The grey seal has a torpedo-shaped body, with thick layers of fatty blubber under the furred skin. The flippers are also covered in fur and undergo an annual moult. Like other pinnipeds, they cannot turn their hind flippers, and movement on land is restricted and cumbersome as they pull themselves forward with the front flippers, dragging their hindquarters behind. When swimming and diving, however, they are highly skilful, moving in an undulating motion of the hind portion of the body and the hind flippers. These seals do raise their heads and necks out of the water, giving the appearance of elongated neck and small head which is typical of many sighting reports. They also have a tendency to roll in forward diving motion in order to submerge. They are a legally protected species in Britain, although culling does occur to get rid of the surplus population.

The hooded seal (*Cystophora cristata*) can grow up to 9 ft in length and averages around 880 lb in weight and can live for up to twenty-five years. It normally remains in the North Atlantic and Arctic Oceans, but has been spotted off the British coastline, in the Orkneys, Suffolk, the east coast of Scotland and the west coast of England. These creatures spend much of their time in the open sea diving deeply for fish and squid, making regular migrations to Greenland and areas of pack ice, particularly in the Denmark Strait where the adults moult. After this, the seals return to different breeding grounds the following spring. The males are extremely vocal, with the noise amplified by a huge inflatable nasal sac, which is clearly visible on top of its snout. The species gets its name from the enlargement of the nasal cavity, found only in the male, which can be inflated to form a hood or crest. The male hooded seal can blow from one nostril a curious, bright red balloon-shaped object which is formed in the nasal septum. They are grey/silver and black in colour. When they haul themselves out of the sea onto pack ice, they look intimidating beasts.

The walrus (*Odobenus Rosmarus divergens*) can grow to anywhere between 8 and 14 ft. It is the largest pinniped found in European waters. It has a short rounded head and large tusks which are elongated and are, in fact, upper canine jaw teeth. These tusks can reach a length of almost 4 ft in some adult males. Their skin can be a grey-yellow or a red-brown colour and is wrinkled, rough and hairless, except for a few hairs found on the muzzle, which form a distinct moustache shape. The walrus has been found in the North Sea and off the Scottish coast, in the Orkney and Shetland Isles especially. Ungainly on land, they are expert swimmers and they tend to dive when approached by man. They can remain submerged for thirty minutes and can dive to a depth of 300 ft. During the dive, blood drains from their skin surface to supply the internal organs with oxygen.

Walruses have a peculiar habit of sleeping vertically in the water; this is managed by inflating a pair of air sacs in the neck, which act as a life jacket, keeping the head above water. Adult walruses require about 100 lb of food a day, but they can starve themselves for seven or eight days during the periods of good weather. Young walruses often ride on their mothers' backs, clinging on with their fore-flippers.

Members of the pinniped species provide a plausible explanation for many sightings; the actions of seals in water resemble some of the sightings from lakes. They are not uncommon in Loch Ness, and they do raise their head and necks above water, which to the unwary might give an impression of a lake monster. I have no doubt that many lake, loch or lough sightings relate to pinnipeds, particularly if several such creatures are playing on the surface, rolling and diving.

The Eurasian otter (*lutra lutra*) is to be found in rivers, lakes and sheltered coastlines. It can grow to a length of almost 4 ft including the tail. It is an agile creature and is equally at home in water or on land. It has a slim mustelid body, a tail which is fleshy and thick for propulsion in the water and webbed feet. The nostrils and ears can be closed when it is swimming in the water. The fur is short and dense and is a brown, black and white colour.

When in the water, it moves with strong undulations of its body and tail, stroking its hind feet. Its diet consists of, among other things, fish, frogs, water birds, and voles. It is a solitary elusive creature, which, while not being purely nocturnal, is generally most active at night. As it dives, it produces an audible gasp and special valves close off its crescent-shaped nostrils. It swims low in the water, with its nose and upper head protruding just above the surface, creating a V-shaped wake. It possesses the ability to dive silently, causing minimal surface-water disturbance. When feeding, it often makes a loud splash, arching its back and diving with the tail whipped upright until the last moment of descent. It can remain underwater for up to seventy seconds.

On land, it walks with its head held low and outstretched and its body naturally inclined, as its fore-limbs are shorter than the hind ones. Moving faster, it arches its back and holds its tail off the ground as it breaks into a gallop. It can live for up to twenty years.

The otter has been nominated by some researchers as an explanation for serpent sightings, particularly those in the highlands of Scotland. Swimming with its head out of the water, it creates a V-shaped wake as it propels itself. It could easily be mistaken for a strange creature, especially when playing with its young. By virtue of the fact that very few people see otters in their natural habitat, they could account for some sightings. One argument against the otter theory, however, has to be its physical attributes; its size alone would make it extremely difficult to escape attention during its forays on land.

The leatherback turtle (*Dermochelys coriacae*) is the largest reptile and can weigh up to 1 ton and grow to a length of just over 5 ft. Normally found in warm and temperate climates, it is adaptable and has a thick layer of fat which insulates its body. Because of this, it is also be found in colder, more northerly waters. With two large fore-flippers, which have an average span of 9 ft and two smaller rear ones, the turtle is a strong swimmer, but somewhat cumbersome on dry land.

The carapace (upper shield) does not have scales like those of other sea turtles; instead it consists of a thick leathery and oily skin with three longitudinal ridges. The head is also large in comparison to the body. It can stay under water for long periods and can also convert saltwater to freshwater by ingesting seawater and excreting the salt. Its main diet consists of jellyfish. It is now officially, an endangered species.

The turtle swims on the surface, and historical records of sightings elsewhere in the world (notably that reported by the Royal Yacht *Osborne* in 1877) do indicate that it may have been mistaken for a sea serpent. It is a common visitor to coastal waters surrounding the United Kingdom, and may well account for a small percentage of similar sightings in these waters.

No account of sea serpents and lake monsters could be considered complete without a survey of the prehistoric reptiles, which could account for sightings. Although they are generally not accepted as an explanation, some of these creatures were similar to those reported, and are worth mentioning. The main problem with all these creatures is that they are believed to have been extinct for several million years. It is most unlikely – but not impossible – that they occupy lakes, lochs or loughs. During the Ice Age such locations were frozen solid and anything in them would have died. If, however, they survived at sea and entered the lakes after the Ice Age, then such a notion becomes more reasonable.

The geosaurus (*'earth reptile'* or *'earth lizard'*) was a 'sea crocodile' with a long snout. It reached a size ranging between 2 and 4 m. It had four paddles and a fin on its tail. It could swim rapidly by swinging its tail and lived in Europe during the Jurassic Period. As we know it from fossilized remains, it does not bear much resemblance to the archetypal sea serpent, although the sighting allegedly made off Fastnet Rock, Ireland, does make mention of a similar-looking creature (see pages 207–9).

The plesiosaur (*'ribbon reptile'*) is by far and away the most popular candidate for the sea and lake monsters. Amateur identikit techniques, which, it has to be said, are far from accurate, would have us believe that the plesiosaur is the answer to all our questions, but in fact, we know very little about this creature. We do know that it grew to a length of about 50 ft, of which more than half was taken up by its long thin neck. It also possessed four paddle-like, oar-shaped flippers on a broad, flat body. It had no fins on its back or tail and often swam into bays or swamps. Its neck was more than 20 ft long and its jaws were filled with sharp teeth.

Plesiosaurs first appeared during the early Jurassic Period, and soon evolved into two distinct groups: the long-necked plesiosauroids with small heads, and the short-necked pliosauroids with broad, flat heads which allowed them to consume larger prey. Fossilized remains have proved that both types were known to frequent British shores.

The largest of all these creatures was the liopleurodon ('smooth-sided teeth'), which was common between 165 and 150 million years ago. A carnivore, this beast reached up to 80 ft in length and weighed up to 150 tons, making it the biggest carnivore ever to exist. It had four paddle-shaped limbs and was a powerful swimmer. With a mouth reaching around 10 ft long, this creature would eat plesiosaurs and ichthyosaurs. Other pliosaurs include the peloneustes, the kronosaurus (which had a head nearly 8 ft long) and the dolichorhynchops.

Of the long-necked variety, cryptoclidus ('hidden collar

bone') could reach lengths up to 26 ft and weighed up to 8 tons. At least 6 ft of its entire body length was taken up by its small head and extended neck. It, too, had four paddle-like limbs and a bulky body. Its teeth were like thin curved needles, and all were about the same length. Other types of long-necks common to British shores were the plesiosaurus, the microcleidus and the kimmerosaurus.

If, it did survive, the plesiosaur is a major contender for many sightings both at sea and on inland waters. However, the last of the plesiosaurs are believed to have died out 75 million years ago. This is a long time for it to have survived unnoticed. There is also the question of why it seems to frequent lochs and loughs and none is seen in tributaries.

The icthyosaurs (*'fish lizard'*) were dolphin-like animals, which lived in the seas and were very strong-swimming reptiles. They would surface periodically to breathe air through their nostrils, which were situated close to the eyes, near the top of the snout. Found in the seas of Europe, they lived from the early Jurassic to the Cretaceous Period. Ichthyosaurs had streamlined bodies, and ranged in length from 7 to 30 ft. The head consisted of long jaws with sharp teeth (they were carnivores) and two large eyes. They also had four fin-shaped flippers, a tall dorsal fin and a fish-like tail. The smooth skin was dark on the back. Unlike other reptiles, they gave birth to their young in the water; fossilized bones of young ichthyosaurs have been found inside the skeletal remains of adults.

One type of ichthyosaur was the ophthalmosaurus. This creature had the largest eyes of any known vertebrate. Fossil remains have indicated that the eyeball was surrounded by bone, perhaps to provide support under great water pressure, which would indicate that it hunted in dark, deep oceans. Its diet consisted mainly of fish, but they would also eat cephalopods, such as squid. The ichthyosaur does not represent a good likeness to the archetypal sea serpent as it has no long, thin neck.

Tylosaurus was of the order of mosasaurs, which were

aquatic lizards which lived and evolved during the Cretaceous Period. They lived in the seas and were predators, searching for similar food sources to the plesiosaurs and ichthyosaurs. They had snake-like bodies, with short necks, large skulls and long snouts. The fore and hind limbs were described as paddles, and were used for steering. The tail was long and tapering and was the main swimming aid. Some mosasaurs could reach a length ot between 15 and 30 ft. It is believed that they are related to the modern monitor lizards, due to their bone arrangements. The skull, for example, is very similar to that of the monitor lizard, as is the structure of the lower jaw, with an extra joint half way along its length. If we believe that it could have survived, the tylosaurus's food resources in the sea would ensure its nourishment. It has to be classed as another candidate for the sea serpent.

The zeuglodont (yoke-toothed whale) is an early form of whale which lived mainly in the Eocene Epoch. It had a long snout and short hind-limbs, and incisor and canine teeth for feeding on crustaceans or molluscs. By the Miocene it was believed to have become extinct.

The recording and analysis of sea and lake monster sightings of the British Isles is but a small step, it is impossible to provide the ultimate solution to this age-old mystery at present. All I can do is provide the evidence and leave the final decision to the reader. The reports are recorded as they were originally penned. Whenever possible, I have inter- viewed eye-witnesses. None of the accounts has been added to or altered in any way. They are true and authentic records as described by those fortunate (or unfortunate) enough to have encountered something which can be regarded as very special, a meeting with a most unusual creature. I have, where possible, indicated known species which could account for the sightings. This is not to deny the possible existence of an unknown species, but simply an effort to provide as much information as is possible. My opinions should not be viewed as solutions to the individual mysteries, merely as options, which should be assessed with the overall evidence.

All I can ask is that you maintain an open mind and do not simply dismiss this phenomenon as unreasonable. We know very little about the oceans, seas and lakes of the world, and they will continue to throw up mysteries, as they have for time immemorial, mysteries, such as the Devil's Hole in the North Sea. According to author and researcher *Harold Wilkins*, some years ago the British Admiralty survey vessel *Fitzroy* was called to an area in the North Sea where fishermen had complained of losing their fishing gear in what seemed a bottomless part of the sea. They claimed that the area was not marked on their charts nor mentioned in the Sailing Directions for Mariners, or the *North Sea Pilot*. The *Fitzroy*, to their surprise, did find a great hole in the ocean floor, which by use of hydrophones, was measured at over 150 fathoms deep! The *Fitzroy* then located a further chasm, some 10 miles long and deep. It was thought that this marked the site of an old sea estuary dating from the age of long-vanished land bridges. Now that really does make me think!

Sea Serpents and Lake Monsters in Myth and Legend

Many local legends throughout the United Kingdom and Ireland tell of huge dragon-like creatures which terrorized local communities before meeting brave souls who slew them. This reflects the basic human need to believe in the power of good over evil. Records of mankind's encounters with these creatures depict them as the ultimate evil, devouring maidens, wrecking communities and destroying wildlife. In most cases, the creature is represented as a dragon or a huge worm-like object, and the dragon does bear a more than passing resemblance to the dinosaur (although there are those who believe dragons are more similar to crocodiles).

Tales of the dragon, which is derived from the Greek word *draken*, meaning serpent, are countless throughout our folklore and legends. Perhaps the best known is that of St George. This story is an adaptation of an older tale. St

George, who is the patron saint of England, did not apparently ever visit these shores, but the dragon-slaying incident is nevertheless very prominent in many religious buildings. Many church murals were covered or destroyed during the Reformation, but there are still a number which portray this epic encounter. At Hardham Church in Sussex, there is an image of St George on horseback, killing a dragon with his lance, and a similar image can be found at Stedham Church, in the same county. He is mounted on a blue steed at Westfield, Sussex, where he is seen killing a red dragon, while St Michael fights a green dragon at Withyham Church.

The story is in fact simply a Christian version of events which were originally attributed to a Babylonian god, Marduk, who slew the first such beast ever recorded, which was in fact his mother, Tiamat. The prophet Isaiah, however, claimed that it was actually Jehovah who was the first to kill the dragon. The common denominator in all of these tales is that it was good which overccame evil; the dragon, serpent, leviathan, monster, has been regarded as a symbol of evil since time immemorial. The first recorded story of mankind, that of Adam and Eve, and the ultimate demise of paradise in the garden of Eden, includes a serpent; which was of course, the devil.

In the British Isles, accounts of sea and lake monsters began to surface in various communities. Bearing in mind the lack of any real communication between neighbouring counties, let alone between England, Scotland, Ireland and Wales, these tales possess striking similarities when it comes to descriptions of the creatures themselves. These similarities raise the question, how was this so if they were but figments of people's imagination and tales of myth and legend? Unless something did exist, how could these descriptions be so similar? As far back as AD 565, there are records of an encounter between St Columba and a water monster in the River Ness, near Inverness. According to this account, written by Adamnan, St Columba banished the beast back to the depths. This has led to a belief that perhaps this beast was an early ancestor of the modern Loch Ness monster.

Dragons are well known in folklore throughout the world, with similar legends being heard from Britain and Europe to China and America. The dragon may well be an ancestor of the more recent sea serpent or lake monster phenomenon. Many lived in or near water so it is only right to include some of the accounts of them in this work. However, it would take several volumes to cover the whole spectrum of dragon folklore, so it only covers a few of the most notable instances.

1
England

In England dragons, sea serpents or lake monsters generally have no other names, although they have also occasionally been referred to as fire-drakes. Curiously, English lakes are devoid of any known monsters or serpents and it is only in recent times that reports of unknown creatures inhabiting rivers have emerged.

The North-east

One of the earliest recorded serpents of the north-east of England is the Lambton worm, a curious creature that ravaged the beautiful countryside of County Durham, and made its first appearance in 1420. On Easter Sunday that year, John Lambton, heir to Lambton Castle, close to the village of Penshaw, was fishing in the River Wear when he hooked something which was described as a cross between an aquatic worm and a leech. Landing his catch, he saw that the weird creature had the head of a dragon and the face of a devil, elongated jaws filled with long pointed teeth and nine gills on each side of its neck, from which oozed a foul fluid. The creature's black, cold-looking eyes glittered, almost causing Lambton to fall into a hypnotic trance as he gazed into them. Initially deeming it an object of curiosity, he felt he would keep it, but as he made his way home he felt uneasy about its ugliness and cast it down a nearby well.

Time progressed, and a few years later John Lambton left the area to go on a pilgrimage to the Holy Land. Unknown to him, the creature he had tossed down the well was still alive and flourishing. It grew and prospered in its environment, until it eventually slithered from the dank and miserable surroundings of the well basin. It then wreaked havoc in the district, killing man and beast as it encountered them. Efforts to destroy it failed miserably; each time it was sliced in two by the blade of a brave swordsman it simply joined together again.

In 1427, John Lambton returned to learn of the carnage the entire community had been subject to and resolved to kill the creature once and for all. Visiting a local witch, he asked how to destroy the giant worm-like beast. She told him to cover his armour with blades and to fight the creature in the middle of the River Wear. However, in return for her advice, she said that he was to kill the first living creature he encountered after slaying the worm, and he agreed. The duel took place in the middle of the River Wear. The worm coiled itself around its foe, but each time it did so the blades on Lambton's armour sliced pieces from its body. As these fell into the river, the current washed them away, thus permanently disabling it and preventing it from reattaching them. The Lambton worm was no more.

John Lambton must have felt some pride; now he simply had to kill the next living thing he encountered, which was to be no problem as he had already arranged for his father to let loose a dog at the sound of his triumphant bugle. Sadly, Lambton senior, in his excitement, forgot to do this and went running to his son himself. The son refused to kill his father, and the witch placed a curse on the next nine generations of the family. It is claimed that John's son drowned in a freak accident, and his grandson and great grandson died in the battles of Marston Moor and Wakefield. Henry Lambton, the ninth Lord of Lambton, an MP, fell from his horse while crossing New Bridge and drowned. The tenth Lord of Lambton died of natural causes at a very good age, so the curse had ended.

Also recounted in the north-east is the saga of the Linton worm, a twelfth-century beast which lived in a hollow on the north-east side of Linton Hill (the spot is still known locally as the Worm's Den). The worm was described as being 'in length three Scots yards, and somewhat bigger than an ordinary man's leg'. A man known as Somerville took it upon himself to destroy this creature, and amid great public interest he thrust a blazing lance down its throat The attack took place with the creature still partially inside its lair, and as it died in extreme agony its writhing body loosened the earth above it, which duly fell on top of it, speeding its demise.

Another serpent of ancient times was that of Handale, which lived in woods around Loft house-in-Cleveland. This huge creature was said to have powers of deception and would lure young maidens into its lair, whereupon it devoured them. A young man named Scaw confronted the serpent at the entrance to its cave and skewered it with his sword. Inside the cave he found the daughter of an earl, rescued her and was rewarded with her hand in marriage. It is claimed that his coffin is to be found close to the site of a small Benedictine priory whose ruins remain close to the woods.

At Longwitton, Northumberland, there is a legend of a dragon-serpent type beast, with a warty skin, a long black tongue and a long tail like a lizard's. It also possessed sharp claws which it used to tear up the ground. This creature, unlike others, was shy and somewhat reclusive, and it caused no physical harm. It was, however, possessive of the wells where it drank and bathed. Anyone trying to get near the wells was frightened off by its anger. A knight eventually slew this creature, but only after three attempts. The wounds he inflicted on the creature at first had no effect, then he realized that it always had its tail in the water when he attacked it, so this must have some magical effect. Finally, in his third encounter, he lured the creature away from the well where he could lance and skewer it. As he did so, blood oozed from its wounds and fell onto the grass, burning it.

The town of Warkworth is on the north-east coast of England, close to Amble and near the mouth of the Coquet, and is built on a rocky spur. The coast is lined with dunes and has a sandy beach, which can be particularly busy during the summer months. It is an area devoid of any sea serpent tradition, but in 1998, Helen Hadley, an experienced canoeist who is well versed in the natural wildlife of the seas and waterways of the British Isles, had an unusual encounter there. It is Helen's belief that many of the strange objects seen on rivers and estuaries may well be otters, the male species of which can grow to the size of a medium-sized dog. However, an otter could not account for the sighting she had off Warkworth. In private correspondence, Helen told me:

It was the last week in August, I can't be sure of the date and we [Helen and her friend] had taken my boss's dog out for a walk. We walked down the path to the dunes, then over the top, onto the beach. It was a calm, warm evening and the light was still very good.

Rafts of birds had settled a short distance from the beach, there was no swell and the sea was like a mirror. Suddenly, something large and black surfaced right in the middle of one of the rafts of birds and they all lifted into the air. The something was large, I can't be sure of the exact size but it was big in relation to the birds, it was very dark in colour and made no noise. As soon as it had surfaced it dived again, much in the fashion of a whale gulping air. The thing continued to do this for a good fifteen minutes, other people on the beach saw it too.

This area of the British Isles is popular with the seals, and it is quite possible that a species of pinniped may explain Helen's sighting. But she is a sensible witness who appears to have a good practical knowledge of wildlife. She later told me: 'The thing was pretty large, bigger than a seal (I know how long they are as I see them every day), black and long, not short and fat.' What she and her friend saw remains a mystery.

Further down the north-eastern coastline we come to Cullercoats, a suburb of Tynemouth. It is a popular seaside resort, along with the neighbouring town of Whitley Bay. In 1849, however, it was but a fishing village. It was frequented by many artists, including Winslow Homer. *The Zoologist* magazine, on 26 March, published the following account of a curios sea creature which visited it:

A strange marine animal, of great size and strength, was captured off Cullercoats, near Newcastle. By the enclosed handbill, which has been enclosed to me, it seems to be quite unknown to the neighbouring savants. The honest fishermen who drew the struggling monster to land are not, however, over scrupulous about the name, provided it be attractive enough to extract from the pockets of "ladies and gentlemen 6d, working people 3d, each'; they therefore boldly announce him as 'the great sea serpent caught at last'. My correspondent very judiciously observes that, whatever the animal maybe, it adds another to the many evidences constantly occurring that there are more things in heaven and earth than are dreamt of by the experienced practical observers. Some thirty-five years since, the distinguished anatomist Dr Barclay was fain to reproach his contemporaries with the folly of affecting to suppose that they knew everything. What additions have five and thirty years not given to science! As the animal in question must be at least a local visitor, may we not hope that some resident naturalist will favour us with a notice of it?

The same magazine commented in a later issue; (21 April 1849):

This most wonderful monster of the deep was discovered by a crew of fishermen about six miles from the land, who, after a severe struggle, succeeded in capturing this, the most wonderful production of the mighty deep. This monster has been visited by numbers of the gentry and scientific men of Newcastle, and all declared that nothing hitherto discovered in Natural History affords any resemblance to this. As an object of scientific inquiry, this 'great unknown' must prove a subject of peculiar interest. Many surmises as to its habits, native shores, etc., have already been made, but nothing is really known. The general opinion expressed by those that are best able to judge, is, that this is the great sea serpent, which hitherto has only been believed to have a fabulous existence, but which recent voyagers have declared they have seen. Now exhibiting, at the shop, 57, Grey Street, opposite the High Bridge.

The story of the Cullercoats creature remains something of an enigma, and is unique among British sea serpent and lake monster records, since it would seem to be the only record of a serpent being pursued, captured and killed. Generally, such pursuits resulted in the creature evading capture and returning to the deep. It is interesting to note that the catch was put to commercial use, with a fee requested before the catch could be viewed. Unfortunately, without a great deal of descriptive detail it is impossible to assess just what this creature may have been. From all the evidence available it would appear to have possessed all the characteristics of a sea serpent, since it was so described by 'those that are best to judge' (presumably local naturalists) as 'the great sea serpent'. One would also think that local fishermen, having encountered many types of fish and sea creature would have been able to determine the identity of something like a porpoise or a walrus. For many hundreds of years, decomposed carcasses have been recovered from British coastal waters or found stranded upon beaches, which tend to be misidentified as sea serpents; more often than not, they are later identified as decomposed basking sharks. However, the

Cullercoats specimen was pursued whilst alive then killed and brought back to shore, so we are dealing with an entirely different scenario; decomposition does not come into the equation, and we are left with something of an enigma.

The East

The village of Nunnington, is situated on the River Rye in North Yorkshire, curiously close to a village named Ness. Here there is evidence of a further encounter between man and monster. On an ancient tomb in the church is a carved figure of a knight, lying with his legs crossed and his feet resting on a dog. In his hands there appears to be a heart. There is no inscription to indicate who this fellow and his dog actually are, but tradition claims that it is Peter Loschy, a knight who slew a dragon which was wreaking havoc in the countryside of nearby East Newton, where its lair was, in woodland on a hill, aptly named Loschy Hill.

Like John Lambton, Peter Loschy fought the beast wearing a bladed suit of armour, and as the creature coiled itself around him it was sliced into countless pieces. To his horror, however, Loschy saw that the pieces immediately rejoined. A fierce fight ensued until a piece of the creature's body again fell to the floor. Loschy's brave dog then retrieved it before it could heal and carried it for a mile. It then returned and carried the other slivers away. Finally, it took the creature's poisonous head. The knight was delighted with his dog and made a great fuss of it. The happy animal licked him in return, but sadly, having absorbed some of the poison, it passed it onto to Loschy, and both died.

Filey Brig is a mile-long rocky reef on the North Yorkshire coast, which juts out from the Carr Naze headland at the top of Filey Bay. One half lies under water, the rest provides a platform for fishermen or those who simply want a closer look at the sea without getting too wet. On a good day you can see Flamborough Head to the south and Scarborough Castle to the North. The *Daily Telegraph* of

1 March 1934 carried the following report of a mysterious encounter there:

> When fishermen in Filey told us a fortnight ago that they had seen a monster of unclassified, but awe-inspiring species, about three miles out to sea, we were sceptical. The fishermen, perhaps discouraged, said no more and we concluded the monster had gone off to the same retreat as its Loch Ness relative.
>
> Now, however, Mr Wilkinson Herbert, a Filey coastguard, says he was on Filey Brig, a long low spur of rocks running out into the sea, when, 'Suddenly I heard a growling like a dozen dogs ahead. Walking nearer, I switched on my torch, and was confronted by a huge neck six yards ahead of me, rearing up eight feet high.
>
> 'The head was a startling sight – huge tortoise eyes, like saucers, glaring at me, the creature's mouth was a foot wide and its neck would be a yard round. The monster appeared as startled as I was. Shining my torch along the ground, I saw a body 30 feet long. I thought – This is no place for me, and from a distance I threw stones at the creature. It moved away growling fiercely, and I saw the huge black body had two humps on it and four short legs with huge flappers on them. I could not see any tail. It moved quickly, rolling from side to side, and went into the sea. From the cliff top I looked down and saw two eyes like torch-lights shining out to sea three hundred yard away'.

It has been suggested that Mr Herbert saw a member of the pinniped family, and that the poor light and viewing conditions caused him to identify it incorrectly.

Hilston is a small community, which overlooks the North Sea. It is a somewhat quiet location, often frequented by birdwatchers and other wildlife enthusiasts. The *Skegness Standard* of 26 October 1966 published a letter from Mr and Mrs B. M. Bayliss of Spilsby, Yorkshire, one of many sent to the newspaper as a result of a spate of sightings of a sea serpent off the coast.

On an afternoon in early August 1945, we were sitting on the edge of the low mud cliffs at Hilston, between Hornsea and Withernsea. There we saw a creature with a head and four or five round humps, each of which was leaving a wake. It was moving rapidly but quite silently along the shore northwards in face of a northerly wind.

Clearly, this sighting cannot be ascribed to low-flying birds, as the witnesses claimed that they could see a wake being created by the movement of the creature in the water. The fact that each hump is described as creating its own wake would seem to indicate a number of different objects, since water displacement caused by the first object (the head and neck) would create a wake through which any following 'humps' would pass, rather than creating their own wakes. The only way that this could have been a single creature was if the humps were a considerable distance apart, allowing displaced water to settle before they passed through it. It seems more likely that Mr and Mrs Bayliss saw a number of creatures (four or five), each moving through the water and causing further agitation of the surface, perhaps a school of porpoises.

Easington is close to the sandy hook-like finger known as Spurn Head, which looks as though it is pointing the way from the North Sea into the Humber ports. In the late 1930s, Mrs Joan Borgeest from Skiffing (Skeffling) was looking after some children on the beach. The weather was good and she was looking out over the North Sea, when, about 100 yd from where she stood, she spotted something, as she recalled on the 1961 BBC Radio broadcast, *Loch Ness Monster Investigated*, 'Suddenly I saw a huge creature rise, it was green in colour, with a flat head, protruding eyes, and a long flat mouth which opened and shut as it breathed; it was a great length and moved along with a humped glide.'

Excited, she shouted out to some other people who were also on the beach, and pointed to the place in the sea where she had seen the creature. When she herself turned to look back at it she realized that her cries appeared to have scared it, as it immediately dived from view.

Clearly, this sighting is of some unknown creature. The 'green' coloration and brief description prove little to indicate its possible identity (it does however, give the impression of the archetypal comic-book dragon, or Loch Ness monster). If Mrs Borgeest gave an accurate representation of the incident, and we have no reason to doubt her integrity, then we must consider all the facts we have. The lack of any indication of size clearly presents a problem, but Mrs Borgeest stated that from a distance approaching 100 yd, she could see its mouth opening and closing as it breathed. Therefore we must assume that it was of immense size, since it would be difficult to see an average-size creature breathing in the sea (which would create its own disturbance) from a distance of 100 yd. Yet, if it was more than average in size, why did she have to draw their attention to it? Surely something so large would have immediately caught the eye as soon as it appeared?

We shall never know, as all efforts to trace witnesses have so far failed to provide any information. We cannot deny the existence of the Easington creature, but it may well have been a known species which was misidentified, especially as sightings of the Loch Ness monster were being heavily reported in the press at that time.

Hull has always been an industrious area, perhaps the busiest on the east coast, although today, ferries replace the ships which used to travel to the port from all around the globe. According to the writer Harold Wilkins, in his *Monsters and Mysteries*, an incident occurred close to Hull which is worthy of consideration:

A seaman on board a ship bound for Hull saw something in the water, which he described to a friend as being '30 feet by four feet, slimy black in colour with a big eel-like head'. The creature was lying out on top of the water. The seaman, who claimed to have been at sea for some 40 years, stated, 'It was no whale or shark', adding that should he encounter another such creature he would quit the sea and remain on land.

Another Hull incident is recorded in the same work:

In the summer of 1927, a steamship travelling from Hamburg to Hull ran into dense fog as it sailed towards the East Yorkshire coastline. The fog slowly lifted and the captain in the wheelhouse saw immediately in front of the ship's bows what appeared to be a 10–12 foot mast sticking out of the water. He rushed to the engine-room telegraph to warn them and to order them to move astern. As he did so the 'mast' moved and swam round to the port side. Here, it reappeared with a second mast curved round like an elephant's trunk of astounding girth. The object rose a little higher and passengers on board saw what appeared to be a black coloured body. It then submerged.

Could these incidents be linked? Unfortunately, no date is recorded for the first of these accounts, so it is impossible to know whether they occurred at about the same time. Certainly, it would appear from the small amount of data available that both sightings were of a similar creature, since the mention of an 'eel-like head' and a 'round, mast-like' object indicate a slim cylindrical neck and head. It should be noted that the appearance of a second 'mast', curved like an 'elephant's trunk and of astounding girth' is typical of the archetypal sea serpent, and descriptions which, six years later, were applied to the Loch Ness monster. It is also the common image of the snake-like reptile of the Cretaceous Period, which of course, was believed to have become extinct at least 65 million years ago. There can be no doubt that this appearance is most common in both lake and sea serpent sightings; many previous commentators have ascribed the plesiosaur shape to the influence of the Loch Ness phenomenon, but clearly such sightings were occurring long before interest in Loch Ness became so intense.

Trusthorpe is now a district of the coastal town and seaside resort of Mablethorpe, Lincolnshire. A popular tourist area since the 1950s and earlier, it has fine beaches and views across the North Sea. The *Skegness Standard* of 6 November 1966 published a letter from Mr R.W. Midgeley of Boston, Lincolnshire, who wrote of an encounter he had had during the summer of 1937 or 1938, and which continued to puzzle him.

One summer, when on holiday at Trusthorpe, Lincolnshire, I was walking along the sea wall when, probably no more than 400 yards from the water's edge, I saw what I can only describe as a sea monster. No head was visible, but I saw quite clearly what appeared to be four or five half links of a partly submerged, huge snake-like body. It disappeared after about five minutes. I am quite certain I had not witnessed a school of porpoises, dolphins or the like.

Mr Midgeley seems positive that what he saw was a solid, living creature, yet he provides no further evidence to support this conclusion. Could the 'half-links' to which Mr Midgeley refers, have been the remnants of a passing boat wake, which does give the appearance of 'humps' moving through the water? These would disappear after a short period of time, giving the false impression of a long, sinuous creature submerging. The witness seems to have some knowledge of marine life, as he is sure that the creature was not porpoise, nor dolphin swimming in a line, so would he be likely to mistake water movement for a living creature? We shall never know.

Further sea serpents sightings occurred down the Lincolnshire coast at Chapel St Leonards, north of Skegness.

The *Skegness Standard* published a letter on 19 October 1966 from Mr George Ashton. The 49-year-old shot blaster from Sheffield and his wife, May, were on holiday at Chapel St Leonards on 16 October, and were out walking along the beach when they saw a sea serpent less than 100 yd away offshore.

It had a head like a serpent and six or seven pointed humps trailing behind. When I have been out at sea, I have seen seals and sea snakes swimming about and what I saw was neither of these. At first I thought it was a log but it was travelling at about 8 mph and going parallel with the shore. We watched it for some time, coming from the direction of Chapel Point, until it disappeared out of sight towards Ingoldmells. I just didn't believe in these things and tried to convince myself it was a flight of birds just above the water. I even thought of a miniature submarine but after watching it for sometime I knew it couldn't be.

Later, speaking to local people, Mr Ashton said; 'I used to laugh at the thought of there being a monster in Loch Ness, but now I believe that something might well exist, especially as I am confident about what I saw. I would swear on oath as to what I saw.' His wife said:

It was an incredible sight. I really don't know what it was, people have tried to persuade us that it was nothing unnatural, but these people did not see what we did. I cannot understand why some people cannot accept that we would not openly claim to see something uncanny if it hadn't actually happened, especially with the amount of ridicule such a sighting creates. I will never be dissuaded that what we saw was not a flock of birds, a submarine, a torpedo or anything like that. It was something extremely large, a living creature of the sort which neither my husband nor I have ever before seen.

With a visible head followed by a number of humps, there can be no doubting that what Mr and Mrs Ashton saw was genuinely an unusual creature which was like no species known to inhabit the area.

A seaside resort in its own right, Ingoldmells is located just to the north of Skegness, Lincolnshire's main resort. Shortly after the outbreak of the Lincolnshire coast 'monster fever' of 1966, the newsroom of the *Skegness Standard* received a curious telephone call from two Sheffield schoolboys who were holidaying there. One of them, 13-year-old Denis Simpson, told a reporter that 'two black coloured snake things' had been seen in the sea off Butlin's holiday camp. 'We saw the things fly through the air and drop into the water. They wriggled for a while, then sank. It looked as if they came from a red and white boat out there. They were long black snakes wriggling in the water.'

This description is somewhat vague, indicative of two children reporting what they believed to be a suspicious incident. The most baffling aspect of this report is that the witnesses believed that the two creatures came from a boat, and had flown through the air before dropping into the water. This raises the question whether they were eels thrown away from a fishing boat? However, more questions remain unanswered, such as how either of the boys saw the creatures wriggling in a constantly moving sea far enough offshore for a fishing boat to operate. There is no indication of the size of the two creatures, and no reports were received from any fishermen or boat crews operating in the area. Whatever it was the two boys saw, it seems to have been a 'one-off' event, perhaps caused by the heightened awareness that sea serpents had previously been reported in the area.

Winthorpe is almost a district of Skegness. It has a long seafront promenade which allows wonderful unobstructed views of the sea. On Sunday 14 August 1960, something was seen in the sea opposite the Derbyshire Miners' Welfare Holiday Centre. As reported in the *Skegness Standard*, August 1960, Len Booth was the first to see the creature.

I was looking out to sea watching two small yachts tackling the rough sea. I thought it was a whale and called John Dutton. We both watched it for about half an hour. It was not going very fast and kept heading in a northerly direction, but swerved out to sea and back to within about half a mile of the shore as we watched it. It was black or dark coloured.

The creature repeatedly submerged and surfaced all the time they had it in view, but they did not see a head or tail.

Sightings continued. Mrs Joan Betts, Councillor J.D. Williamson and Rosina Stubbs, all local people were looking at the Derbyshire Miners' Welfare Holiday Centre boat, which was about 800 m out to sea when they saw something strange. Joan Betts said:

I saw it twice on either Monday 15 August or Tuesday 16 August, I cannot recall. The first time was mid-morning and I saw a long black thing hurtling along but not disturbing the water. I called Rosina to look, and we both watched it for a few seconds before it was lost to view behind camp buildings. It was travelling south to north and was long, dark and curved.

The *Skegness Standard* had a monopoly on these incidents and was full of enthusiasm in its reporting them. Most of the articles were pro-serpent, but some correspondents were critical of the testimony, and claimed that the witnesses had seen natural events, such as a flock of birds skimming the water prior to taking off, or a shoal of porpoises, or even a wave pattern. The low-flying bird theory would seem to offer the most logical explanation, as some of the witnesses thought that the object was skimming the surface. Others mentioned the fact that no wake could be seen, which also suggests that it was not actually in the water, since it is impossible for a solid object to move in water without creating some water disturbance.

The sighting aroused a good deal of attention as casual visitors flocked to the area in the hope of viewing the 'Skegness thing'. Most were, of course, disappointed. Then later in 1966 came news of a further sighting off the coast, this time from a local Skegness man, John Hayes. He wrote to the *Skegness Standard*, informing them of an incident which had occurred at the beginning of the summer season 1966.

Hayes had been cycling along the front of the Derbyshire Miners' Welfare Holiday Centre at Winthorpe. It was a clear moonlit night. Suddenly he heard a loud crack that seemed to emanate from the sea. He stopped and looked out. There, in the water, he could see a huge, dark shape moving at about 20 mph and approximately 500 yd from shore. Could this have been the noise which seals often make by slapping their fore-flippers on the water surface to attract the attention of their fellows? Without further details, it is impossible to interpret this incident. It could, of course also have been the slapping of a large heavy body hitting the water surface as something dived.

Prior to the excitement of 1966, Skegness had received other reports of strange and mysterious creatures off its coast, as a report from the *Skegness Standard* of Wednesday, 10 August 1960 reveals:

On Sunday, 7 August 1960, five witnesses saw something in the water off Gibraltar Point, Skegness, between four and five in the afternoon. The weather was good and the sea reasonably calm. One witness, Ray Handsley, a Wainfleet butcher said: 'When I saw it, I had no idea what it could be. It was difficult to judge how far out it was, maybe a mile or two, but it looked as though it was travelling along the edge of the deep water. It was just a long black line on the surface about nine or ten feet long. It was travelling a dead straight course towards Skegness. It's hard to say what speed it was doing, but it was very fast. I'd say about forty or fifty miles an hour. The thing looked perfectly

flat. The curious thing was there was no wake after it.'
His wife, Ruth Handsley, claimed that whatever it was,
it was curved. 'At first I thought it was a whale. It was
very long – about twelve feet, and it was going very
fast. I can't say that I've ever seen anything like it
before.'

Another witness, Mrs Vera Digby, believed it was a
torpedo; she thought it was 6–9 ft long, with about 1 ft showing above the surface water line. Her husband, William, was
the first of the group to spot the object. 'It was coming from
the Barton area and heading north in an absolutely straight
line. I couldn't really tell what shape it was.' The fifth witness
was an 11-year-old boy, Peter Handsley, the son of the
Wainfleet butcher. To his mind the object reminded him of a
submarine.

With so many different witnesses seeing the same creature,
one can only accept the accounts as genuine. Gibraltar Point,
near to which the creature was seen, is a nature reserve, a
somewhat desolate area consisting of sand dunes, mud flats
and sea, ideal for the naturalist to study the local habitat. This
creature once again takes the form of an archetypal sea
serpent.

East Anglia

Just south of Cromer on the Norfolk coast is Overstrand, the
scene of a sighting by a reputable witness. The Reverend
Abercromby described an incident which occurred on 31
July 1891 while he was watching the sea from the cliffs close
to his home at Overstrand Rectory. The story appeared in the
East Anglia News on 3 August 1891.

As my daughter and I were standing half way down the
cliff overlooking the sea this morning, we saw a most
extraordinary sight. At first there appeared, what
looked to be, the wings of large brown birds just on the

surface of the water which, in a moment or two, proved to be the fins or large spines along the back of a sinuously moving creature of immense length.

Immediately afterwards, a head was reared up for a few seconds, looking about the size of a very large man's head, having shaggy brown hair or mane flowing back from it. The sun was shining on it, so we both saw it most distinctly. What added to its uncanny appearance was the tremendous speed at which it was going; it travelled in a straight direction and then suddenly disappeared. The time was 1 o'clock and the beach was being just cleared of people and bathers, and no fishing boats being then in sight, all was very quiet and still.

Some forty-five years later, again off the Norfolk coast, the following report describes a creature of a similar type. Mr Alec Enkel, informed Tim Dinsdale, author of *The Leviathans*, of an incident which occurred during an angling holiday at Mundesley:

The year was 1936, and the month August when on a touring holiday we drew our caravan to a parking site at Mundesley, on the Norfolk coast. The party included a Mr and Mrs Savage, my wife Marjorie and myself. After having an evening meal, Leslie [Savage] suggested we had a final stroll on the beach while our wives were tidying up. Off we went down the cliffs, onto the beach. All of a sudden Leslie said, 'Alec, look out there! What do you think it is?'

Being quite a distance out to sea, and the evening closing in, it was three or four seconds before I caught sight of it, but there it was, the outline plain to see. There were the five curved humps, and the long neck, with a head pointing forward at right angles to the neck, like the head of a large snake, travelling at a terrific speed, and going south-east diagonally from us. Its colour was a dark brown – almost black. None of the humps moved nor changed shape at any time during the sighting.

Recently I heard someone discrediting this and several other land-to-sea sightings as being nothing more than the misidentification of sandbanks. This is an easy assumption to make, but it does not explain the clarity of the description of a head, neck and humps, nor is it clear how a stationary sandbank could appear to be moving fast in a south-easterly direction.

The appearance of the five curved humps, which, according to the witness, maintained their shape throughout the incident, tends to indicate an archetypal sea serpent, a large snake-like mass moving through the water. Since there is no report of 'undulating movement' of the body, we can also glean that the creature must possess some other method of propulsion through the water. Clearly, whatever the creature was in this case, it cannot be dismissed as mistaken identity. The extended neck and head indicate the established plesiosaur-like creature, yet the five humps present a problem to this explanation since as far as we know, plesiosaurs did not have several humps.

The *Eastern Evening News* of Friday, 7 August 1936, carried the following report of a strange creature which was seen by a number of witnesses off Eccles, also on the Norfolk coast:

A sea serpent well over 30 feet long, swimming at a mile a minute, has been seen off the Norfolk Coast at Eccles. This is the strange story contained in a letter from no less a person than H.E. Witard, a former Lord Mayor of Norwich. It is authenticated by Mr Charles Ammon, MP, his wife and two daughters, and by Mr A Gosling, former MP for one of the Birmingham divisions and now resident at Eccles.

Witard says: 'I am positive that what we saw was a sea serpent. We were all on the beach together on Wednesday evening [5 August 1936] when we saw the creature. It was a perfectly clear evening. The suggestion that we mistook a shoal of porpoises for a serpent is ridiculous. I am an old sailor, and I know something about the habits of porpoises. It was at least a mile out to sea, and was swimming parallel to the coast. Its speed was terrific, 90 to 100 miles an hour is not an exaggerated estimate. It disappeared very quickly on the skyline in the direction of Happisburgh.'

The national press picked up the story, and shortly after the event, Henry Witard found himself being interviewed by a journalist representing the *Daily Mirror*, who was no doubt very keen to expand upon this most newsworthy event, especially as the witnesses had some public standing. The newspaper managed to extract a more detailed account of the incident from the former mayor.

We were standing on the beach at 7.25 in the evening when I noticed an unusual form travelling swiftly, about one mile from the shore, in a northerly direction. I am an old sailor and could not be deceived by a shoal of porpoises. It was a serpent beyond question.

Looking at it from a distance, it appeared to be about thirty or forty feet in length and was skimming the surface of the water in a worm-like movement. Its speed was terrific. It would not be an exaggeration to say it was anything from ninety to one hundred miles an hour. It was a perfectly clear evening and six of us watched it take a straight line parallel with the coast.

The article prompted several replies from local naturalists, the majority of whom dismissed Witard's claims, and suggested that what they had witnessed was simply a flock of bids flying close to the water's surface. As an MP, Charles Ammon may have been concerned for his public credibility, so he attempted to distance himself from the sea serpent theory. Within days of the initial press coverage of the event, he told the *Irish Daily Telegraph* (10 August 1936) that the creature he had seen was 'probably a whale'.

However, the *Eastern Evening News* received further letters from other members of the public, who confirmed seeing a strange creature in the vicinity. Mr Colin N. King of Wroxham wrote:

On Wednesday afternoon [5 August 1936] I was sitting with my wife and daughter on the sand hills at Eccles, when I pointed out to them a black snake or worm-like object travelling at a terrific speed on the surface of the water, about half a mile or so out, going in the direction of Happisburgh. We remarked about the great speed it was travelling. It must have been well over 30 feet in length. The time we saw it was between 2 and 3 p.m., and Mr Witard saw it at 7.15 p.m. (We left the beach at 4.30 p.m.) I have been wondering if there were more than one, or, if this creature is still in the vicinity.

On 11 August 1936, another correspondent, Stanley D. Cooper of Sheringham, also wrote to the *Eastern Evening News*.

At 4.36 p.m. on Sunday [9 August 1936] I saw the sea serpent which was recently seen at Eccles. It was about two miles out from shore, and was travelling at a terrific speed, which, I can safely say, was over a mile a minute. The serpent was at least 40 feet long, and the suggestion that it was wild ducks in flight is ridiculous. The sea was very calm, and it could be followed quite easily with the naked eye for about a minute and a half. It was going in the direction of Cromer and judging by its great speed it would pass Eccles again in time for tea.

Local naturalists would have none of it, and dismissed every sighting as either a shoal of porpoises swimming in a row or wild ducks in flight just above the waterline, creating an image of a long serpent-like creature! There was nothing to support these claims and none of the self-proclaimed experts had seen anything themselves, nor had they interviewed the witnesses. The low-flying wild duck theory is hardly a reasonable argument in this case, since the witnesses watched the creature for some considerable time, and flying ducks could be expected at some stage of the flight to rise above the surface, or at the very least to change their pattern of movement. It is also difficult to explain how they would give the same impression as Charles Ammon's 'whale'.

A shoal of porpoises would be a better explanation, but Henry Witard himself stated that he was aware of the habits of porpoises, so would he really propose the sea serpent theory without first trying to rationalize what he saw as porpoises?

The witnesses' perception of the great speed of the creature, for example Witard's '90–100 mph', seems to be over-estimated. The distance would exaggerate the speed unless there was something with which to compare it. This then was, in all probability, a mistaken estimation. But if an error in speed could be made, then can the rest of the testimony be trusted? It is true that Henry Witard was in no position to make any estimation of the creature's actual speed, but perhaps his excited state, or a desire to make the creature seem more fantastic than it actually was, made him guess. Nevertheless, it should be remembered that every witness claimed that the object they saw moved with great speed. There can be no doubt of their sincerity: they certainly did see something unusual, something which, to date has never been satisfactorily resolved.

Lowestoft was the site of the first recorded lighthouse in England and is an important fishing port. On 30 October 1896, the crew of the fishing boat *Conquest* arrived in the harbour, and told of a sea serpent they had seen off the coast. (H.T. Wilkins, *Monsters & Mysteries*).

The thing was seen by the lugger *Conquest*, off Banff, Scotland. All the crew of eight men were on deck at about 6 p.m., when a mile or so on their lee quarter they heard a loud noise, likened to a big steamer cutting her way through the water. Looking in that direction, they saw a huge serpent, which now rose only 20 yards distant. They said the monster was fully 300 feet long and moved at about 8 miles an hour. It resembled three enormous half circles in line, each being 10 feet high and 50 feet long, and there was room between each circle for the lugger to have passed. Still making the same noise, it passed close under the lugger's stern. All the men watched it fully for 15 minutes. They describe it like a fishing-boat turned upside-down and equally large in girth.

It is difficult to understand how a creature, which, when it rose, was only 60 ft from the vessel, could manage to expose three semicircular humps each measuring 10 by 50 ft then completely submerge in order to pass under the lugger. Estimates of size and speed are difficult for experts to assess, let alone the layman, who may be in a state of shock or surprise as a result of an unexpected confrontation with a large creature.

It is interesting to note the 'upturned boat' appearance of this creature, something which is now commonly associated with sightings of sea serpents and lake monsters. It is generally believed that this appearance occurs when the creature's body is seen from directly in front or behind. There may be a ridge (dorsal fin?) on the peak of the back, at the highest projected point out of the water, which enhances this appearance. The report gives insufficient detail to determine a great deal about the creature, other than it was of typically 'monstrous' proportions. It is likely that its dimensions were exaggerated, which casts doubt on what may well have been an authentic sighting of an unknown sea creature.

Reports of a sea monster off the Kessingland coast of Norfolk appeared in *The Gentleman's Magazine* of December 1750. 'The creature was about five feet long from what could be viewed of it above water, with a head like a dog and a beard like an alien. The skin was spotted like that of a leopard. It passed in a leisurely fashion, finally disappearing beneath the waves to the great amazement of all those watching from the shore.'

Some 162 years later, on 20 July 1912, another sighting occurred, this time by Miss Lilias Haggard, daughter of Sir Henry Rider Haggard, author of *King Solomon's Mines* and owner of Kessingland Grange. Haggard himself was at the time working on a novel at his home in Ditchingham and received a letter from his daughter, part of which read:

We had great excitement here this evening. And we are convinced we saw a sea serpent! I happened to look up when I was sitting on the lawn, and saw what looked like a thin, dark line with a blob at one end, shooting through the water at such a terrific speed it hardly seemed likely that anything alive could go at such a pace. It was some way out over the sandbank, and travelling parallel with the shore. I tore into the morning room and got the glasses and though it had, at that moment, nearly vanished in the distance, we could make out it had a sort of head at one end and then a series of about 30 pointed blobs, which dwindled in size as they neared the tail. As it went along, it seemed to get more and more submerged and then vanished. You can't imagine the pace it was going. I suppose it was about 60 feet long.

Perhaps a little suspicious as to what was occurring in Kessingland, Haggard went there immediately. His daughter had always been a sensible girl, not prone to fanciful tales or untruths, and he wanted to confirm her opinion as to what it was she and the household staff (Phoebe Haggard and Beatrice Carter) had witnessed. He spoke separately to Lilias, the gardener and the cook, all of whom had seen the object. Their descriptions corroborated each other.

Lost for an explanation, Haggard sent his daughter's letter to a local newspaper, the *Eastern Daily Press*, in the hope of finding a solution to the mysterious sighting. The letter was printed in full on Wednesday, 14 July 1912, along with a note from Haggard himself.

In the hope that it may elicit an explanation, I enclose a portion of a letter received from my daughter who is staying at my house, Kessingland Grange, near Lowestoft. May I ask:

(1) Has anybody else seen a peculiar creature in the sea off the East coast? and,

(2) Could what my daughter and her two companions saw have been a school of porpoises travelling at a great rate?

The response was overwhelming and it seemed that the waters surrounding the Norfolk coast must home some unusual creature of the sea serpent type. Mr C.G. Harding, an employee of the Lowestoft Water and Gas Company, wrote to the paper, explaining that he too had seen something unusual in the waters off the local coast early on the morning of Sunday, 21 July 1912. He described what he saw as being black or dark-coloured, and it moved 'as if it were a torpedo which had been discharged along the surface of the water.' Mrs Adelaide J. Orams of Mundesley had also seen a dark object moving rapidly through the water as she stood looking out to sea at Mundesley with her young daughter.

Another correspondent, with the curious signature of 'SHE', told of a sighting which had occurred three weeks prior to the Haggard incident, at Gorleston. Apparently, many visitors to the beach that day had seen a large creature travelling in a northerly direction with 'lightning rapidity'. It was about ½ mile offshore, and when it was almost opposite the harbour mouth, it turned seaward and disappeared. The sighting lasted about fifteen seconds in total.

Mr W.H Sparrow of East Runton told readers how he and

his wife were on the promenade at Cromer on Saturday, 19 July 1912, at around 7.15 p.m., when they saw, about 2–3 miles out to sea, a 'dark-coloured line' about 30 ft long travelling at not less than 40 mph. Mr Sparrow claimed to see the shape rise and drop into the water as it moved along (an inference of undulations). It moved towards Sheringham and submerged.

It is clear that Rider Haggard had personal knowledge (or had received information from someone) of the deceptive appearance a school of porpoises can create. However, from the description provided by Lilias Haggard and other witnesses, it is difficult to see how this explanation could withstand scrutiny. Each witness describes a 'long' creature. Lilias Haggard claimed that it appeared to have a head at one end, and up to thirty pointed blobs tapering towards what she assumed to be the tail. This is hardly like a school of porpoises swimming in line. Indeed, it would take an incredible feat of synchronized swimming for porpoises to submerge in sequence. Flotsam, ducks, seals, sandbanks or other theories also fail to provide an adequate explanation for these sightings.

In 1972, an anonymous letter from a holidaymaker was received by the *East Anglian Magazine*. The writer stated:

> The sea was quite calm when my attention was suddenly drawn to what I can only say looked like the head of a seal on a long neck sticking up out of the water. There seemed to be some humps behind the head, but the creature only remained visible for a matter of a few seconds before diving beneath the surface. I would be inclined to think that I had imagined everything if I had not read the story of the Kessingland Sea Serpent.

Built on cliffs, Southwold is a picturesque town on the Suffolk coast. The first mention of a mysterious sea creature there came, by the witness's own admission, as a result of mistaken identity. In a letter to *The Times* of 15 December 1933, Mr C.W. Limonzin of Ealing wrote:

A few years ago I was fishing from the beach north of Southwold, when my attention was drawn to an object coming down tide, which I thought was an empty oil drum. But as it drew nearer, almost opposite to me, and some fifty yards out to sea, the oil drum raised its head about two feet of neck out of the water and appeared to be seeking for something to devour. As it drifted past, I followed it with my rod cast in its direction, hoping, as I desired a nearer view, that it might spot a meal at the water's edge and come towards me, so that I might get a glimpse of the submerged body. It did come a shade nearer and I recognized at once a member of the Phocidae – a common grey seal.

The same mistake was not, however, made in 1938, when the following sightings were reported in the national press. On the morning of Friday, 21 October 1938, Ernest Watson and William Herrington went out in their 18 ft fishing boat *Fisher Girl*, trawling for sole near South Barnard buoy, 4 miles east of Southwold. The sea was dead calm and both men were returning to land when they were startled by a huge animal which thrust out a 'long neck' from the water, about 40 yd from them The creature was estimated to be about 50–60 ft long and shot off at a speed of some 30 knots, eventually diving amidst a swirling wash. It was dark grey in colour. Ernest Watson said of the incident (*Daily Mirror*, 22 October 1938):

I have never seen anything like it in my life and I've been nearly all round the world. Everything was quiet at the time, and we had our trawl out when all of a sudden I saw a head come out of the water. Then something flashed past like a torpedo, I never saw its head again. It gave us a look, as it seemed to be cutting toward

Covehithe Cliff, and then, I fancy, it heard our engines and turned eastward and out to sea. We watched it for over five minutes.

It kept its neck bent, and showed its camel-like back, which stuck out of the water so far that we could see right under it. It was dark grey in colour, and the nearest it was to our boat was about forty yards. I've heard all about people seeing such things as the Loch Ness monster, and I've laughed: but this was no laughing matter. My word it was going! You ought to have seen it, and then you would have realized what a fright it could give anybody. I am only glad it did not come up nearer to our boat. It seemed to be towering right over the top of us as it was. I shouldn't like to think that we were any nearer to it than we were, in such a small boat.

William Herrington, a former Southwold town councillor said (*Daily Mirror*:)

I should never have believed it if I hadn't seen it with my own eyes, and even if the other fishermen whom we have told laugh at us, they wouldn't laugh if they came across it. I wondered what was up when Ernie shouted, 'Look at that great head!' I just turned round and caught one glimpse of the head, and then afterwards all I saw was a humped back ... It wasn't a thresher or a blower. I know what these fish are, and I haven't been to sea all the time I have and then imagine these things. Why, it wasn't as if we just saw it at a glance; we watched it right out of sight, although that wasn't for long because it was going so fast.

Ernie says forty miles an hour was the speed, I say it was more than that. This was really something very strange and I can tell you I was mighty glad when I saw it going away from us instead of coming towards us. The wash alone would have swamped us. Anyhow, I shouldn't like to think we were ever coming across it again, and

I shouldn't like to think of it coming up out of the water anywhere nearer our mates than it did to us. But all the same for that, I should just like some of the other men to see it. Yes, I confess I was really frightened.

Herrington did not have long to wait to discover that the creature had indeed been sighted by another witness prior to their own encounter. On 23 October 1938, the Reverend R.N. Pyke, Vicar of Southwold, told reporters that while he was standing outside his home with his wife and the Reverend W.N. Welch of the Southwold Mission for Seamen, they saw a huge creature moving in a sort of undulating way about twice the length of the pier away from shore (*Sunday Referee*, 23 October 1938).

I could not see its head. Mr Welch knows all about strange fish of the sea, and he declared he had never seen anything like it in all his life. The creature was dark, but not black, and there were several parts of it sticking out of the water. We watched it go out of sight, and I quite believe the fishermen thought it was travelling at over 40 miles an hour, because it appeared to be going faster than the quickest motor-boat I have ever seen. There is no doubt that the two fishermen gave a perfectly fair account. We said nothing at first about our experience, but now I am glad that somebody else has seen this monster.

Mrs Pyke said that the part of the monster sticking out of the water was larger than the biggest motor car. These reports of a monster in the Southwold waters brought a healthy number of visitors for several weeks after the initial sightings. Miss A.M. Jenkins, in private correspondence, described another sighting of the Southwold sea serpent in 1938.

I saw the sea monster off Southwold one autumn day in 1938. It was fine and the sea very calm, with a slight sea mist. It was travelling south about 100 yards from me; I judged its length to be about twenty feet, it seemed to be raised from the water, but I could not estimate how high it actually was. It was travelling in a southerly direction at a speed of about 30 mph. I saw several humps and watched the creature until it was out of sight.

One cannot ignore the testimony of so many independent witnesses giving the same description of the Southwold creature. There can be no doubting the certainty of each witness of what they saw. A sketch drawn by Ernest Watson and William Herrington shortly after their sighting shows an extended neck and small head, with what appears to be a bulky, bulbous body behind. Herrington was so convinced by the creature he saw, that he made a small model of it, which was at one time displayed in Southwold Museum. Clearly, if this was still available it would provide marvellous potential for identifying the species. Sadly, all efforts to find it have failed.

Mrs Sybil Armstrong and her sister, Mrs Hamilton, made contact with author Tim Dinsdale (*The Leviathans*) to inform him of an encounter they had in June 1931:

I had rented a bungalow for a month at Thorpeness in Suffolk, built on the edge of a low sandy cliff with nothing between us and the sea. The weather had been set fair for some days and the evening we saw the creature was a particularly clear and brilliant one – not a cloud in the sky and the sea dead calm – it was about 8 p.m. – the beach deserted.

Our governess, the cook and I were eating supper in the sitting room, which had French doors opening out onto the beach with, of course, a full view of the sea. I was looking vaguely at the view and noticed what I took to be a man's head swimming. I remarked he was bathing late, but as I said it, I saw that it was coming at a great speed and was much too big to be a man's head.

I went outside for a better view and saw there was a great length of snake-like body behind. I exclaimed in surprise and the other two came out to see – we were astonished – forgot the sleeping children and ran along the cliff trying to keep up with it and see all we could. It was then at the Aldeburgh end of the beach, a large sandbank which I was told afterwards was a quarter of a mile out, but I do not think it could have been so much – people used to swim out, and you could distinguish them by their bathing dresses if brightly coloured. Anyway, when the monster got level with the sandbank, which was now between it and the deep sea, it turned and drew itself up on it. It was now with its back to us. It went over the crest and on reaching the water on the far side, raised up its front part and beat on the sea with enormous oyster-coloured fins (I suppose) making such a volume of spray – it made me think of a swan beating the water with its wings – meanwhile the length of its body was across the sandbank with the tail end still in the water on the beach side – it then ceased beating on the sea and the whole body was pulled over. It was incredibly long. I don't remember what the tail end was like – it all happened so quickly, but whereas in the water it looked black, when on the sandbank it was a tawny sandy colour. It was a marvellous sight and the agility with which the monster crossed the sandbank makes me realize they are not completely helpless on land.

The next evening I looked most carefully at fishermen's rowing boats coming along to collect lobster pots at approximately the same distance out, and came to the conclusion the monster was about five times as long.

It is possible that this creature was of the pinniped species, possibly a misplaced walrus. They are known to frequent the North Sea, but usually in much more northerly waters.

Colour-wise, the creature would seem like a walrus. The systematic beating of the front flippers on the sea is also common amongst pinnipeds. The one fact which does not fit with the pinniped explanation, however, is the body shape, which was described as long and snake-like. It is possible, however, that the witnesses' description may have been inaccurate, perhaps due to the distance involved and their incredulity at what was unfolding before their eyes.

Another sighting off the Suffolk coat at Aldeburgh occurred in 1985. Nigel Howse, in private correspondence explained:

In 1985 my Shetlander friend James Thomason and I had an exhibition of our paintings at Gallery 44 in High Street, Aldeburgh. We co-hosted our own show for two weeks that last fortnight. That is quite a long time ago now. All I know was that I had broken off at lunchtime to have a portion of fish and chips. I sat down on the edge of the concrete wall beside the footpath next to the road.

As I sat looking out to sea – the day was sunny and the visibility was very good – I saw on the horizon a black-coloured moving shape. There were, I remember, very few other boats or ships about. This object, it occurred to me at the time, was really quite large and, unlike a boat, it disappeared and reappeared! It was like the Loch Ness monster, coiling up out of the water, then moving forward along the far distant horizon. This event has stuck in my mind as special all this time.

Mr Howse has been unable to confirm his impressions of what he saw, other than a mysterious creature of the deep. Natural phenomena such as porpoises or seals, do not account for coil-like shapes (humps), but associated wave patterns could give that impression to the naked eye. Yet a wave pattern would not disappear then reappear. As very few boats or ships were about, a wake is equally as unlikely. The witness was certain that the 'black' object was not part of the water, but something *in* the water.

The South-east

According to Adrian Gray's *Tales of Old Essex*, two water dragon incidents are recorded in Essex. Both were the result of the creatures being imported from abroad. The first story relates to a beast brought to London by Barbary merchants which managed to escape and headed down the river Thames, eventually coming ashore and taking up residence on land between East Horndon and Herongate, south of Brentwood. Sir James Tyrell did not appreciate the terror this creature was causing among the local people, as it took to eating many of them. So, early one morning, Tyrell, knowing that serpents were vain creatures, strapped a mirror to his chest of armour, then went off to slay the beast. The serpent saw Tyrell approaching and prepared itself for battle. But it caught sight of itself in the mirror and was mesmerized, allowing Tyrell time to cut off its head and return home with it.

The second tale relates to the town of Wormingford, in north Essex and occurred some time between 1189 and 1199. According to legend, this serpent was brought home to London by King Richard I from the crusades. It was called a cockadrille, and was at first quite a small creature. As it grew it managed to escape to Wormingford. On this occasion, the beast was slain by Sir George de la Haye.

A more recent encounter occurred in an area of the Thames estuary known as Black Deep at a time when the area was closed to shipping. The captain and crew of HMS *Kellett* were surveying the area at some time around 9.00 a.m. one August morning in 1923, when they saw a strange creature. (Rupert T. Gould, *The Case for the Sea Serpent*).

Captain Haselfoot and Commander Southern both saw a long neck rise out of the water at a distance of about 200 yards from their position on HMS *Kellett*. The object rose to a height of about seven feet and then submerged only to reappear again and once more reared itself up out of the water for a period of about five seconds on either occasion. Captain Haselfoot drew a sketch of the creature.

It is worth noting that, however, that the same Captain Haselfoot, also claimed to see a creature in Loch Ness in July 1934, as he wrote in a letter to *The Times* on 16 July 1934: 'What I saw in Loch Ness was a living creature, the likes of which I have never before witnessed.' The Loch Ness creature also showed a head and neck which stood proud of the water at a height of about 4 ft. It seems that Captain Haselfoot had a rather short memory, as his Thames estuary sighting had, seemingly been forgotten by this time! Could one truly forget such an incident?

In 1935, an incident occurred at Herne Bay, to the west of Margate. Being a seaside resort, it is one of Kent's busiest towns, and still has a typically Victorian seaside appearance. According to author H.T. Wilkins, in his impressive book *Monsters and Mysteries*, that summer, crowds of excited onlookers lined the cliffs and watched a number of speed boats and motor boats moving at a good speed (an estimated 40 mph) as they chased a strange monster for half an hour. The creature was thought to be about 20 ft long and evaded capture. It was first seen churning the water into foam about 1½ miles beyond the pier. Witnesses who saw it said that it travelled with an undulating motion and appeared to have smooth skin, dark on top, and yellow below. In a scene reminiscent of the film *Jaws*, bathers spilled from the water and onto the beach in panic. The entire incident was also witnessed by a crowd of several hundred holidaymakers from the esplanade. None of the pursuing boats ventured closer than ¼ mile from the creature.

Cliftonville is a suburb of Margate, a seaside resort which annually attracts millions of holidaymakers. It is located on the most easterly peninsula of Kent. A Londoner, Mr John

Handley, was on holiday in the area (July, 1950) and swimming in the sea close to the Lido Baths at Cliftonville. The sea was calm and the weather described as good, when suddenly Handley noticed a curious water disturbance. Without further warning, 'a two foot long head, with horse's ears, rose out of the water' (*Fate*, vol. 3, no. 8) less than 200 yd from where he was swimming.

In a state of panic, Mr Handley rushed to get out of the water, swimming to shore without looking back. Later, he admitted that due to the shock of it all, he did not have much opportunity to take a long look at whatever it was, but he was sure it was an unusual and ugly creature which was foreign to him. The whole incident was witnessed by another holidaymaker, a woman who was sunbathing on a nearby beach and saw the object surfacing in the water close to where Mr Handley was.

One of the most picturesque areas of Kent is St Margaret's Bay, north-east of Dover. It is most popularly known as the starting point for cross-channel swimmers. Reached by a steep winding road which leads down the chalk cliffs, it has a peaceful and somewhat secluded beach. In 1912, a long sinuous body was seen in the bay, by a Mr Stone, along with two other unnamed people. The group had first spotted a dark object moving rapidly in the water. As they looked at it, they believed that it was moving in an undulating manner. None of the group could positively identify what it was, other than that it seemed to be a large living creature. As they continued their observations, a sailing vessel moved towards the object, which seemed to cause the creature to sink from view immediately. (This incident was described in the *Week-end Natal Advertiser* Durban, 8 March 1924.)

The South

The eighth-century *Anglo-Saxon Chronicle* mentions 'Wondrous Adders that were to be seen in the land of the South Saxons'. *Ethelward's Chronicle* of AD 770 records:

'Monstrous serpents were seen in the country of the Southern Angles that is called Sussex.' And there are other early tales about serpents.

A small area of the ancient Wealden forest, near Horsham, is called St Leonard's Forest, so named after one of the dragon legends that is set there. It is said that St Leonard, a sixth-century French hermit, once lived there, and during a long battle with a dragon which frequented the forest, which he eventually won, St Leonard was injured. It is said that God made white lilies spring forth from the ground where the saint's blood fell. He also asked what reward St Leonard wanted for freeing the local people from the dragon; the saint asked that snakes should be banished from the forest and nightingales, which had disturbed his prayers, should be silenced. Dr Andrew Borde, in the sixteenth century, confirmed that the nightingales did not sing because they disturbed the devotions of a forest hermit. There is no proof that St Leonard, a French Saint and Martyr, ever visited Sussex. Another version of the tale says that he asked for the snakes to be made deaf, and this is echoed in another piece of superstition in Sussex: that, on their bellies, adders have written the words:

> If I could hear as well as see,
> No mortal man should master me.

There is a second, much later story about a dragon in St Leonard's Forest. An unusually detailed account is given in a pamphlet produced in 1614 and, like so many scary tales, it is thought by some to have been concocted by smugglers to keep people away from the area. A copy can be found in the Library of the Sussex Archaeological Society, in a document called *The Harleian Miscellany*.

A Discourse relating a strange and monstrous Serpent (or Dragon) lately discovered, and yet living, to the great Annoyance and divers Slaughters both of Men and

Cattell, by his strong and violent Poyson. In Sussex, two miles from Horsam, in a Woode called St Leonard's Forrest, and thirtie miles from London, this present month of August, 1614. With the true Generation of Serpents.

In Sussex, there is a pretty market-towne, called Horsam, neare unto it a forrest, called St Leonard's Forrest, and there, in a vast and unfrequented place, heathie, vaultie, full of unwholesome shades, and overgrowne hollowes, where this serpent is thought to be bred; but, wheresoever bred, certaine and too true it is, that there it yet lives. Within three or four miles compasse, are its usual haunts, oftentimes at a place called Faygate, and it hath been seen within halfe a mile of Horsam; a wonder, no doubt, most terrible and noisome to the inhabitants thereabouts. There is always in his tracks or path left a glutinous and slimie matter (as by a small similitude we may perceive in a snaile's) which is very corrupt and offensive to the scent; insomuch that they perceive the air to be putrified withall, which must needes be very dangerous. For though the corruption of it cannot strike the outward part of a man, unless heated into his blood; yet by receiving it in at any of our breathing organs (the mouth or nose) it is by authoritie of all authors, writing in that kinde, mortall and deadlie, as one thus saith: *Noxia serpentium est admixto sanguine pestis* – *LUCAN*. This serpent (or dragon, as some call it) is reputed to be nine feete, or rather more, in length, and shaped almost in the forme of an axeltree of a cart; a quantitie of thickness in the middest, and somewhat smaller at both endes. The former part, which he shootes forth as a necke, is supposed to be an elle long; with a white ring, as it were, of scales about it. The scales along his backe seem to be blackish, and so much as is discovered under his bellie, appeareth to be red; for I speak of no nearer description than of a reasonable ocular distance. For coming too neare it, hath already beene too dearly payd for, as you shall heare hereafter.

It is likewise discovered to have large feete, but the eye may be there deceived; for some suppose that serpents have no feete, but glide upon certain ribbes and scales, which both defend them from the upper part of their throat unto the lower part of their bellie, and also cause them to move much the faster. For so this doth, and rids way (as we call it) as fast as a man can run. He is of Countenance very proud, and at the sight of men or cattel, will raise his necke upright, and seem to listen and looke about, with great arrogancy. There are likewise on either side of him discovered, two great bunches so big as a large foote-ball and (as some thinke) will in time grow to wings; but God, I hope, will (to defend the poor people in the neighbourhood) that he shall be destroyed before he grow so fledge. He will cast his venome about four rodde from him, as by woeful experience it was proved on the bodies of a man and a woman comming that way, who afterwards were found dead, being poysoned and very much swelled, but not prayed upon. Likewise a man going to chase it, and as he imagined, to destroy it with two mastive dogs, as yet not knowing the great danger of it, his dogs were both killed, and he himselfe glad to returne with hast to preserve his own life. Yet this is to be noted, that the dogs were not prayed upon, but slaine and left whole: for his is thought to be, for the most part, in a coniewarren, which he much frequents; and it is found much scanted and impaired in the encrease it had woont to afford. These persons, whose names are hereunder printed, have seene this serpent, beside divers others, as the carrier of Horsam, who lieth at the White Horse in Southwarke, and who can certifie the truth of all that has been here related.

John Steele. Christopher Holder. And a Widow Woman dwelling nere Faygate.

As a point of curiosity, Iguanodon bones have been found in Tilgate Forest, not too far from St Leonard's Forest. Finally, it should be noted that there is a small place called Dragon's Green just to the south-west of the forest. While this may be a reference to the legend of the dragons in St Leonard's Forest, it may also be a reference to the personal name of Dragon. A family so named lived in nearby Cowfold, and gave their name to Dragon's Farm there, which can be traced back to 1682.

A famous dragon called a knucker lived in a pool near the village of Lyminster, which is still known as the Knucker Hole. The word 'knucker' can be traced back to the Saxon word *nicor* which means a water monster and can be found in the poem *Beowulf*. In Iceland, the word *nykur* means a water horse, and the German *nickel* is a form of goblin found underground in mines. A similar creature, though decidedly more friendly, could be found in Cornish mines, and was known as the knocker. In Scandinavia there are the *nacken* (water men) and *neck* (water spirits), in Estonia the *näkineiu* (mermaid) and *näkk* (singing water animal), in Finland the *näkki* (fearsome water spirit) and many more. It has also been suggested that the word comes from the Celtic *cnuc* or the Saxon *cnucl*, meaning a joint or junction. This also seems to be a reasonable conclusion, as pools were once seen as entrances to the underworld.

The Knucker Hole was for many years believed to be bottomless, and it was said that the six bell ropes of Lyminster church were tied together and let down without touching the bottom, although it is now known to be just 30 ft deep. The hole is fed from a strong underground spring which keeps the pool clear and the temperature of the water relatively constant throughout the year. The Knocker Hole dragon was a rampaging beast, noted for killing livestock and human beings (though some say only fair damsels), much to the annoyance of the local community, many of whom had lost maiden daughters to the creature. A water-based creature, it is also said that it could fly. One version of the story says the monster aggravated the King of Sussex to such an extent that he offered the hand of his daughter to anyone who could kill the beast. A journeyman knight slew the creature in bloody combat and afterwards settled down in Lyminster with the king's daughter. His gravestone can still be seen at Lyminster Church; it has been moved inside the church to avoid further weathering. The stone is medieval and bears no markings to suggest the identity of the owner, but there is a cross which overlies a herring-bone type pattern. Folklore claims that this represents the knight's sword lying on the ribs of the dead dragon. Another version says that the pattern was caused by the dragon's claws as it tried to dig down to its slayer. It is said that a local child in the 1930s was sufficiently convinced of the truth of the tale to leave snapdragons on the grave.

Another version has it that it was a local Sussex man who killed the dragon, not a wandering knight. He was a farmer's boy, Jim Pulk from the village of Wick (others claim he came from Arundel). He dispatched the dragon by baking a huge pie laced with poison, which he put on the back of a cart and left by the Knucker Hole. The creature ate the lot, along with the horses and the cart that delivered it. It soon died and brave Jim cut off its head with a scythe and removed it to the Six Bells Inn, where he and the local community could celebrate. Sadly, Jim died during the celebrations, allegedly from poison, either from the dragon's blood or from when he baked the pie.

Another story from Wick, this time involving one Jim Puttock, is similar, but in this case the dragon's death is attributed to both poison and an axe. The story is retold by an old hedger (Lillian Candlin, *Tales of Old Sussex*).

They do say, that at Dunna many years ago there was a gert dragon lived in that big pond there, Knucker his name was, and Knucker Hole we calls it to-day. And thisyer ole dragon, you know, he uster goo spannelling about the Brooks by night to see what he could pick up

for supper, like few horses, or cows maybe, he'd snap
'em up soon as look at 'em. Then bimeby he took to
sitting top o' Causeway, and anybody come along there,
he'd lick 'em up, like a toad licking flies off a stone. So
what with that, and him swimming in the River other-
while and sticking his ugly face up agin the winders in
Shipyard when people was sitting having their tea,
things was in a tidy old Humphrey up Arndel way, no
bounds.

So the Mayor of Arndel, as was then, he offered a
reward for anyone as ud put an end to en. I misremem-
ber ho much t'was, but something pretty big, I reckon.
Howsumever, everybody was so feared on en, that they
was unaccountable backward in coming forward, as you
might say.

So Mayor, he doubled the reward; and this time a
young chap from Wick put up for it. Now some people
says he was a Arndel man; but that an't true. Young
Jim Puttock his name was, and he came from Wick.
I've lived at Toddington all my life, so I reckon I
oughter know. Sides, my great-aunt, Judith, what lived
down along there where you turns up by they gert
ellum trees, just t'other side o' the line, uster say that
when she was a gal, there was a marn lived 'long o'
them as was courting a gal that 'ventually married a
kind of a descendant of this Jim Puttock. Let be how
t'wull, this Jim Puttock he goos to Mayor, and tells
him his plan. And Mayor he says everybody must give
en what he asks, and never mind the expense, 'cause
they oughter be thankful, anyway, for getting rid of the
Knucker.

So he goos to the smith and horders a gert iron pot
'bout so big. And he goos to the miller and asks en for
so much flour. And he goos to the woodmen and tells
'em to build a gert stack-fire in the middle o' the Square.
And when t'was done he set to and made the biggest
pudden' that was ever seen. And when t'was done – not

that t'was quite done, bit sad in the middle, I reckon, but that was all the better, like – they heaved en on to a timber-tug, and somebody lent en a team to draw it, and off he goos, bold as a lion.

All the people followed en as far as the bridge, but they dursn't goo no furder, for there was ole Knucker, lying just below Bill Dawes'es. Least his head was, but his neck and body-parts lay all along up the hill, past the station, and he was tearing up the trees in Batworth Park with his tail. And he sees thisyer tug a-coming, and he sings out, affable-like:

'How do, Man?'

'How do, Dragon?' says Jim.

'What you got there?' says Dragon, sniffing.

'Pudden,' says Jim.

'Pudden?' says Knucker. 'What be that?'

'Just you try,' says Jim.

And he didn't want no more telling – pudden, horses, tug, they was gone in a blink. Jimmy ud agone, too, only he hung on to one o' they trees what blew down last year.

'T'wern't bad,' says Knucker, licking his chops.

'Like another?' says Jim.

'Shudn't mind,' says he.

'Right,' says Jim. 'Bring ee one Sadernoon.'

But he knew better'n that, surelye. Fore long they hears en rowling about, and roaring and bellering fit to bust hissel. And as he rowls, he chucks up gert clods, big as houses, and trees and stones and all manner, he did lash about so with his tail. But that Jim Puttock, he weren't afeared, not he. He took a gallon or so with his dinner, and goos off to have a look at en. When he sees en coming, old Knucker roars out: 'Don't you dare bring me no more o' that 'ere pudden, young marn!'

'Why?' says Jim. 'What's matter?'

'Colly wobbles,' says the Dragon. 'Do set so heavy on me I can't stand un, nohows in de wurreld.'

'Shudn't bolt it so,' says Jim, 'but never mind, I got a pill here, soon cure that.'

'Where?' says Knucker.

'Here,' says Jim.

And he ups with an axe he'd held behind his back and cuts off his head.

Lyminster is not the only place with a Knucker Hole. The *Sussex Dialect Dictionary* tells us that they are 'springs, which rise in the flat lands of the South Downs. They keep at one level, are often 20 feet or so across and are reputed to be bottomless. The water is cold in summer but never freezes; in a frost it gives off a vapour, being warmer than the air. Knuckerholes are found at Lyminster, Lancing, Shoreham, Worthing and in many other "Flats".' The hole at Lancing was also believed to be bottomless. It was near an old inn called the Sussex Pad, which stood on the banks of the River Adur. Local belief held that the countryside was filled with such holes, and some believed that they continued down to the other side of the world.

Herm, to the east of Guernsey in the Channel Islands, is a small and unspoilt isle. In 1960 Mrs Hilda Bromley of Kensington, London, made contact with writer and Loch Ness monster author Tim Dinsdale, and told him of an incident which occurred there.

My husband, young sons, two governesses and myself were guests of Lord and Lady Perry (then Sir Percival and Lady Perry). It was August 1923, I think. It was an amazing 30-foot tide and at lunch we said how we would like to see how far out we could walk following the outgoing tide. Lady Perry said we must take a sailor or fisherman out with us, therefore Sir Percival put Mr Bannister in charge. Soon, 14 of us set out walking quickly each with a stout stick with a hook at the end, hoping to dislodge and catch lobsters. After walking and running for some time, we came to a large pool –

but what held us spellbound were marks on the seaweed as though something huge had come out of the pool and had dragged itself over the seaweed-covered sand to our right – we one and all turned, and followed the drag marks, (if I can remember rightly) for some considerable distance and then we came to an enormous pool – far larger than the first one, into which drag marks 5–6 feet in width, disappeared! [Mrs Bromley described these drag marks as looking like those from a farmer's harrow – the type towed behind a tractor]. We all stood amazed, 14 of us, what could it be? Then slowly, away in the middle of the pool, a large head appeared and a huge neck – but we did not see the body; there it stayed with its great black eyes gazing at us without fear – then slowly it sank back into the water. It was evident it had never seen a human being before. We joined hands and all stepped into the pool, to see if we could disturb the creature, but it was too large and deep for us to make any real impression.

Then Bannister said we would have to return as the tide was coming in rapidly – we asked to stay a little longer, but he insisted. On the way back he said he had been by the sea all his life and so had all his family, but he had never seen or heard of anything like it!

On our return, there was much talk and interest about the 'Monster' – and on visiting Loch Ness some years ago, the memory of it came back to me.

Mrs Bromley gave a brief description of the creature, saying that it had a neck 3–4 ft long and thick, and its mouth was like a sea lion's. The head was reminiscent of a seal's in shape, but was too heavy. She knew what a seal looked like and said that it was not a seal. The creature moved in a slow and ponderous manner and did not at all seem concerned by human attention. Mr Toby Bromley, claimed that, to him, 'it looked like a gigantic eel'.

The South-west

Berry Head is 1 mile east of Brixham on the south Devon coast, in the broad sweep of Torbay. In the summer of 1906, Mr A.J. Butler was fishing in his small sailing boat off the coast there. The weather was warm, visibility was good, and the water was reasonably calm – perfect conditions for a relaxing day's fishing. He noticed something of a commotion in the water close to his boat. Casting a fisherman's expert eye on the disturbance, he expected to see a surfacing fish. Instead, he was shocked to see a creature which he could only describe as 'a buff-coloured baby monster'. The creature, which he thought was at least 6 ft long and 5 in wide, wriggled past his boat. He described it as having serrated edges, and had the impression that these were 'set along with tiny fins'. The creature was quite flat 'like a broadsword blade'.

From this description, the creature would appear to resemble a young eel, although at 6 ft it was quite a size. Young eels are olive brown, which could appear as a 'buff colour'. The conger eel is a uniform grey-brown colour and does grow to a considerable size, well over the 6 ft Mr Butler estimated. It is not often known to swim close to the surface, but on occasion it may do so.

On 5 July 1912, at 6.30 a.m., Captain Ruser and the first mate of the German ship *Kaiserin Augusta Victoria*, saw a 20 ft eel-like creature thrashing about on the surface of the water near Prawle Point, close to Salcombe. He later said that he thought that the creature was about '20 ft long, 18 in thick and was a blue-grey colour on its back, white below'. It seemed to be in conflict with another sea animal, as it was violently whipping the water with its tail as though agitated by something below the water. Captain Ruser also claimed that the whole of the serpent's body had been in view during the sighting, and that there was no mistaking its reptilian form. This indicates some form of giant eel, although the term 'reptilian form' is somewhat confusing and does not tie in with his description.

Until the late nineteenth century, Salcombe was in the business of building schooners, an industry which provided the majority of the town with employment. It now has only a few thousand inhabitants, although it is rather more developed as a tourist area. The monster of Salcombe first made its presence known in August 1970, when four skin-divers who were about 40–80 ft under the water off Lannacombe Bay suddenly heard strange barking noises, the like of which they had never previously encountered. The noises became so persistent over the following couple of months that it became known as the 'Lannacombe bark'. Despite their frequency, no one encountered anything strange.

Around this time, the Salcombe Shark Angling Society reported that anglers had hooked something large in mid-channel. They had played it for a while before losing contact, but when the lines were reeled in, they found that their large and formidable hooks had been bitten in two! However, the strongest species of shark known to be found in British waters was incapable of such a bite.

News of the mystery quickly spread, but still no one had seen any sort of strange creature. As a result there was some scepticism, with many people dismissing the entire episode as pure nonsense. The Torbay branch of the British Sub-aqua Club attempted to make some sense of the mystery and expressed the opinion that the object encountered by the Shark Angling Society was, in all probability, nothing more than a giant conger eel. They had received reports of such a creature in the area from other experienced fishermen. Estimates of the creature's size were 8 ft long and approximately 120 lb in weight.

This seemed to be the end of the matter, but in June 1971, several independent reports were received, from both holidaymakers and local people, of a large and fearsome animal, which had made several appearances on the sea between Start Point and Lannacombe Bay. The witnesses accepted that there might well be a giant conger eel in the area, but the creature they saw bore no resemblance to any conger eel they had ever seen, and this was much bigger in both length and circumference.

Stephen Smith, an experienced fisherman from Leeds, was holidaying in the area in July of 1971. He had heard rumours of the monster, but did not believe them. He also found it difficult to accept the conger eel theory, as it seemed extremely exaggerated in size. As Mr Smith described to me, he was forced to change his mind when he saw the creature himself.

The weather was fine and the sea calm, I don't wear spectacles and have no problems with my eyesight, nor had I been drinking alcohol before or during the sighting. I am also in good physical health. The thing I saw must have been about twenty feet long, and was dark in colour; it gave the impression of having an oily skin. Its head was like the giant serpent-type you see in old drawings, or like a conger eel's, only four times the size. The neck was long and about the same thickness as the head from what I could see. There was a substantial body beneath the water. I knew this because every so often, parts of is back would break the surface as it moved forward. I would say that this was in an undulating or slithering-like motion. It created an incredible wash and commotion in the water.

I'm a keen fisherman, and am proud to say that I have fished all over the world, but never have I seen something like this. If it didn't sound so stupid and I didn't know better, I would say that it was a form of hybrid eel, but at twenty feet? It can't have been, there's no eel on record that size, there must be a more rational explanation, but I'm damned if I know what it is!

Harold T. Wilkins, author of *Monsters and Mysteries*, was out on the coastal waters of East Looe, Cornwall, on 5 July 1949, when, at around 11.30 a.m. in the company of another man, he saw two remarkable saurians, each measuring about

19–20 ft long. The creatures had bottle green heads, and swam one behind the other. Their middle parts remained under the water during the sighting, but Wilkins claims that the dorsal parts he saw were ridged or serrated, similar to old pictures of Chinese dragons. It seemed to him and his friend that the creatures were apparently chasing a shoal of fish up a tidal creek. Gulls swooped down towards the one in the rear, which had a piece of orange peel on its dorsal parts. Wilkins believed from what he saw of the monsters, that they resembled the plesiosaurus of Mesozoic times.

An article in the *West Briton* in 1875 carried the following report:

Portscatho. The sea serpent was caught alive in Gerrans Bay. Two of our fishermen were afloat, overhauling their crab pots about 400–500 yards from the shore, when they discovered the serpent coiled about their floating cork. Upon their near approach, it lifted its head and showed signs of defiance, upon which they struck it forcibly with an oar, which so far disabled it as to allow them to proceed with their work, after which they observed the serpent floating about near their boat. They pursued it, bringing it ashore yet alive for exhibition, soon after which, it was killed on the rocks and most inconsiderably cast into the sea.

The same newspaper reported another incident in 1926:

Mr Reese and Mr Gilbert, two fishermen, were trawling three miles south of Falmouth and caught themselves a sea monster. It was twenty feet long, had an eight-foot tail and a beak, which they thought was 2 feet long and 6 inches wide. It also had four scaled legs attached to the body, which had armour-like joints, and a wide flat back, which was covered in a matted brown hair. The creature managed to escape by tearing the nets and leaving a great gobbet of blood. It was reported that the two men had brought some of the hair ashore, and that the Plymouth Biological Observatory was consulted but were unable to offer any opinion.

Some forty-nine years later it was the *Falmouth Packet* which published another report of a sighting off the Falmouth coast. This creature, it is claimed, has continued to make frequent appearances ever since. It is so well known in the region that local people have provided it with a name – Morgawr, meaning 'Sea giant'.

On a sunny September evening in 1975, Mrs Scott of Falmouth and Mr Riley saw a huge creature off Pendennis Point. They described it as having a small head with two stumpy horns, and a long neck with what looked like coarse hair or bristles on it. As they watched, the creature dived for a few seconds and then reappeared, clutching what looked like a conger eel in its jaws. Mrs Scott said she would 'never forget the face on that thing' as long as she lived.

On 28th December 1975, Mr Gerald Bennett of Seworgan, wrote to the *Falmouth Packet*:

I myself, during the last Christmas holidays, witnessed the sighting of a similar creature [to that seen by Mrs Scott and Mr Riley] although until now I have remained reticent about it. It was off the shore at Durgan, Helford, about 4 p.m., near dusk. When I first spotted it, I thought it was a dead whale, but as I drew nearer it started to move away, smoothly, and I could see it was not a whale, nor like any creature seen round here. I judged that the part of it I could see above water was about 12 feet in length with an elongated neck.

Another similar sighting occurred here (on 14 July 1977), when it was reported to the author that a witness (Trevor

Hopliss) saw a strange creature swimming in the mouth of Helford River one afternoon. He described the creature as having an 'elongated neck' and that the visible part above the water was about 12 ft in length.

In January 1976, Mr Duncan Viner, a dental technician from Truro, saw something swimming in the water a few hundred yards off Rosemullion Head. Initially, he saw a dark hump, which he thought was the back of a whale, then a long neck reared up out of the water. He estimated the entire length of the creature to be around 30–40 ft. He monitored it for a few moments before it submerged.

Later that same month, Mrs Amelia Johnson, a holiday-maker from the London area, was out walking near Rosemullion Head when she saw a large creature rise to the surface in Falmouth Bay. She believed it had two humps and closely resembled 'a sort of prehistoric dinosaur thing, with a long neck, which was the length of lamp post' (*Falmouth Packet*, 13 December 1975). Then towards the end of January, a strange and mysterious carcass was washed up on the shore of Durgan Beach. It was found by Mrs Payne of Falmouth, and baffled those who saw it, since it was of no identifiable shape. Unfortunately, it was washed back out to sea before it could be officially examined.

On 5 March 1976, the *Falmouth Packet* received a letter and two photographs which were said to show a sea monster in Falmouth Bay. The letter, signed by Mrs Mary F., stated that the photographs were taken in early February 1976, when she had seen the monster off Trefusis Point. The mysterious correspondent, who never supplied her full name or address, nor the original negatives of the photographs, described the creature as being about 18 ft long, with a humped back, long neck and small head, and a blackish-brown colour. She sent a second letter to the *Falmouth Packet*, explaining that she had sold the original negatives to an 'American gentleman'.

The photographs caused a worldwide sensation and many visitors toured the coastline in the vain hope of catching a glimpse of the creature. Eventually, when the excitement had dwindled, researchers got on with the task of trying to assess the pictures' provenance. Many believed them to be authentic, but without a witness or the original negatives, there was some doubt as to how the claims could be substantiated.

Sea serpent sightings and incidents continued in the Falmouth region. Miss M. Jenkins told local people how a friend had seen a large snake-like creature swimming in the sea at Mylor some years previously. And on 4 May 1976, two London bankers, Tony Rogers and John Chambers, were fishing from the rocks off Parson's Beach, at the mouth of the Helford River when, 'suddenly, something rose out of the water about 150–200 yards away. It was greeny-grey in colour and appeared to have large humps. Another smaller one also appeared [this second creature was not witnessed by Chambers]. They were visible for about ten seconds and looked straight at us.'

In July or August 1976, George Vinnicombe, a Falmouth fisherman, and his friend John Cock of Redruth had an encounter with a strange sea creature which they claimed resembled a prehistoric monster with a back like corrugated iron (*Cornish Life*, August 1976).

We were fishing over wartime wrecks in the channel [25 miles south, off the coast at Lizard Point]. It was a beautiful calm, clear day. I looked over the starboard side and saw this thing in the water. I thought it was a boat upside down. We went over to investigate and it looked like the back of a dead whale but with three humps, and was about 18–20 feet long. The body was black but a lighter colour under the water. Then suddenly this head came out of the water, about three feet from the body. It just looked at my mate and we just looked at one another. He said 'What the hell have we got here?' Then the head vanished and the body sank away. I've been fishing for 40 years and it's the first time I've ever seen anything like that. Folk have told me about monsters and I always took it with a pinch of salt, but now I'm prepared to believe anything I see out there.

Another report (*Cornish Life*, October 1976) which was not taken too seriously at the time (presumably because children were the witnesses), occurred on Sunday, 12 September 1976. Brother and sister Allan and Sally Whyte, were exploring Grebe Beach when they came across a long brown living object, which was about 15–20 ft long. The creature slithered from the beach into the sea before anyone else could see it.

An incident which was taken rather more seriously occurred on Wednesday, 17 November 1976, when the witness was the editor of *Cornish Life*, David Clarke, accompanied by Anthony 'Doc' Shiels. Clarke later reported in the December issue:

After discussing Morgawr with Doc Sheils, he agreed to my taking some photos of him standing by the Helford River 'invoking' the monster by magical means! Early in the morning of Wednesday 17th last, we drove to the village of Mawnan and clambered down the cliffs onto the rocky beach below the church. I duly took pictures of Doc waving his stick at the waves and a few more of the river, as fishing boats left the Helford on a rising tide. Doc also took some colour photos of areas where Morgawr had previously been seen. While I was waiting for him, trying to keep warm by throwing stones for my dog to chase, Doc drew my attention to an object half way across the river – a small dark head poking out of the water. We both stood on large rocks for a better view and I attached a telephoto lens to my camera. The object slowly moved nearer and I could see that it was definitely a head, probably a seal. It came within seventy or eighty feet and started to move very slowly up and down the river in a zig-zag pattern. It was only when I saw its side that I observed that the greenish black head was supported on a long arched neck, more slender than that of a seal. In the wave troughs at least four or five feet of neck were visible. There was a slow movement of water stretching back behind the head and neck for about ten feet, and at one point, a gently rounded shiny black body broke the surface. (Doc later said that he had earlier seen two humps.) The head was rounded with a blunt nose and on top of the head were two small rounded buds.

Doc and I were both busily shouting to one another as we took photos and I must admit to feeling rather afraid as the creature surged back and forth. It had obviously seen us. At this point my dog, demanding more stones to be thrown, began to bark. The head of the creature turned to us and its mouth opened as it slowly sank and vanished in a swirl of water. We stood for another half an hour looking for more signs, but nothing else appeared.

On Friday 13 May 1977, Mr and Mrs Arthur Wood of Plymstock were taking an early morning stroll along Pendennis Point when two strange incidents occurred within an hour of each other (*Western News*, 24 February 1980). The couple first saw a bright orange ball of light in the sky with green fire emanating from it. As if this was not enough for them to ponder over, an hour later they saw a dark, strange creature heading out to sea. Neither of them could positively identify just what it was, it seemed too large to be a seal or any other sea creature known to frequent the area. They were never fully able to explain what it was.

On 20 February 1980, Geoffrey Watson, a sociology undergraduate from the Thames Polytechnic and a member of the Loch Ness Monster Association of Explorers, was patrolling cliffs and beaches in the Trefusis and Mawnan areas. He had made a special visit to the region in the hope of catching a glimpse of Morgawr, and of photographing it should it rise from the water. Watson could not believe his luck when he had a one-minute sighting of a black object which surfaced about 300 yd from shore. He told the *Western News*: 'The first protrusion was about nine inches above the surface. Farther back, there was what might have been a hump and then another hump at about equal distance. Of course, it might have been a log, but it certainly moved closer and closer to the shore and then disappeared.'

Watson returned to London where he had his film developed, thinking that he might have caught Morgawr on camera. He was to be disappointed, as the developed photographs were far too indistinct to make out any definite shape or object in the water. It is interesting to note his cautious approach to what he had seen; this is typical of those involved in Loch Ness research, a reluctance to state the obvious, and a need to apply rational reasoning to what must have been an irrational situation. Presumably the incident must have excited him, and he must have spoken of it to others, as someone contacted the press. Yet when questioned by a reporter he appeared doubtful about what it was he actually saw. As someone who was used to watching the waters of Loch Ness, he must have had some idea as to whether it was a genuine sighting or not. Could it be that when confronted by the press, he became concerned about the stigma attached to those who claim to have seen sea serpents?

In July 1985, two girls, Jenny Halstead and Alice Lee of Hebden Bridge, Yorkshire, were on a cycling holiday in the Falmouth area when they claimed to have a sighting off Rosemullion Head. Jenny said, as reported in the *Falmouth Packet*, 26 July 1985:

At some time between 6.30 and 7 p.m., from a position at Rosemullion overlooking the sea, we witnessed a genuine living monster of the deep, which we believe must be your legendary monster Morgawr. The creature's back broke the surface and looked rather like a massive overgrown black slug. We both watched the animal for about ten seconds as it wallowed in the water. Then the creature sank beneath the waves and did not surface again. Even though we had a camera to hand, we were too astounded by the sight of the monster to think of taking a photograph until it was too late.

On 24 August 1999, at around 4.30 p.m., Josh Tomkins, a fisherman, was out with his son in a boat off the Falmouth coastline, he told me, when they both saw:

... a huge semi circular shaped mound rise from the water, we were about a mile off shore. Initially I thought it was a dead body rising to the surface. As we watched the mound, it dropped back under the water, causing a terrific swell. Moments later it resurfaced, about fifty yards from our boat. I could now see that it was no dead body, but a large creature. My son thought it was the back of a whale as this was the most logical explanation we could find. Our opinions altered when, about ten yards in front of the mound, a small head appeared above the surface. The head lifted out of the water only very slightly but sufficient for us both to see part of what seemed a long slender neck. It then dropped back down and the whole thing submerged in a colossal water disturbance.

We were both shocked by the immense size of the creature; it was like no fish I have ever seen, in fact, it wasn't like anything I had ever seen before. I am pretty sure it must have been 'Morgawr' the sea monster. I didn't believe in this before and I am still not certain now, but that thing sure did look like a dinosaur-like creature. I would think it was dark brown or black, but its coloration was not evenly distributed, it seemed to be patchy in parts, slightly lighter in areas. We both saw its eyes, no ears and no mouth. It made no noise, just created a huge wash as it submerged. After seeing it, I would not be too happy about going out into open

101

water after dark in a small boat; it's very large and could inflict some serious damage to a small vessel.

In late August 1999 (possibly the same time as the Tomkins sighting), Mrs Elsie Moran of the Keighley area in West Yorkshire saw something remarkably similar in the water off Falmouth. She told me:

I was sat enjoying the afternoon sunshine looking out to sea and not particularly thinking about anything, when I saw about one hundred yards seawards a black object suddenly appear in the water. It appeared before my eyes and seemed to be stationary. I would estimate that it was about ten feet long and, at its highest point out of the water, about two feet. As I watched, something rose out of the water close to the 'hump-like' mound. It appeared to rise to an angle of about 45 degrees and looked a bit like the curved end of a question mark, but more angular. I then realized that it was either the tail or the head and neck of some large marine animal. This dipped in and out of the water several times, its highest point appeared to be moving from side to side, like the head of a snake looking around. It remained in sight for about a minute or so before sinking from view. I could see white foam on the sea surface where it disappeared. It wasn't like any sort of animal or fish I had ever seen, nor could I imagine what it looked like as a whole, but it was very large and looked quite cumbersome.

The most recent sighting off Falmouth, which was reported to the author, occurred on 16 May 2000, when Derek and Irene Brown were touring the area in their caravan and had stopped to have refreshments overlooking the sea.

The sea was quite calm, not choppy or heavily disturbed, and the weather was reasonably good, by that I mean that no mist or rain was falling and visibility was clear for some considerable distance out to sea. As we sat next to our caravan overlooking the sea, I saw something appear in the water, perhaps 200 yd away, certainly no more. I took no notice of the object as the sea does throw up debris and driftwood and I had no reason to concentrate on the object. I looked away and then heard Irene ask me 'What is that out there?' I looked again and she was pointing to the object I had glimpsed a few moments earlier. The object now took the form of defined humps, two of them very close together. I would think that overall they measured about 15 ft. I estimated this from my height, I am just over 6 ft tall. The humps were still, and as I sat searching for an explanation to give to Irene, a periscope-like object came out of the water very close to these humps. It was moving in a flexible manner, not at all rigid. I would think it looked close to the stance a cobra or a python takes, raising its head and neck, before it strikes. Irene shouted 'It's an octopus', but it clearly wasn't. I took the humps to be the back of a large body, the periscope-like object being a head and neck. I told Irene that I thought it was a monster and to get the camera from the car as we should take a picture of it.

As she got up to leave me, the creature seemed to roll forward, dipping head-first into the water. There was a huge commotion as it disappeared. Irene came back with the camera but it had gone. We stayed to look out for the creature for about another hour, but it never resurfaced.

I cannot begin to explain how we felt about what we saw. We decided to keep it to ourselves, as no one would believe us and we would look stupid. I think the creature you are looking for is not one known to zoological science, but more to archaeologists who search for fossilized remains of creatures that existed many millions of years ago. This may sound stupid and far-fetched, but somehow I believe that some of them have lived on and exist in our waters. It wasn't a fish, more like a water-based dinosaur, like something you see in those 1960 films about prehistoric times.

I am not a storyteller, nor do I wish to capitalize upon what my wife and I saw, but felt that I should report this to someone, as it genuinely happened.

I am now aware that a number of the reported Falmouth sightings were concocted as a hoax. The information I have received indicates that the majority of the 1975 and 1976 sightings were part of the same conspiracy. One person has privately confessed to a part in the hoax, and in particular the forgery involving the 'Mary F.' photographs. It also seems that several other hoaxers played a part in producing false evidence of Morgawr sightings. Doubts have been expressed in the past about the authenticity of some of the photographs of Morgawr, but these have always been vehemently denied. Now, sadly, it seems that the majority of the documentary and illustrative material relating to the mid-1970s sightings of Morgawr, should be dismissed as irresponsible testimony. I should point out that I am not casting doubt on earlier and more recent sightings of the creature, the majority of which have been reported by genuine witnesses. However, for the benefit of future researchers, the sightings of Messrs Clarke, Shiels, Riley, Viner, Vinnicombe, Chambers, Rogers and Bennett, and Mrs Scott, are believed to be complete fabrications.

A curious creature was washed ashore at Prah Sands, Cornwall on 7 June 1928. The creature went largely unrecorded, until 11 December 1933, when *The Times* published the following account by Mr E.J. Garmeson:

I saw the dead body of a very curious animal washed up on shore at Praa [local spelling] Sands in the Spring of 1928. It had been killed by the storm which threw it up and the head had been torn off, but it must have been not unlike the Loch Ness 'monster' as described by

Commander Gould. Several feet remained of the snake-like neck and what remained of the body measured from neck to tail approximately 30 feet, while it was some 3 to 4 feet in diameter at the thickest part of the body barrel. There were four feet-like flippers for swimming and the tail tapered to a point. The colour was a dirty white with some traces of pink, the skin was coarse and covered in places with hair or bristles, while the bones, which were of considerable size, were more fish-like than animal.

Unfortunately, the position was such that it was impossible to get a satisfactory photograph, and the situation was too out of the way for any proper investigation to be made.

Mr Garmeson estimated the creature to be about 20 ft in length and the neck portion from which he believed the head had been torn off, was about 2 ft 6 in long and some 6 in in diameter. It had continuous skin around it, and no vertebrae at the torn end.

Garmeson also noted coarse hair or bristles, light in colour, in patches on the body. The skin texture resembled that of a pig, and the bristles were pig-like, and the skin colour was pinkish white, but tending more to white. There was no trace of a dorsal fin or any flukes on the tail which measured about 4 ft in diameter.

Someone else who saw the carcass, Major Hutchinson, believed it to be longer than 20 ft. He claimed that the neck was like that of a giraffe and tapered, the head end being jagged. At the hind end of the creature were two fins or flippers. He felt there may have been similar flippers at the front end, but he was not certain. Those he saw were 1½–2 ft long and at the outer end were what appeared to be bristles. He too claimed to see thick, coarse hair, although he remembered them as being dark in colour and about 5 in in length. In between the hairs, whose roots might have been ¾ in apart, the skin was light brown. Coastguards who examined the creature on 7 June 1928, reported the stranding to the Natural History Museum, and it was reckoned to be a shark. They noted that the creature was very much mutilated and decomposed and would have to be buried immediately.

Thus the case of the Prah Sands stranding ended, without the creature ever being examined by a qualified zoologist, and yet being classified a shark, possibly a basking shark. Perhaps they were right, but what about the hairs which were seen by at least two independent witnesses? If it had hairs, then it could not have been a shark, but might have been a member of the seal family (pinniped). Yet no pinniped known to British waters can reach such a size. The coast-guard station officer's wife also looked at the carcass but could not recall seeing any hair or bristles, although she admitted that she did not look for them. Could two totally independent witnesses imagine coarse bristly hair on the skin? Sadly, the problem will never be resolved. The carcass was buried close to where it was washed ashore, and was never again removed for full examination. The authorities have it recorded as a basking shark.

In August 1906 the transatlantic ocean liner *St Andrew* of the American Phoenix Line, was passing Land's End, when the first and third officers and a wealthy American passenger, Mr Percy Hopley, a cattleman, saw an 18 ft chunk of animal with a body some 5 ft in circumference and a set of jaws with great 'fin-like' teeth.

The creature suddenly appeared at the surface; it was like no fish or marine creature I have seen. It was serpent-like with a vast body, far thicker in circumference than those we are used to seeing. For a moment it raised its head and displayed a set of powerful jaws, which were armed with great fin-like teeth. I drew it to the attention of Spicer and Cuming, the first and third officers on board the *St Andrew*. They too were shocked by what they saw. Cuming later told me that he believed it to be the great Sea Serpent, a creature who lived at great depths. He had never before seen such a creature. We discussed the reluctance of natural history to accept that this creature exists; how they can do so when it is there, I do not know.

After a few moments, the creature rolled forward and dived back beneath the water, leaving a huge surface disturbance. Mr Spicer asked me not to discuss the sighting with other passengers as it could make some nervous.

As a result of an article in *The Times* of 9 December 1933, Mrs C.J. Adkins of Uppingham wrote in to describe a sighting she had off Padstow in 1907, along with her cousin.

What we saw, about half to three quarters of a mile away, corresponds closely to sketches 1 and 4 of your article today. There was a long neck ending in a smallish head, but not reared quite so high out of the water as in sketch 1. Then, a space of water and a long series of small humps, separated by spaces of water exactly as in sketch 4. I flew into the house for field glasses, but by the time I returned with them, the creature had sunk.

Of course, we got mercilessly teased and told that it must have been a school of porpoises. But I know a school of porpoises when I see one, and we were quite convinced that we had seen some extraordinary monster, though I cannot give a definite date. We thought the creature was at least 50 feet long, it was moving very lazily across the bay towards the estuary of the Camel River.

The *Western Morning News* of Saturday, 14 September 1907 reported the following story of a sighting at Tintagel:

Mr Edward S Dodgson of Jesus College, Oxford, who is staying at Clifton House, Tintagel, says: 'At 11.45 am., today [Thursday] I was seated with the Reverend T.C.

Davies, MA, of the Queen's College, Oxford, Chaplain of an almshouse at Sheffield, who is now staying at this hotel, on the edge of the cliffs of the cove known as Gulla Stem, at Tintagel, when he called my attention to a black object that was moving at a distance of about 200 yards very rapidly along the calm surface of the sea towards Tintagel Head.

In about a minute, it had disappeared behind the cliff that bounds the cove on the west. It was a sea serpent, at last 20 feet long, holding its large head, with apparently some kind of crest or mane upon it, aloft. Unfortunately, we had no telescope with us, less still a Kodak wherewith to take its likeness. We are told that no such beast is known to have been seen here. I have, however, seen a large yellow and green snake swimming quite close to me in the sea at Curunna in the north-west of Spain, and smaller ones like it in Spanish rivers. This fact may be worth recording as a contribution to the Natural History of North Cornwall.

The report provoked a response from an A.C. Mason of Tintagel, who supported Dodgson's claim in correspondence to the paper on Monday, 16 September 1907.

I write to tell you that on Thursday morning last at 11.45 am., I was sitting with a friend, Miss Hawley, on the north-east cliff of Gulla Stem Cove, Tintagel, when we distinctly saw the black object which Mr Dodgson has described in your columns today as a sea serpent. His description exactly tallies with what we saw, but his words hardly give the impression of the extreme rapidity with which the beast moved through the water, which was very calm at the time.

In the same newspaper, Mr T.V. Hodgson of the Museum and Art Gallery, Beaumont Park, Plymouth, dismissed the Dodgson sighting. He felt it was more likely to be a ribbonfish or oarfish. He further claimed that some twenty-five specimens of this species had been caught in British coastal waters. But it is doubtful that the creature was a ribbonfish, since these fish are not black, but virtually transparent. So such a creature would therefore not be clearly visible at a distance of 200 yd. Furthermore, the creature seen by the witnesses held its crested head high. Granted, ribbonfish do have a crested head, but they do not have the muscle tissue to support them above the water.

The Times of 17 October 1882 contained the following letter from the Reverend E. Highton, Vicar of Bude, written on 12 October 1883. Previous reporters, initially Heuvelmans but others after him, have claimed that this incident occurred on 11 October 1882, but research indicates that this is not so.

Yesterday at 4.30 p.m., a remarkable sight was seen from Sommerlease, Bude, [an open down]. I saw a long low dark object about a mile and a half from shore, skimming along the surface of the sea, the back of the creature being a little above the top of the water. It kept on its course at a rate which I calculated to be about twenty-five miles an hour, never once disappearing entirely the whole time it was in sight.

It was watched by seven friends who were with me and myself for about ten minutes and by that time it had passed over a considerable space of water, between four and five miles, I should think. The creature's length was variously guessed by us to be from fifty to eighty feet. Just once a larger mass appeared out of the water than at any other time, but for not more than a couple of seconds. This was at the end, apparently, of the creature but it scarcely looked like a tail. It seemed more like a curl in some long thin monster.

In 1911, William Cook was taking three ladies by boat from Instow, where the Rivers Taw and Torridge meet to Westward Ho!, further to the south in Bideford Bay. He changed course to avoid going on some rocks, but suddenly found that the rocks were moving. They were part of a living creature. Concerned for his and his passengers' safety he at once headed for shore.

> The thing then stretched itself out in an undulating coil, lashing the water. We calculated its length from 60–90 feet, and its head did not appear. The body was round, and about the size of a 30-gallon cask. Almost black fins, with short intervals, ran the entire length of its back. Its body was of a brownish grey, with scales, very similar to a gigantic snake.
>
> The creature made off on to the other side of the bay, in the direction of Clovelly.

The West

An incident that occurred in the Bristol Channel was recorded in the *Liverpool Echo* on Tuesday 30 April 1907 and the *Daily Chronicle*, on the same date.

A Clevedon (Somerset) correspondent forwards the following story to the *Daily Chronicle* of a strange adventure, which he says befell Mr McNaughton, a Scottish visitor to the town. The incident, which occurred on Sunday last [28 April 1907] was, he says, witnessed by many spectators.

> Mr. Mc Naughton was quietly rowing in a little skiff about a mile off the Clevedon Pier when a long snake-like object, which he describes as being 'like a huge mummy with large sunken eyes enveloped in a sort of hairy flap', suddenly appeared at the rear of the boat, about twenty yards away. It approached by a series of leaps and dives, causing the sea to be greatly disturbed. Mr McNaughton says, that by plunging the oars into the surf, he endeavoured to keep his antagonist at bay. But his efforts were only momentarily successful. In a few seconds it had reached within a few yards of the boat.

'I can only dimly recollect what happened,' he continued. 'The flabby monster seemed to leap straight out of the water – straight as an arrow at me. I hardly know what I did. I think I must have ducked and crashed the oar into the creature; at any rate I was flung violently into the water. When I regained the surface I managed to clamber into the boat. My terrible antagonist was nowhere in sight. In a dazed condition, scarcely knowing what I did, I succeeded in reaching Portishead.'

Mr McNaughton's account is quite incredible, not only because he apparently suffered a physical attack from an unknown sea creature, which to most people would be a horrific event, but also because our intrepid hero not only fought off his foe, but continued on his journey, soaking wet and presumably in a state of shock, rowing several miles to Portishead in what he describes as a 'dazed condition'. Most people would simply have headed for the nearest shore and abandoned their voyage as impossible in such conditions.

The description of the creature, first described as 'snake-like' then later 'flabby', also seems contradictory. Likewise, its movements were unnatural, leaping and diving forward, then leaping straight out of the water towards him 'straight as an arrow'. The account does not give the statements of the 'many witnesses'. The occurrence cannot be denied, nor disproved, but it is fair to say that the report may not be a true representation of events.

This was not the first sighting of a strange creature in the Bristol Channel. *The Graphic* of 20 October 1883, in a column titled 'Scraps', revealed:

The inevitable sea serpent has turned up again. This time he has been seen going down the Bristol Channel towards the Atlantic at a rate of twenty-five miles per hour, and afterwards he was noticed on the north coast of Cornwall. The monster was about half a mile long, and left a greasy trail behind him.

Kilve, in Somerset, can boast a tale of a creature whose existence can be supported by fossilized remains. Blue Ben, as it was known, resided in a tunnel beneath Kilve and Putsham. The thick mud which surrounded the tunnel where he lived created a dangerous obstacle as it was so deep that it would permanently trap anything or anyone who stepped or fell into it, so Blue Ben built a causeway to allow him easy access to the cave. According to the tale, one day he slipped off the causeway into the mud, which instantly trapped him. Unable to move he was sucked deeper into the slime and drowned. Curiously, a fossilized icthyosaurus (a reptilian fish-lizard believed to have died out in the Cretaceous Period) was found near this location in the last century and is now on display in Taunton County Museum. Many people claim these remains are of Blue Ben, and their presence does of course raise the question of whether there might be some truth in the tale of Blue Ben. Could it be that some form of subspecies of the icthyosaur survived the passage of time and was seen by eye-witnesses, thus creating the legend, which transformed it into an evil dragon-type monster?

Lancashire too had its problems with such beasts. The Dragon of Wantley allegedly had forty-four iron teeth and a long sting in its tail. A brave knight named More, of More Hall, slew this creature in a two-day battle in a local well, by lancing it with a spike. The Vurm (Worm) of Shervage Wood was another such beast, destroyed on this occasion by a woodsman who chopped it in two. Confused, the two halves failed to join up and moved in opposite directions, so the creature died. There is a Dragon's Cross at Bilbrook, believed to have been named after this creature.

In June 1999, a correspondent, Miss Sheila Smith, informed me of the following incident which occurred whilst out walking with her brother, Edwin, in the late spring or early summer of 1994. It was a warm sunny afternoon and visibility was very good.

We were out walking with our two dogs on a very fine day, along the banks of the River Ribble, in Preston, Lancashire. From quite a distance up the river, I cannot say just how far, I saw a very tall thin object protruding from the water. At that point I was only casually glancing and joked to my brother, 'Look, the Loch Ness monster', and we thought no more of it.

Nevertheless I kept my eye on it, and as we walked on – we were gradually getting closer to it – I was still trying to make out what it could be, my thoughts being that it was probably a tree or the branch of a tree stuck in the river. Then just about thirty seconds later as we drew level with it, this thing just completely submerged into the river. It created a cascade of ripples, it even made the dogs curious, and we were nearly speechless.

When we both drew breath, our conversation was like, 'Good God, what was that?' The both of us felt it would not have been a tree because it was quite a flowing current on that day and we did not feel a tree would have made all those ripples like it did.

A couple of minutes later, two men were walking our way, and they kept glancing down into the river; at this point we did not say anything to them about what we had seen. I think we both felt silly to mention anything and we were not entirely sure what we had seen. We resumed our walk somewhat behind these two men, and noticed how they continued to keep peering down into the river, obviously looking for something.

Eventually they headed back towards us, when we asked what they were looking for. The reply was 'elvers', but we did not mention what we had seen, and neither did we know at that time what an elver was.

On our return home, having found out an elver is a baby eel, it stands to reason I suppose if there are young there must also be adults in the same river ... I feel certain that it was a living creature, which must have stood all of 4 ft, possibly a bit more.

Sheila Smith went on to describe the creature as being black or possibly dark brown in colour and measuring about 1 ft in circumference, with no visible head. The exact location of the sighting was close to Preston docks and Marina, although she states that this particular of the River Ribble is particularly quiet.

Looking at the information provided and speaking to fishermen, it seems that this area is a popular venue for eel fishing, and this may provide an explanation to the mystery. An eel, though, is not known for its ability to stand upright in the water. It could have been an otter, or even something lifelike dropping from a nearby tree, although Miss Smith recalls no trees in the area.

According to local folklore, the River Ribble requires one human life every seven years in order to quell its power.

Further up the west coast there is a tale of the sea-worm of the Solway, which apparently made its way up the Solway Firth from the sea. It was attacked by the entire community who lanced it with sharpened stakes, and finally became grounded, taking three days to die. It was eventually devoured by birds and fish.

Maryport, on the coast of Cumbria, was once an industrious fishing town and has a community of fishermen, many of whom have fished the seas off the Maryport coast for many years. Tommy Graham was born and bred by the sea, and much of his life has been spent in the waters off Maryport. In the afternoon 14 August 1993 whilst out in a small boat off Silloth, Tommy saw something which he had only heard other fishermen speak of during his fifty-three years at sea. He told me:

'It was about 2.15 p.m., and I was out enjoying a pleasant afternoon doing a bit of private fishing from my

small boat. I reckon I was about half a mile from the
Silloth shoreline. I have always been one for being a bit
sceptical about tales of monsters and sea serpents. Many
of my fishing mates over the years have told me of their
personal experiences. I always thought it a bid odd that
folk would talk of such things when they know people
will laugh at them. Monsters of any description could
not have been further from my mind when I suddenly
saw a commotion in the water about fifty yards out to
sea to my right. Thinking that it might be a porpoise or
something, I watched. A bloody great disturbance of the
surface water followed, but for a few seconds nothing
happened. Then, all of a sudden, up came this great dark
hump, about five feet long and 18 inches out of the
water; honestly I thought it was a whale it was so big.
My heart missed a beat or two, as I realized I was too
close to this thing, and that it could cause some damage
to my boat if it inadvertently collided with me. I hardly
had time to think about it, when up popped a submarine-
periscope-like head and neck; this was about three foot
in front of the breaking body I just described. I'm not
trained in these sort of things but the thing I saw resembled more of a dinosaur-like creature than any fish I've
ever seen, and I think I've seen just about everything in
my time. I have been on boats where we have mistaken
floating seaweed for a sea monster before. Only when we
got near did we realize what it really was.

The thing I saw could not be mistaken for anything
but a large living creature. There seemed to be some
kind of water disturbance on the side of the hump or
breaking body I could see. From the size of body parts
I saw, it must have been about thirty feet long, dark
brown to black in colour, and had a neck which stood
about three feet tall of the water. This seemed to have a
sort of eel-like head on the top, by that I mean the head
looked like that of an eel and was the same circumference and size as the neck. It seemed to look round, and

in one movement flopped forward, dropping its neck and head into the water, disappearing in a huge foam of water. I got out of the area as quickly as I could and made for the safety of the shore.

I can still see it in my mind now and, as sure as the light of day, I am not exaggerating one little bit. The sea was reasonably calm and the sun shining through a light cloud. My eyesight is good, I couldn't really mistake this creature from such a short distance. Later, I told my wife of what I saw. I told her that it was something that shouldn't be living in this day and age, but it was. I'm no fool and don't want the hassle of being the object of public amusement at my stage of life, so I have kept quiet about it until now.

Asked if he could place the creature into any category, Tommy replied, 'Dinosaur.' He also said that the 'upturned boat' shape of the hump is the most common description among his fishermen friends who had also seen these creatures.

Fishermen do not talk about sea serpents, they are too busy concentrating on finding fish, a basic necessity for the occupation and making money. Every so often you meet with other crews who have seen strange objects rise out of the sea, too high to be waves in calm seas, these they describe as looking like the exposed hull of a small upturned boat, or tyre-shape, they sink from view. No one has ever described to me a moving submarine periscope object rising in front of the hump, like the creature I saw. I've never heard of any stories about sea monsters off this stretch of water, other than those told privately by fishermen. I don't know what else I can add, other than I know what I saw and I didn't imagine it.

A correspondent of mine, Miss Wendy Ferguson, related an incident which occurred off Skinburness, about 20 miles south of Carlisle on the coast of Cumbria, in the Irish Sea.

My friend [David Alderson] and I were looking out towards the sea at Skinburness, it was 17 April 1979 at around 3.00 p.m. It was a cold afternoon, cloudy and the sea looked brown in colour. We were stood on sand dunes and the sea was, I would guess, half a mile away. David carries binoculars with him as he is a bit of an ornithologist.

As we were looking out across the water, we both saw a curious long curly shape emerge on the surface, about a mile away from us. Through the naked eye it seemed to wriggle. David looked through the binoculars and shouted out, 'It's Nessie, honestly, look.' He handed me the binoculars and it took a few seconds for me to focus on anything, but when I did I saw an animal, which I think must have been thirty to forty feet long, with what looked like three humps and a hook-shaped neck, which stood apart from the humps. The neck was standing above the water at an angle of about 45 degrees, perhaps four feet tall. I could not describe any head, as the thing was too far away. David took back the binoculars, and watched it for about two minutes before it submerged; it was moving in the direction of Silloth. I did question my sanity as I tried to assimilate it to a known object. I really don't know what was going through my mind at the time, as I was excited and shocked. I keep asking myself what the tall hook-like object was at what we took to be the front of the creature; this was in view throughout the entire sighting. As we watched it, the hook-like neck seemed to fall forward and the entire thing submerged. The only justifiable conclusion I can draw from the sighting is that it was the neck and head of some living creature.

David continued to watch the area where we last saw the object. He must have studied the water in that area for about fifteen minutes, but nothing more was seen, just the brown-coloured water. We tried to see if it could have been a wave formation, but nothing remotely similar could be seen. Later that night, I told some people about our sighting. They said it was probably birds flying in a row close to the water surface, but that doesn't explain it either, as there was not a single thing in the area after the object had submerged, no bird, no floating debris, not a thing. I now know that it must have been a large living creature; it's just a shock to see something like that at Skinburness. People have since made jokes about it, saying it must have been a lost Nessie, or a Russian submarine, which is strange, as one of my initial thoughts was that it might be a submarine, but when I looked closer, this was impossible, it was nothing like a submarine. If I had to say it looked like anything I would say a huge snake or an eel.

The earliest report we have from the Isle of Man comes from a 1924 edition of *Worldwide* magazine and recalls a sighting which occurred some time around 1910. It came from Vice-Admiral Robert Anstruther, who at the time was on board HMS *Caesar* between the Isle of Man and the northern coast of Ireland.

In the first dog watch I was standing on the bridge, when suddenly something shot out of the water right in front of me, about half a ship's length off, straight up in the air to about the height of the foremast ahead, about fifty feet.

I, of course, had my Galilee-glasses handy, and quickly fixed them on the quadruped – for a four footed or, at any rate, four-legged, beast it proved to be. In appearance it gave me the impression of a skinned chow-dog, such as one sees hanging up in the butchers' shops of Canton. In shape it reminded of a chameleon, though a shortened one, the head and short tail, also chameleon-like in appearance. With outstretched neck and legs it fell, or rather dived, into the sea again.

Anstruther immediately called to his navigating officer and, as he reached the bridge, the creature shot clear of the water for a second time. 'It did not appear to have scales, but rather the shiny skin of a reptile. Its feet seemed like the claws one sees represented in figures of Chinese dragons. We waited and waited but it never rose again.'

Another sighting was recalled in a letter published in the *Daily Mail* on Monday, 23 October 1937, by Major W. Peer-Groves, who explained how, five years previously, with other members of his family, he had been visiting the Isle of Man on holiday, when he saw a strange creature in the sea. 'The beast was obviously large, many feet in length, though only the head was visible. The head was about as big as that of a large bull, but rather broader between the ears, ending in a dog-like snout.'

A type of seal? Not according to the sketch drawn by Major Peer-Groves which fails to throw any light on the mystery, as the creature depicted in his sketch has more of a 'muppet' appearance than anything else.

2
Scotland

In the Highlands of Scotland lies Loch Garten, in the midst of the Abernathy Forest. According to ancient legend, an area of the loch which flows through thick woods was haunted by a large, carnivorous water monster, a cross between a horse and a bull, with a jet black mane, a huge head and burning eyes. It had a blood-curdling roar, which would echo through the trees and round the loch at night. A crofter volunteered to capture the creature, and tied a long thick rope around a large stone, weighing many tons, which he placed on the shore of Loch Garten. On the other end of the rope he tied a hook and a young lamb as bait for the creature. The bait was then taken out into the water, weighted and dropped over the side of the boat. That night, a fierce storm blew, but still the howls and roaring of the monster could be heard. The following morning, the crofter visited the loch and saw great grooves on the shore where the huge boulder had stood, leading straight into the loch. The monster has never been seen or heard of since.

Many Highland lochs are supposed to be inhabited by beasts, fairy dogs, little people, or of course, the Devil. At Loch Assynt, the Devil, it is claimed, played a major part in the building of Ardvreck Castle, and both Loch Achilty and Loch Guinach are particular favourites of his.

It is the water horse, water bull, water kelpie or *each uisge* which is generally associated with the lake monster tradition. These creatures take different forms: those found on the west coast are black, and those on the north and east coasts golden or yellow. In the Shetlands the creature is known as Shoopiltee, and in the Orkneys, Tangie. According to legend, the water horse is an associate of the devil and can change its form. It can be a beautiful tame horse with exquisite saddlery, calmly grazing by a loch or river. Yet when mounted, it turns into a wild stallion and gallops off into the water, where it drowns its victim and devours the flesh. It is also believed to take the form of a handsome young man who entices maidens to a watery grave.

The River Spey had a yellow water horse, which curiously had a preference for married couples. It would lie in wait until its victims made an effort to cross the river, then offer to carry them across. Once they had mounted, it would carry them off into the Spey. Loch Shin, a long narrow loch, was also home to a yellow water horse, which in the early days of Christianity persuaded a local priest to trade a soul for assistance in building a church. The horse purloined stones and carried them across the loch to the place where the church was to be built. Unfortunately, the stones were from the home of a fairy dwelling, which angered the little people who ordered him to return them, and made him suffer for his crimes. Needless to say, the agreement with the priest was also negated.

Some of these creatures, demand annual human sacrifice as a form of tribute to their power. According to folklore, the River Dee needs three, the River Don needs one and the River Tweed needs one. The water horse of Loch Pityoulish takes the form of a white Highland pony, with an ornamental saddle and bridle. This particular beast is said to be keen on young children who play near the Loch. It is claimed that on one occasion it carried nine into the loch, none of whom was ever seen again. One man is said to have escaped the fate of the Pityoulish water horse by cutting the fingers from his hand, thus releasing his grip upon the creature's reins and destroying its power.

The beast of Loch Borrolan has no particular preferences; it is said to have taken two fishermen to their deaths. When a search for the missing anglers was carried out, all that were found beside the loch were their rods and some fish which they had caught. Nearby, large hoofprints could be seen in the soft ground, leading into the water.

At Loch Garve, near Strathpeffer, it is claimed that a beautiful girl was carried off into the loch by a water horse. There she lives now in the beast's home. She complained of how cold the home was, so the beast captured a mason, dragging him into its watery lair. The unfortunate man was forced to build a fireplace and chimney. According to the legend, the heat from this fireplace and chimney prevents the eastern end of the loch from freezing over.

Loch Awe has a beast, which occasionally takes to land in winter when fish are difficult to catch. The creature's growling and panting is said to be frequently heard as it searches for food on land.

The West Coast

Girvan is a small port on Scotland's west coast, 22 miles from Ayr. In August 1935, it was reported that a sea creature measuring 35 ft in length with a 'giraffe-like neck, and a camel's head and a tail', had been washed up on shore. The tail alone measured 12 ft, and those who saw the remains claimed that the carcass was entirely covered with bristles. Local naturalists could not agree what it was; some believed it to be the partially decomposed remains of a basking shark, while others claimed that a basking shark would not be covered in bristle-type hair. Two people who saw it, Archie and Gwen Wilson, were horrified by the sight.

We saw the thing laying on the beach close to some rocks; it was horrible to look at, like some eerie relic from our past. A man was taking measurements and making sketches of the remains; he looked like some sort of official. We asked him what it was, he told us that he 'wasn't sure, but the one thing it wasn't, was the Loch Ness Monster'. We asked if it was the same sort of creature as that reported in Loch Ness; he said that he didn't believe in monsters. It was an irresponsible sort of thing to consider.

We pointed to the carcass and said to him, 'If you don't believe in monsters, what is that thing?' The man shrugged his shoulders and replied, 'Yes, you are probably right, this is a monster, a dead one, but all the same a monster. I think I should try to get rid of it before it causes too much of a sensation.'

We tried to get a close look at the remains, but the stench was awful, and caused us both to feel sick. After a while we got used to the smell, and I [Archie] approached the dead beast. It looked as though it had a tiny head on a long neck, a wide thick body tapering down to a long tail. It was a brown or cream sort of colour, lighter underneath. It seemed to have two flippers, but it was laid on its side so I could not get to see both sides of it. Presumably, there would have been two flippers on its other side. I could not make out a mouth, although I think I could see the eye socket. The thing was very badly decomposed with bits of its insides hanging out all over the place.

We walked away from the carcass and could still smell it from some distance away, I think we must have been one of the first to see the creature after it was washed up. Very few people knew about it when we later talked of it. Some who went to see it the following day, found it had gone.

Mr Wilson was correct; locals burnt the carcass due to the stench and the health risk it presented.

The story of the Girvan sighting is similar to that of the

Stronsa carcass of 1808 (see page 170) with public disbelief that a basking shark could take the form of a plesiosaur-type creature, although we know from experience that they can. Whether the Girvan carcass is just another such case, or whether it was a genuine stranding of a sea serpent, we cannot be certain.

Glasgow doctor, John Paton, reported an incident, which occurred to him and his daughter in the summer of 1931 on the Isle of Arran.

On the 28th July 1931, my daughter (aged 14) and myself were returning from a cycle ride. It had been a glorious, warm day with bright sunshine, and about seven o'clock in the evening we were cycling close to the sea on the shore road, at an almost deserted part of the island, between Imachar and Dourie. The beach here is rocky. There was no one in sight, and everything was still.

I thought it rather strange then, that I should see a few hundred yards further on, what I was certain must be an upturned boat lying on a rock in the water, a few yards from the beach. I determined to find out what boat it was, to report the matter if necessary. Immediately I came opposite to it, I dismounted and proceeded to make my investigation.

I had not gone more than a few yards when, to my astonishment, a head turned and looked at me from what I had thought to be the bow of the boat. I waved my daughter's attention to the creature, and made an effort to get as close as possible. The legs or flippers could not be observed, and I wanted to be sure of just what kind of extremities it had. I was disappointed, as the movement evidently frightened it, and it wobbled off the rock into the sea. It made off at a good pace, and left a considerable wake behind it.

The head was parrot-shaped, that is to say that it had a kind of beak. It was of a rather light grey colour. The body was longer than that of a large elephant, of a similar colour, and just as shapeless.

I was certain that the animal would be seen again by someone and reported, but this did not happen. I reported it to the *Glasgow Herald* in August 1931, but the letter was not published.

I am of the opinion that although the head was small, and close to the body when I saw it, it is probable that the creature would be able to extend the head considerably. The head could be turned round so fully that there must have been rather a narrow neck between it and the huge body. I am familiar with seals, sharks, whales, etc. What I saw was unique.

The Cumbrae Islands, Great Cumbrae and Little Cumbrae, are located close to the mouth of the Firth of Clyde. In August 1935, a group of fishermen saw what appeared to be a 'camel's head on a giraffe-type neck' rise out of the water close to them, near Great Cumbrae. The creature remained in view for a few seconds before sinking back under the water. It did not resurface and was not seen again by the group.

At nearby Little (Wee) Cumbrae an incident was reported in the *Sketch* of 30 August 1911. The article took the unusual form of a poem, entitled 'Cuff Comments' by Wadham Peacock, which is quite refreshing, but does not provide the descriptive narrative which is useful to the researcher.

(A visitor to Millport, while fishing near the Wee Cumbrae, observed a monster of the deep about one hundred yards away.)

Bless you, sea serpent! I'd begun to think
That, what with strikes and heat waves and the rest
On the seafloor you had continued to slink
Basely away from our Autumnal jest.
But now from Millport comes the cheerful news

That, near the lighthouse on the Wee Cumbrae
A fisherman, one hundred yards away,
Has with your coils had several interviews.
Bless you again sea serpent! Had you failed,
As that false Giant Gooseberry has done,
In my disgruntlement I should have railed
Yet more against the blaze of August's sun.
But this has quieted my soul's alarms:
I could not spare that flabby wrinkled skin,
That short, snub nose, that sparsely bearded chin,
Not any one of your disgusting charms.

This creature bears some vague similarities to a pinniped, as witness the 'short snub nose and sparsely bearded chin' and 'flabby wrinkly skin'. However, there is also mention of 'coils'. These do not conform to any kind of pinniped known to mankind, although the continual surface diving motion of a pinniped may produce an impression of an elongated body with several coils rising independently to the surface. The Little Cumbrae sighting offers us very little in the way of positive information, but is worth mentioning, purely because of the manner in which it was reported, indicating that some of the press viewed such sightings with satire and cynicism.

A more curious incident occurred in the summer of 1942, at Gourock on the River Clyde. Charles Rankin, a council officer, noticed a foul-smelling odour in the air. Curious, he and a foreman went in search of the source of the stench, which they described as being like rotting fish. It was quickly traced to an unusual carcass beached on the River Clyde. Neither Rankin nor his colleague could decide what it was; both felt it was the remains of a new or unknown species. Rankin at once rang the Royal Scottish Museum, but they were dismissive of his claims.

Because of wartime restrictions, Rankin was refused permission to photograph the carcass; the area where it was beached was a restricted area, and the Royal Navy forbade him to do anything but remove and destroy it. The creature was chopped up and buried in the grounds of the municipal incinerator. Charles Rankin later recalled (*Arthur C. Clarke's Mysterious World*):

It was approximately 27–28 feet in length and 5–6 feet in depth at the broadest part. As it lay on its side, the body appeared to be oval in section but the angle of the flippers in relation to the body suggested that the body section had been round in life. If so, this would reduce the depth dimension to some extent. The head and neck, the body, and the tail were approximately equal in length, the neck and tail tapering gradually away from the body. There were no fins. The head was comparatively small, of a shape rather like that of a seal, but the snout was much sharper and the top of the head flatter. The jaws came together one over the other and there appeared to be a bump over the eyes – say prominent eyebrows. There were large pointed teeth in each jaw. The eyes were comparatively large, rather like those of a seal but more to the side of the head.

The tail was rectangular in shape as it lay – it appeared to have been vertical in life. Showing through the thin skin there were parallel rows of 'bones' which had a gristly, glossy, opaque appearance. I had the impression that these 'bones' had opened out fan-wise under the thin membrane to form a very effective tail. The tail appeared to be equal in size above and below centre line.

At the front of the body there was a pair of 'L'-shaped flippers and at the back a similar pair, shorter but broader. Each terminated in a 'bony' structure similar to the tail and no doubt was also capable of being opened out in the same way.

The body had over it at fairly close intervals, pointing backwards, hard, bristly 'hairs'. These were set closer together towards the tail and at the back edge of the flippers. I pulled out one of these bristles from a flipper. It was about 6 inches long and was tapered and pointed at each end like a steel knitting needle and rather of the thickness of a needle of that size, but slightly more flexible. I kept the bristle in the drawer of my office desk and some time later I found that it had dried up in the shape of a coiled spring.

The skin of the animal was smooth and when cut was found to be comparatively thin but tough. There appeared to be no bones other than a spinal column. The flesh was uniformly deep pink in colour, was blubbery and difficult to cut or chop. It did not bleed, and it behaved like a thick table jelly under pressure. In what I took to be the stomach of the animal was found a small piece of knitted woollen material as from a cardigan and, stranger still, a small corner of what had been a woven cotton tablecloth – complete with tassels.

This description, if accurate, can hardly relate to the decomposed corpse of a basking shark; it is more like a species of pinniped, yet Rankin must have been aware of what a pinniped looks like, as he says that the head was 'similar to that of a seal', but the snout was much sharper and 'the top of the head flatter'.

With the remains destroyed and no official investigation of the carcass, the Gourock stranding remains something of an enigma to those with an open mind, but to the sceptic it is regarded as nothing more than further evidence of the decomposed stranding of a basking shark.

Further along the Clyde, Mr A.H. Vincent reported seeing a sea serpent sighting to the *Daily Sketch* on Monday, 29 September 1913.

Many years ago, I was living at Ashton, a small seaside place on the Clyde. I was a schoolboy at the time, but my experience has not faded from my memory. I used to rise in the morning before the household was astir and go for a bathe when everything was still and quiet.

On this particular morning, the sea was as smooth as glass and not a soul to be seen anywhere. I entered the water about a mile below Clock lighthouse and was hardly in the water a few minutes when I suddenly saw what seemed to me like a large serpent rise out of the water only a few feet away.

I was so fascinated that although I was shivering with fear I could not help but notice the appearance of the apparition. The head was small and shaped like a hooded serpent with tiny peering eyes that darted hither and thither. The neck was long, I should say quite ten feet. It seemed to be listening intently. The markings I remember were just like a serpent – a criss-cross pattern and of a brown fading into a dirty yellow After a minute that seemed like an eternity, I came to my senses and caused a disturbance in the water. Then the brute lowered its head and neck and shot away like a flash. That the submerged part of its body must have been a tremendous length was proved by the white foam it lashed up fully 50 feet and more behind it. When I got home and related my adventure, I was laughed at by everyone and on the few occasions since when I have ventured to relate this incident my story was invariably received with rigid politeness.

Mr Vincent's recollections were of course those of a child, which may have been distorted with the passage of time, but it seems to be a genuine unknown species he had encountered. The skin coloration and description of the head and neck are indicative of some species of eel, but since no eel of such proportions is known to exist, we are again left to speculate about the creature's identity.

A more recent sighting occurred at Helensburgh, on the Firth of Clyde, close to the entrance of Gare Loch. In February 1962, Jack Hayand his spaniel dog Roy were out walking on the beach when the dog began to whimper and cower behind his master. Mr Hay recalled (*Scottish Daily Mail*, 3 February 1962):

About 40 yards away, I made out a massive bulk with a sort of luminous glow from street lamps on the esplanade. It did not move for about a minute, and then seemed to bound and slither into the water. I saw the thing swim out. It had a long body and neck and a head about three feet long. I watched until it was well out in the water and had disappeared. There was a strong, pungent smell in the air.

He admitted that he was scared, but decided to look at the spot where the creature had slipped into the water. Using a lighted match, he could see a large footprint in the sand, with three pads and a spur to the rear.

The sighting coincided with several reports of strange noises – roaring sounds – which appeared to enamate from the beach area at the eastern end of the esplanade at Helensburgh. Although several independent witnesses reported these sounds, no explanation was ever recorded. Other local residents reported that their dogs were reluctant to go out during the hours of darkness.

Because of poor reporting, this sighting has been the subject of much subsequent misinterpretation. It reads as though Mr Hay indicated that the object had a self-induced luminous glow. However, the eye-witness has subsequently revealed that what he meant was that the luminous glow and reflection from the street lamps along the esplanade actually made the object *seem* to glow in the water. It is quite normal for a shiny wet surface to give such an impression. So, what we have is a large wet creature illuminated by the glow of the street lamps. Whatever the explanation, the incident seems to have been short-lived, as no further reports appeared. Opinions differ among researchers about what may have been the cause, the most popular view being that it was nothing more than a group of seals. However, I know of no pinniped which would reproduce footprints in the sand similar to those described by Mr Hay.

In the summer of 1918, another sea serpent incident

occurred at the entrance to Gare Loch. The account was given to Gavin Maxwell, by author of *Harpoon at a Venture* by Sandy Campbell. According to Campbell, two fishermen in a coble (a flat-bottomed rowing boat) were taking in lobster creels and heading towards Rhu, a small village north-west of Helensburgh and the centre, in years gone by, of the whisky-smuggling industry. The men were apparently stopped in their tracks by the sudden appearance of an object which rose out of the water to a height of about 30 ft. The object was waving to and fro out of the sea and was moving at speed towards them. The two men wasted no time in rowing ashore. They looked back only to see that the object had disappeared.

A curios and unknown creature was seen in Campbeltown Loch, on the Kintyre peninsula, in 1934. The Edinburgh *Evening Dispatch* of Tuesday 6 November 1934 reported the incident:

Another monster has made its appearance in Scottish waters. A creature of unusual shape and of large dimensions was seen disporting itself in Kilkerran Bay, the east side of Campbeltown Loch, on Saturday [3 November].

When John MacCorkindale, a local naturalist, and Charles Keith, rural postman, were standing speaking on the public road, which skirts Kilkerran shore, a loud splash seaward attracted their attention. On turning round, they saw an enormous creature lashing the surface with the fore part of its body, at a distance of about 300 yards from the shore. It would raise its fore part out of the water for fully twelve feet and then flop down with a loud crash. This movement was repeated several times, and then the animal submerged and was seen no more.

Mr MacCorkindale, who is a trained observer, gave a description of this animal or fish. 'The fore part of the body resembled a giraffe, with a thin long neck and small head and ears, like that of a land animal. It was of a glistening silvery colour, with thin streaks of dark bands encircling the body. A faint trace of a dorsal fin could be seen, but no other fins were visible. The major part of the body and tail were not seen, and judging by what was exposed of the creature, it must be about thirty feet long.'

The island of Jura, situated off the Argyllshire coast, is about 30 miles long and 7 miles wide, a rugged and isolated place which is sparsely populated.

Neil MacInnes, a stalker from Craighouse, with whom I was in correspondence, told me of how in early June 1964, he was driving along close to the shore when he saw a strange creature in the sea at a distance of about 250 yards. This he described as looking very much like a box. As he drew closer he could see that it had the appearance of a cow's head. He took his telescope and saw that the head was indeed cow-like, but with white buds on either side rather than horns, and it moved from side to side. There was no sign of eyes, ears, fins or humps and although he could not see the full extent of the body in the water, he believed it to be about 25 feet long and tapering at the tail. It was a grey colour and smooth-textured. It seemed to move faster than the slow tide flow, without a wake or disturbance. He estimated its general speed as being about 6 mph.

The diversity of the descriptions given by witnesses of curious creatures seen in the water continues to puzzle researchers; snake-like, eel-like, cow-like, horse-like and giraffe-like all appear with some regularity. This would seem to cast doubt on the existence of such creatures, as we appear to be discussing not one but countless different species. The presence of 'white buds' on either side of the head is not as uncommon as one might think, although we have no knowledge as to what these may be. It has been suggested that these 'buds' are an illusion, caused by light reflection. However, Neil MacInnes viewed his creature through a telescope and appears to have been certain that they were there.

A further report from the Jura region was submitted to me by Helen Hadley in July 1999.

A group of canoeists, of whom I was not a part, went to paddle around Jura. They could not get out to the island, as the weather was too bad. They changed plans and paddled up the coast. The party was not expecting the weather to be quite so appalling and so most of the gear was wet. One of the party, Jake. decided to go and find a cave that was marked on the nautical chart to allow him a dryer night's sleep. I assume that this cave was in a cliff above the high water mark. When he got into the cave he turned around only to see several rotting dismembered sheep carcasses behind him. He told me that he never moved so quick in his life!

Author Harold T. Wilkins, in his book *Monsters and Mysteries*, reported a carcass, aground on the shore of Loch Fyne.

A 30 foot monster, with girth of 30 feet, was washed ashore on Loch Fyne, Argyllshire. Fishermen swear that it is neither shark nor whale. Its head is in front of its mouth and two huge fins are well forward. The massive tail is powerful looking. The carcass lies in three feet of water at low tide. It is wondered if it is the monster rammed by the turbine steamer *King George V*, three weeks ago, or is the one shot with an explosive bullet, at close range, second week of June, off Inverary.

Due to lack of information, notably dates, it has proved impossible positively to identify these incidents. Yet clearly, if they have been accurately recorded, a number of incidents relating to what may be the same creature seem to have occurred during a short period of time. From the description (both in dimension and tail) it sounds very much like some form of whale, but the presence of two forward fins presents something of a problem if that is the case.

The town of Oban is built on wood-covered hills, which overlook Oban Bay and offer outstanding views of the surrounding area. On 18 November 1873, a long and large black animal was seen in the area. Eye-witness testimony was reported in The *Scotsman* of 24 November 1873.

Near the middle of Belhaven Bay and about a quarter of a mile from where we were standing, there certainly appeared 'a long black animal' in the water, having all the appearance of the Saurian described by Mr Joass (see page 179). When first observed, it was proceeding shoreward, with what seemed to be its head and various undulating portions of the body above the surface. After getting near the shore it turned to the westwards and kept moving about in that position for some considerable time. Sometimes it appeared to stretch itself out to its full length, at which time both its head and tail were seen above water, only a small portion of the middle of the creature being submerged. Most frequently, however, it was the undulations or apparent coils of the body that were observed, two or three of them being occasionally visible at the same time. The foils had all the appearance to the observers at the distance mentioned above, of the coils or folds of a serpent, the sea and the black masses being distinctly separated. Occasionally the creature seemed to take a header and disappeared altogether, but it seldom remained longer than two or three minutes beneath the surface without exposing some part of its body. When fully stretched out, as it appeared several times during the period of observation, it seemed to be upwards to a hundred feet in length, with an apparent breadth of from two to three feet. No doubt the dimensions must have been very much larger. As it was in sight for upwards of a quarter of an hour, ample opportunity was afforded for watching its movements.

Oban had not seen the last of the sea serpent. Four years later, the *Oban Evening News and Star* of 28 April 1877, carried the following somewhat sensational account provided by an alleged witness:

The sea serpent story, always turning up in dull season, has come upon us at the most inopportune moment. At a time when pubic interest is engrossed in the Eastern question and Oban has been suffering from an earthquake, the sea serpent – between whose presence at Oban and the occurrence of the recent phenomenon the prescient will no doubt draw their own inferences – has reared his crest to the height of the proverbial 25 feet above the waves and drawn on himself the fire of those enthusiasts who always perambulate the beach with loaded rifles. According to the remarkably circumstantial narrative, which has been sent to this office, it is the last time the newspaper will be able to utilize the logbooks of American Whalers and the diaries of Chinese residents, for the sea serpent has actually arrived on our shores. Many who read the story below will experience much regret that his progress has been arrested....

Sir. A most extraordinary event has occurred here, which I will give detail, having been witness to the whole affair, i.e. to the stranding and capture of the veritable sea serpent in front of the Caledonian Hotel, Grange Street, Oban. About four o'clock, yesterday, an animal or fish evidently of gigantic size was seen sporting in the bay near Heather Island. Its appearance evidently perplexed a large number of spectators assembled on the pier, and several telescopes were directed towards it. A careful look satisfied us that it was of the serpent species, it carrying its head a full 25 feet above the water. A number of boats was soon launched and proceeded to the bay, the crews armed with weapons as could be got handy. Under the direction of Malcolm Nicholson, our accomplished boatman, they headed out after the monster and some of the boats were within 30 yards of it, when it suddenly sprang half-length out of the water and made for the open. A random fire of several volunteers with rifles seemed to have no effect on it. Under Mr Nicholson's orders, the boats now ranged across the entrance of the bay and by screams and shouts, turned the monster's course and it headed directly for the breast wall of the Great Western Hotel. One boat, containing Mr Donald Campbell, the Fiscal, had a narrow escape, the animal actually rubbing against it. Mr Campbell and his brother jumped overboard and were picked up unhurt by Mr John Hardie, saddler, in his small yacht, *The Flying Scud*.

The animal seemed thoroughly frightened, and, as the boats closed in, the volunteers were unable to fire more, owing to crowds assembled on the shore. At a little past six, the monster took ground on the beach in front of the Caledonian Hotel in George Street and his proportions were now visible. In his frantic exertions with his tail sweeping the beach no one dared approach. The stones were flying in all directions, one seriously injuring one Baldy Barrow and one breaking the window of the Commercial Bank.

A party of volunteers under Lieutenant David Menzies now assembled and fired volley after volley into the neck according to the direction of Dr Campbell who did not wish for scientific reasons that the configuration of the head should be damaged. As there was a bright moon this continued till nearly ten o'clock, when Mr Stevens of the Commercial Bank waded in and fixed a strong rope to the animal's head and by the exertions of some 70 folk it was securely dragged above the high water mark. Its exact appearance as it lies on the beach is as follows:

The extreme length is 101 feet and the thickest part is about 25 feet from the head, which is 11 feet in circumference. At this part is fixed a pair of fins, which are 4 feet long by nearly 7 feet across at the sides. Further back is a long dorsal fin extending for at least twelve or thirteen feet and five feet high in front tapering to one foot. The tail has a more flattened termination to the body proper than anything else. The eyes are very small in proportion and elongated, and gills the length of two and a half feet behind. There are no external ears, and Dr Campbell did not wish the animal handled till he communicated with some eminent scientific gentlemen. We could not ascertain whether there were teeth or not.

Great excitement is created and the country people are flocking in to view it. This morning Mr Duncan Clark, writer, formally took possession of the monster, in the right of Mr McFee of Appin, and Mr James Nicol, writer, in the name of the Crown.

I am, sir, your obedient servant. John B. Anderson.

This entire incident aroused the interest of the Manager of the Royal Aquarium who, having read the article, at once telegraphed John B. Anderson (the writer of the Oban article) and asked to buy the carcass for exhibition. The following reply was received. 'The whole thing is a shameful hoax deserving no attention except to punish the author.' But in a private letter of 1921 which is in my possession, Mr Brian Murray, a local resident, recalls the incident.

A good deal of attention was caused by the sea monster of Oban when it was caught and killed before many witnesses. I recollect the activity of it all very clearly, the capture and killing of the serpent caused a procession of visitors to the town, many who fainted at the sight of this beast in the depths of the sea. As young ones we were told not to tread near it, in fear that it may be feigning death and could spring to life at any moment.

My father, a seafarer, would later speak of how it caused many a seaman to cease seagoing activities when alone.

The serpent was of giant proportion. I cannot say how long but I would claim, from my vivid recollection, over 80 feet from head to tail. The head was small compared to the rest of its dimensions, it sat aloft a narrow snake-like neck. It was very much similar to how I imagine the plesiosaurus gave appearance; it was very real and unlike any fish or marine creature I have seen since. I am appreciative of the whale and the shark in appearance; this was not of that type, but of a kind uncommon to most folk, other than fishermen and those who are acquainted with the power and wonders of the sea. The serpent was cut into pieces and removed back into the sea; for many week after, fishermen had wealthy catches. It was widely held that smaller sea creatures were attracted to the area to feed upon the monster's remains.

The island of Tiree is part of the Inner Hebrides group. It is about 11 miles long and 6 miles wide, and is more commonly noted for its variety of bird life than for sea serpent sightings. The following account, however, is taken from the log of the Latvian motor schooner, *Elsa Croy*, the crew of which encountered a strange creature there.

July 19, 1934, time 12.15 p.m. Weather calm and sunny. Off the island of Tiree, in the Gulf of the Hebrides, Scotland, we saw in the sea an unknown monster like a large lizard. He was a giant in size. Length about 50 feet and had an immensely long neck and vast mouth. Also, a long tail with fins underneath and on top. He had the body of a dray horse. We put the ship on course, and when he saw we were following him, he turned and charged us at great speed. Our gunner fired his harpoon at him, but the monster escaped with a part of the ship's rail.

The physical attack upon the schooner is quite unusual in such encounters, as is the 'lizard-like' description. Just what species this creature belonged to is a mystery; with the body of a dray horse, a long tail and fins it does not easily fall into any known specific group.

The island of Coll, is also part of the Inner Hebrides group, measuring just 12 miles by 4 miles. Its east coast is rocky, its west coast filled with sandy coves and beaches. In 1809, the Reverend Donald M'Clean, a parish minister of Eigg, made the following report to Mr Patrick Neill, the Secretary of the Wernerian Society, Edinburgh.

I saw the animal of which you inquire in June 1808, on the coast of Coll. Rowing along that coast, I observed, at about the distance of half a mile, an object to windward which gradually excited astonishment. At first view it appeared like a small rock, but knowing that there was no rock in that situation, I fixed my eyes closely upon it, then I saw it elevated considerably above the level of the sea, and after a slow movement, distinctly perceived one of its eyes. Alarmed at the unusual appearance and magnitude of the animal, I steered so as to be at no great distance from the shore. When nearly in a line between it and the shore, the monster, directing its head, which still continued above water, towards us, plunged violently under the water. Certain that he was in chase of us, we plied hard to get ashore. Just as we leapt out on a rock, and had taken a station as high as we conveniently could, we saw it coming rapidly under water towards the stern of our boat. When within a few yards of it, finding the water shallow, it raised its monstrous head above water, and by a winding course, got, with apparent difficulty, clear of the creek where our boat lay, and where the monster seemed in danger of being embayed. It continued to move with its head above water, and with the wind, for about half a mile, before we lost sight of it. Its head was somewhat broad, and of a somewhat oval form, its neck somewhat smaller, its shoulders, if I can so term them, considerably broader, and thence it tapered towards the tail, which last, it kept pretty low in the water, so that a view of it could not be taken so distinctly as I wished. It had no fins that I could perceive, and seemed to me to move progressively by undulations up and down. Its length I believe to be between 70 and 80 feet. When nearest to me it did not raise its head wholly above water, so that the neck being under water, I could perceive no shining filaments thereon, if it had any; its progressive motion under water I took to be very rapid. About the time I saw it, it was seen near the Isle of Canna. The crews of thirteen fishing boats were so much terrified at its appearance that they in a body fled from it to the nearest creek for safety. On the passage from Rum to Canna, the crew of one boat saw it coming towards them with the wind, and its head high above water. One of the crew pronounced the head as large as a little boat, and its eye as large as a plate The men were much terrified, but the monster offered them no molestation.

Kilchoan is situated on Ardnamurchan point, the most westerly point of mainland Scotland. Mingany Pier looks eastward across the water towards the ruins of Mingany Castle. In a letter to author Tim Dinsdale in 1965, Mrs Lilian Lowe of Birmingham recalled the following events:

Three of us, my husband, my cousin and myself, were standing on the end of Mingany Pier, Kilchoan, Ardnamurchan, looking out to sea, which was mirror like, with not a ripple on the surface. My husband was looking through binoculars (Taylor Hobson ex-army x 6), at the old ruined Mingany Castle. I saw what I thought to be a seal appear above the water, about one hundred yards off shore. Then another hump appeared, directly behind it and a few feet away. As it moved, I came to the conclusion that the two humps belonged to one object. I said, 'What's that?' My husband immediately sighted the creature but was silent. He said afterwards he was too amazed to speak. He could see a huge shape about forty feet long beneath the water, and after a few moments said, 'A submarine, I think.' He then noticed what seemed to be legs or flippers paddling at the side of the body, creating turbulence beneath the water.

My cousin and I could only see the two humps moving steadily along and waited for a decision as to the identity of the creature, but all my husband could say was that he had never seen anything like it in his life. The two humps were very solid and dark and shiny, and the skin seemed to be like hide. I was anxious to see it through binoculars ... but just as I had it in view the creature submerged. I must state that my husband has exceptionally keen eye-sight and has seen basking sharks off the Cornish coast and is convinced the creature was something he had never before encountered.

Further inland is the freshwater Loch Shiel, 18 miles long and 1 mile across, between Inverness and Argyll. Dom Cyril Dieckhoff, a monk at St Benedict's Abbey on the shores of Loch Ness, who kept notes about sea and lake monsters, received information from a Highlander, whom he had known for some twenty-five years, of incidents there.

The Loch Shiel beast had been seen in 1911 by two men, one of them a former head keeper of the Inverailort Estate. Using a keeper's telescope they had seen its three humps, each separated by water. In 1925, there was a further report of a creature with three humps, the central one being the biggest and the overall length 'longer than the little mail steamer *Clan Ronald*'. They also saw a head on a long neck. An old woman was said to have seen the three humps travelling very fast. The creature was also alleged to have been seen on land.

Loch Linnhe is a sea loch which extends some 35 miles from Loch Eil to Duart Point on the island of Mull. It splits into two natural divisions, an inner and an outer loch, separated by the Corran Narrows. The inner stretch of the loch, to the north-east, is overlooked by Ben Nevis. In the 1940s Mrs B.F. Cox saw a long-necked creature there from a distance of about 20 ft. It was summer and the creature surfaced as she looked out across the water; it was dark brown in colour and seemed to have small eyes, stumpy tube-like horns on its head, just above where one would imagine its ears should have been. The creature submerged in a slow diving manner before she could make out any further detail. On 21 July 1954, Mr Eric Robbins of Doncaster, South Yorkshire, told BBC radio reporters that he once also saw a monster in Loch Linnhe. Sadly, no further details have ever been forthcoming relating to this sighting.

At the sea entrance of Loch Linnhe is the island of Shuna. In 1887 the following sighting was recorded off the island. Professor Matthew Forster Heddle and J.A. Harvey Brown were cruising in the loch on board the yacht *Shiantelle* on the morning of 30 July. They and two members of the crew saw a monster appear in the water about 500 yd from the yacht. After the beast had disappeared, each of the four men wrote down a description of the sighting and placed it in a sealed envelope. These were opened a few days later and the circumstances surrounding the sighting matched; however, the descriptions of the creature did not. Heddle claimed that it had a low flat head, much like a large skate's, and a series of ten humps that increased in size towards the middle. He estimated that the size of the creature was 60–65 ft and that the body was rushing through the water. 'My impression was that, setting aside the quiescent low head, I did not see a solid substance at all – except when the tail hummocks momentarily appeared – and that what I did see was water being thrown over laterally by the undulous lashings of a long black fin of a dark colour, which gave opacity.'

Brown wrote: 'I came to the conclusion and feel very certain still, that it was simply a tide rip or tidal wave coming from the direction of Corrievreachen between Scarba and Jura running easterly and then north-easterly along smooth water where surroundings showed the meeting of the shallow and the deep.' It is worth noting that the Strait of Corrievreachen, which separates Scarba from Jura, is well known for its whirlpool and powerful tide formations, which is clearly what Mr Brown felt was the source of this strange sighting.

A monster in Loch Eil, at the head of Loch Linnhe, is mentioned in the book *September Road to Caithness* by 'BB.'. It is an unsubstantiated sighting at an unspecified date. 'BB' claimed to have seen it on a bright October morning. He was watching some mallard when they suddenly rose out of the calm water. A big black shiny object, which resembled the 'blunt, blind head of an enormous worm', rose out of the water.

It was, I suppose, some fifty yards from where I was standing, and it kept appearing and disappearing, not moving along, but rolling on the surface. The water was greatly disturbed all around the object. It had a shiny, wet-looking skin, but the head (if head it was) was quite unlike a seal's and had no face or nose, nor eyes. It rose quite a long way out of the water, some three feet or more, before sinking back.

Hurriedly leaving the scene to fetch some binoculars from his nearby van, the author was disappointed to find upon his return that the creature had gone, disappearing into a swirl of water. I confess to being somewhat dubious about such accounts, where dates and authors' names are omitted; they are not of much use to a researcher, as they are unverifiable. Hence the creature of Loch Eil is rather unconvincing.

Loch Morar is 17 miles long and less than 2 miles wide and

is well known as the haunt of a lake monster. At its eastern
end it is the deepest inland water in Britain (180 fathoms).
Records of the monster, which is known as 'Mhorag' go back
a long way, but sightings continue to occur with almost as
much regularity as those of the Loch Ness beast. The *Sunday
Post* newspaper of 31 May 1934 reported:

Mr Alec Patmore a company director of Chalfont St
Giles, Buckinghamshire, and his wife Carol, spotted a
strange creature in Loch Morar near Fort William,
described as a huge fish-like creature about 40 feet long
with three humps. They stood spellbound as the creature rose from the depths of the loch about 100 yards
away like a surfacing submarine.

Mr Patmore said: 'We saw the monster move down
the loch at high speed. It was definitely a living creature
for it writhed continuously, and churned up banks of
foam. It was a fine day, no boats in the area and the
surface of the loch was placid.'

A few months ago, crofter Duncan Gillies of Bracara
saw something, which moved down the loch against the
current with the speed of a motorboat. Years ago, two
crofters vanished while out fishing on Loch Morar.
Their upturned boat was found later, but their bodies
never recovered.

The *Glasgow Herald* of 31 July, 1948, related a further
history of strange encounters at Loch Morar.

Reported on 30 July 1948 on Loch Morar, by a party of
nine who were cruising in a motorboat on the loch.
Though none of the nine people in the motor boat was
prepared to say outright that what they saw in the loch
was, in fact, a 'monster', all were convinced that the
creature they had seen was something extraordinary and
out of the category of known fish or animals.

They saw no head on the object – only five humps moving fairly slowly above the surface. The humps were not the undulating coils of a sea serpent, they declared, but appeared to be ridged. They covered a length of about 20 feet of the loch surface. Mr James Doig of Glasgow was one of the party. He initially thought it to be the backs of salmon; there was a slight wash coming from it. 'When I took the binoculars it was just disappearing. I can't say whether it was a monster or not, but it was certainly something unusual.'

A strange creature has been seen in the loch before. Three years ago, two girls from Bracara, a hamlet on the north of Loch Morar, reported they had seen a 'queer' animal in the water which seemed to be neither fish or amphibian.

On 16 August 1969, Duncan McDonnell and William Simpson were returning from a day's fishing. McDonnell was at the wheel when he heard a splash or disturbance in the water astern of his boat (*Glasgow Herald* 31 July 1948).

I looked up and about twenty yards behind us this creature was coming directly after us in our wake. It took only a matter of seconds for it to catch up with us. It grazed the side of the boat. William Simpson came out of the cabin to try to fend the beast off with an oar. To me, he was wasting his time. I seen the oar break and I grabbed my rifle and quickly putting a bullet in it, fired in the direction of the beast. I then watched it slowly sink away from the boat.

Neither witness saw any blood, nor confirmation that the bullet had struck its target. They believed that the creature was between 25 and 30 ft long. It had three shallow humps or undulations and a snake-like head, about 1 ft across with rough and dirty brown skin. McDonnell believed that it might well have been an overgrown eel.

Since 1887, there have been around fifty independent sightings of the creature of Loch Morar. Investigators at Loch Ness also carried out research into Morar, but found very little evidence of any creature other than anecdotal sighting reports. The loch is full of brown trout. A short river (the Arkaig) connects the loch with Loch Lochy. Salmon and sea trout enter it via the river and by a remote connection with the sea. The eastern end of the Arkaig is said to contain treasures hidden by the Jacobites. It was once home to Lord Malmesbury, who recorded in his memoirs:

October 1857. This morning my stalker and his boy gave me an account of a mysterious creature, which they say exists in Loch Arkaig, and which they call the 'Lake-Horse'. It is the same animal of which one has occasionally read accounts in newspapers as having been seen in the Highland lochs, and on the existence of which Lord Assynt, the late Lord Ellesmere, wrote an interesting article, but hitherto the story has always been looked upon as fabulous. I am now, however, nearly persuaded of its truth. My stalker, John Stuart, at Achnaharry, has seen it twice, and both times at sunrise on a bright sunny day, when there was not a ripple on the water. The creature was basking on the surface; he only saw the head and hindquarters, proving that its back was hollow, which is not the shape of any fish or seal. Its head resembled that of a horse ... The Highlanders are very superstitious about this creature. They are convinced that there is never more than one in existence at the same time, and I believe they think it has something diabolical in its nature, for when I said I wished I could get within shot of it my stalker observed very gravely: 'Perhaps your Lordship's gun would miss fire?'

Loch Lochy is one of the chain of lochs which form the Great Glen and a part of the Caledonian Canal; for the most part its shores are hilly and wooded. The *Northern Chronicle* of Wednesday, 11 October 1933 carried the following report of sightings of a mysterious creature there:

> Loch Lochy – another link of the Caledonian Canal. There is known to live, move and have its being a creature whose bulk, movements and speed closely resemble those characteristics of the monster of Loch Ness.
>
> In the summer of 1933, a man who lives at Loch Lochy side, on returning from a fishing trip one evening, told his wife to stop her usual practice of washing her household linen on the shore. His wife, on seeking an explanation was told only that he had seen a beast in the water, refused further details, and said it may be harmless.
>
> Two gamekeepers obtained a view, four years before, a scene described as follows:
>
> The Loch lay calm and still under the brilliant sunshine of a summer afternoon when suddenly the surface of the water was stirred by a curious commotion, caused, as far as the watchers could discern, by a huge log of wood slightly rounded at the middle. With the aid of a telescope the keepers quickly realized that this was no floating tree trunk, but some mysterious creature whose movements they were able to follow for about a mile.
>
> Both refrained from telling of their experience, because they thought they would not be believed.

James Butler, a historian, made a record of the experiences of nine witnesses, who in 1960 saw a large black creature, thought to be between 30 and 40 ft long, roll over and expose a flipper and a light underbelly, before seemingly righting itself and sinking below the surface.

At 2 p.m. on 30 September 1975 Mr and Mrs Sargent from Fort William, were motoring along the southern shore of the Loch in their van, accompanied by their three children. As they turned the corner by the Corriegour Lodge Hotel, they saw an unusual wave in the water. A few seconds later, a gigantic creature rose to the surface. It was moving through the water in a gliding manner, showing a great black back about 20 ft long. Mr Sargent slowed his van, allowing his wife, who had a camera, to jump out. But before she could take a photograph, the creature had submerged. Moments later, a terrific surge of water broke the shore below her. Leaving his wife a few yards back, Mr Sargent continued a short distance along the road, where he stopped his van. Looking out across the loch he noticed a second hump, which was slightly smaller and sat just behind the original hump. Mrs Sargent failed to see the second hump. He later claimed. 'I was stunned and simply froze to the spot. When I went to my wife, she was visibly shaking. We knew we had seen something quite incredible.' Mrs Sargent said, 'There can be no doubt in our minds about what we saw on Lochy, and, incredible as it seems (we got no sleep that night talking about it!) it was as real as we are today; it will remain one of the most thrilling memories of our lives.'

A more recent sighting was by hotel boss, Andy Brown who, on 13 September 1996, had a first-class view of something unusual which surfaced about 35 yd in front of him. The sighting was also witnessed by Lorna Bunny and several guests at the Corriegour Lodge Hotel, who also saw a three-humped creature rise out of the water. Andy Brown told me:

> It was black or brown in colour, there was no mistaking it was something unusual, I am a keen fisherman and have not encountered a beast like this before. I think I was within about thirty-five yards of it. The water surrounding it was very disturbed; it looked, for all the world, like it had flippers or something on the side of the body in view; the water was extremely agitated at these points. As for size, well I would think the portion we saw measured about twelve foot; there was more of its body, which never actually rose above the surface, its head never came into my view, just the three large

humps which I would think stood 18 inches tall of the water. I don't like to promote supposition, but it looked very much like something that time had forgotten, a relic of some bygone era.

Lorna Bunny later admitted that she had seen a marine animal in the loch three weeks earlier. 'At first I thought it was just the wake from a cabin cruiser, but it was too fast and the ripples were too close together for that. I realized it was some kind of creature.'

Lindsey Burton, from Hornchurch, Essex, explained: 'At first we thought it was an upturned rowing boat, then it started moving backwards and round in circles and we saw that it had three humps. I would think the part we saw was about 12 foot long.' Catriona Allen, a psychology student at Aberdeen University, watched the creature through binoculars. 'I watched this dark shape, with a curved head and a long body, keep turning round and whipping about on the loch's surface. It was moving like no other marine animal I've seen and it certainly wasn't a seal, otter, porpoise or dolphin.'

Also in 1996, staff and guests at the Letterfinlay Hotel saw something which had the appearance of an upturned boat. It surfaced for about a minute before slowly sinking back down into the loch.

In recent times work has been done on Loch Lochy to try to establish the existence of this monster. In September 1997, the *Sun* arranged a trip in a rowing boat equipped with sonar and a small outboard engine. Cameron Turner took the *Sun* reporters onto the loch, along with his four-man search team, and kept the journalist informed of every step of the operation. It was reported that sonar equipment at one stage showed the bottom of the loch to be over 2,100 ft from the surface, deeper than any sea, lake or ocean in Europe. If the reading is accurate, this is over 1,000 ft deeper than Loch Morar, which had previously been accepted as the deepest lake in Europe. After a few hours of cruising the loch, a sonar reading was eventually found of an object said to be swimming about 13 ft from the loch bed. Dramatically, Cameron announced to his passengers, 'She's here, she's 300 ft directly underneath the boat – and she's about the size of a double-decker bus.' Moments later, a second contact, said to be 30 ft long, was made. After a short period the contacts were lost, and despite retracing their movements, the team could not locate them again.

Loch Hourn, which when translated becomes 'Loch Of Hell', is a wild and gloomy loch. Harold Wilkins writes of it in his book *Monsters & Mysteries*:

It is stated that the father of the Duke of Marlborough [in 1934] told the Scottish Inspector of Fisheries, that he and three parsons had seen in Loch Hourn, in the county of Inverness, a creature 96 feet long, with a flat and eyeless head, a black body, which forged through the water, and, as it did so, raised its back in ridges which curved then flattened.

Perched just off the west coast of Scotland, Skye has a history of incidents with sea serpents. A report in the *Illustrated London News* of 4 June 1960 tells of an encounter on the island of Soay, on the south coast of Skye by an experienced fisherman:

On the morning of 13 September 1959, basking shark fisherman, Tex Geddes and engineer James Gavin, who were on holiday on the island, were out mackerel fishing. Visibility was good. The two had seen a basking shark and a pod of killer whales in the distance, however their attention was drawn to a black shape about two miles away across Soay Sound. It approached at a speed of around 3–4 knots and, as it came closer, the men could hear it breathing.

The head was definitely reptilian, about two feet high with large protruding eyes. There were no visible breathing organs, but a large red gash of a mouth which

151

seemed to cut the head in half and which appeared to have distinct lips. There was at least two feet of clear water behind the neck, less than a foot of which we could see, and the creature's back, which rose sharply to its highest point some three to four feet out of the water and fell away gradually towards the after end. I would say we saw 8 to 10 feet of back on the waterline. It came to within twenty yards of the dinghy and was constantly turning its head from side to side. The head was blunt, there were no teeth, the body was scaly, and the mid-line of the back came to a knife edged ridge, which was deeply serrated. The creature seemed to breath through its mouth which opened and closed regularly. Geddes believed it could have weighed about five tons. They watched it travel in a SSW direction towards the island of Barra at the southern tip of the Outer Hebrides.

James Gavin said of the beast, when being interviewed by Dr Maurice Burton, 'At the waterline, the body was 6–8 feet long. It was hump-shaped, rising to a centrally placed apex about two feet high. The line of the back was formed by a series of triangular shaped spines, the largest at the apex and reducing in size to the waterline. The spines appeared to be solid and immobile – they did not resemble fins. I only got a lateral view of the animal but my impression was that the cross-section of the body was roughly angular in shape. Apart from the glide, I saw no movement.

The neck appeared to be cylindrical and, at a guess, about 8 inches in diameter. It rose from the water about 12 inches forward of the body. I could not see where they joined, about 15–18 inches of neck was visible. The head was rather like that of a tortoise with a snake-like flattened cranium running forward to a rounded face. Relatively, it was as big as the head of a donkey. I saw one laterally placed eye, large and round like that of a cow.

When the mouth was opened, I got the impression of a large blubbery tendril like growth hanging from the palate. Head and neck arose to a height of about two feet. At intervals the head and neck went forward and submerged. They would then re-emerge, the large gaping mouth would open (giving the impression of a large melon with a quarter removed) and there would be a series of very loud whistling noises as it breathed. After about five minutes the beast submerged with a forward diving motion – I thought I saw something follow the body down. It later resurfaced about a quarter of a mile further out to sea and I then watched it until it disappeared in the distance. I have heard that crews of two lobster boats, fishing off Mallaig, have also seen this animal – much to their consternation.'

Further sightings continued to be reported from the Skye region. The following incident occurred to Colonel H.B. Donne of Seend, Wiltshire, in the late nineteenth century.

We were nearing the red beacon of Scalpay Island, near the Isle of Skye, when we saw No. 1 monster. He had four humps, slowly waving in different directions. From time to time, a fifth hump appeared, which was perhaps a snout. It measured at least 40 feet in length. What species it was, I know not ... Half mile on, we saw No. 2 monster. My wife, the owner of the yacht (Mrs Kitchener) and I drew up, and the skipper, Robert Molachlan, signed a statement of what we saw.

Perhaps the most detailed account of a sea serpent encounter was recorded in *The Zoologist* magazine, No 92 – May 1873, which gave a first-hand account of a sighting by two church ministers.

Appearance of an animal, believed to be that which is called the Norwegian Sea Serpent, on the Western coast of Scotland, in August 1872, by the Rev. John McRae, Minister of Glenelg, Inverness-shire, and the Rev. David Twopeny, Vicar of Stocksbury, Kent.

On the 20th of August 1872 we started from Glenelg in a small cutter, the *Leda*, for an excursion to Lochourn. Our party consisted, besides ourselves, of two ladies, Forbes and Katie, a gentleman, Gilbert Bogle, and a Highland lad. Our course lay down the Sound of Sleat, which on that side divides the Isle of Skye from the mainland, the average breadth of the channel in that part being two miles.

It was a calm and sunshiny day, not a breath of air, and the sea perfectly smooth. As we were getting the cutter along with oars we perceived a dark mass about two hundred yards astern of us, to the north. While we were looking at it with our glasses (we had three on board) another similar black lump rose to the left of the first, leaving an interval between; then another and another followed, all in regular order. We did not doubt it being one living creature; it moved slowly across our wake and disappeared. Presently the first mass, which was evidently the head, reappeared, and was followed by the rising of the other black lumps, as before. Sometimes three appeared, sometimes four, five, or six, and then sank again. When they rose, the head appeared first, if it had been down, and the lumps rose after it in regular order, beginning always with the next to the head, and rising gently, but when they sank, they sank altogether rather abruptly, sometimes leaving the head visible. It gave the impression of a creature crooking up its back to sun itself. There was no appearance of undulation; when the lumps sank, other lumps did not rise in the interim between them. The greatest number we counted was seven, making eight with the head, as shown in sketch number one [two engravings are given]. The parts were separated from each other by intervals of

154

about their own length, the head being rather smaller and flatter than the rest, and the nose being very slightly visible above the water; but we did not see the head raised above the surface either this or the next day nor could we see the eye. We had no means of measuring the length with any accuracy; but taking the distance from the centre of one lump to the centre of the next to be six feet, and it could scarcely be less, the whole length of the portion visible, including the intervals submerged, would be forty-five feet.

Presently, as we were watching the creature, it began to approach us rapidly, causing a great agitation in the sea. Nearly the whole of the body, if not all of it, had now disappeared and the head advanced at a great rate in the midst of a shower of fine spray, which was evidently raised in some way by the quick movement of the animal – it did not appear how – and not by spouting. Forbes was alarmed and retreated to the cabin, crying that the creatures were coming down upon us. When within about a hundred yards of us, it sank and moved away in the direction of Skye, just under the surface of the water, for we could trace its course by the waves it raised on the still sea to the distance of a mile or more. After this it continued at intervals to show itself, careering about at a distance, as long as we were in that part of the Sound; the head and a small part only of the body being visible on the surface, but we did not again, on that day see it so near nor so well as at first.

At one time Forbes and Katie, and Gilbert Bogle saw a fin sticking up at a little distance back from the head, but neither of us were then observing. On our return the next day we were again becalmed on the north side of Loch Hourn, where it is about three miles wide, the day warm and sunshiny as before. As we were dragging slowly along in the afternoon the creature again appeared over towards the south side, at a greater distance than we saw it the first day. It now showed itself in three or four rather long lines, as in sketch number two, and looked considerably longer than it did the day before; as nearly as we could compute, it looked at least sixty feet in length. Soon it began careering about, showing but a small part of itself, as on the day before, and appeared to be going up Loch Hourn, and when we had nearly reached the island of Sandaig, it came rushing past us about a hundred and fifty yards to the south, on its return from Loch Hourn. It went with great rapidity, its black head only visible through the clear sea, followed by a long trail of agitated water. As it shot along, the noise of its rush through the water could be distinctly heard on board. There were no organs of motion to be seen, nor was there any shower of spray as on the day before, but merely such a commotion in the sea as its quick passage might be expected to make. Its progress was equable and smooth, like that of a log towed rapidly. For the rest of the day, as we worked northwards through the Sound of Sleat, it was occasionally within sight of us till nightfall, rushing about at a distance, as before, and showing only its head and a small part of its body on the surface. It seemed on each day to keep pace about us and as we were always then rowing, we were inclined to think it perhaps might be attracted by the measured sound of the oars. Its only exit in this direction to the north was by the narrow Strait of Kylerhea, dividing Skye from the mainland, and only a third of a mile wide, and we left our boat, wondering whether this strange creature had gone that way or turned back again to the south. We have only to add to this narrative of what we saw ourselves, the following instances of its being seen by other people, of the correctness of which we have no doubt. The ferry-men on each side of Kylerhea saw it pass rapidly through on the evening of the 21st, and heard the rush of water; they were surprised, and thought it might be a shoal of porpoises, but could not comprehend their going so quickly. Finlay McRae, of Bundaloch in the parish of Kintail, was within the mouth of Loch Hourn on the 21st, with other men in his boat, and saw the creature at about a distance of about one hundred and fifty yards. Two days after we saw it, Alexander Macmillan, boat builder at Dornie, was fishing in a boat in the entrance of Loch Duich, halfway between Druidag and Castledonan, when he saw the animal, near enough to hear the noise, and see the ripples it made rushing along in the sea. He says that what seemed four or more lumps, or 'half rounds followed its head' as he calls them, and that they sometimes rose and sometimes sank altogether. He estimated its length at no less than between sixty and eighty feet. He saw it also on two subsequent days in Loch Duich. On all these occasions his brother Farquhar was with him in the boat, and they were both much alarmed, and pulled to the shore in great haste.

A lady at Duisdale, in Skye, a place overlooking the part of the Sound which is opposite the opening of Lochourn, said that she was looking out with a glass when she saw a strange object in the sea, which appeared like eight seals in a row. This was just about the time that we saw it. We were also informed that about the same time it was seen from the island of Eigg, between Eigg and the mainland, about twenty miles to the southwest of the opening of Lochourn. We have not permission to mention the names in these last two instances.

John MacRae. David Twopeny.

P.S. The writers of the above account scarcely expect the public to believe in the existence of the creature which they saw. Rather than that, they look for the disbelief and ridicule to which the subject always gives rise, partly on account of the animal having been pronounced to be a snake, without sufficient evidence, but principally because of exaggerations and fables with which the whole subject is beset. Nevertheless, they consider themselves bound to leave record of what they saw, in order that naturalists may receive it as a piece of evidence, or not, according to what they think it is worth. The animal will very likely turn up on those coasts again, and it will be in that 'dead season', so convenient to editors of newspapers, for it is never seen but in the still warm days of summer or early autumn. There is a considerable probability that it has visited the same coasts before.

In the summer of 1871, some large creature was seen for some time rushing about in Loch Duich, but it did not show itself sufficiently for anyone to ascertain what it was. Also, some years back, a well known gentleman of the west coast was crossing the Sound of Mull, from Mull to the mainland, on a very calm afternoon, 'When,' as he writes, 'our attention was attracted to a monster which had come to the surface, not more than fifty yards from our boat. It rose without causing the slightest disturbance of the sea, or making the slightest noise, and floated for some time on the surface, but without exhibiting its head or tail., showing only the ridge of the back, which was not that of a whale or any other sea animal that I had ever seen. The back appeared sharp and ridge-like, and in colour very dark, indeed black, or almost so. It rested quietly for a few minutes, and then dropped quietly down into the deep, without causing the slightest agitation. I should say that about forty feet of it, certainly no less, appeared on the surface.'

It should be noticed that the inhabitants of the western coast are quite familiar with the appearance of whales, seals, and porpoises, and when they see them they recognize them at once. Whether the creature which pursued Mr M'Clean's boat off the island of Coll in 1808 and of which there is an account in the Transactions of the Wernerian Society, was one of these Norwegian animals, it is not easy to say. Survivors who knew Mr McLean say that he could quite be relied upon for the truth. The public are not likely to believe in the creature until it is caught, and that does not seem likely to happen just yet, for a variety of reasons. One reason being that it has, from all the accounts given of it, the power of moving very rapidly. On the 20th, while we were becalmed in the mouth of Loch Hourn, a steam launch slowly passed us, and, we watched it, we reckoned its rate at five or six miles an hour. When the animal rushed past us on the next day at about the same distance, and when we were again becalmed nearly in the same place, we agreed that it went twice as fast as the steamer, and we thought that its rate could not be less than ten or twelve miles an hour. It might be shot, but would probably sink. There are three accounts of its being shot at in Norway; in one instance it sank, and in the other two it pursued the boats, which were near the shore, but disappeared when it found itself getting into shallow water.

It should be mentioned that when we saw this creature, and made our sketches of it, we had never seen either Pontopiddan's Natural History or his print of the Norwegian evidence, extending through a number of years, which remains after setting aside fables and exaggerations. It seems surprising that no naturalist of that country has ever applied himself to make out something about the animal. In the meantime, as the public will most probably be dubious about quickly giving credit to our account, the following explanations are open to them, all of which have been proposed by me, viz: porpoises, lumps of seaweed, empty herring barrels, bladders, logs of wood, waves of the sea, and inflated pig-skins! But as all these theories present to our mind greater difficulties than the existence of the animal itself, we feel obliged to decline them.

Sandy Campbell told author Gavin Maxwell about an incident which occurred on Loch Scavaig at the southern end of

Skye. Sandy, his uncle and John Stewart were fishing for herring, which used to swim into the loch in their thousands. It was dusk, the sky was still light, but the land was dark – a fine night with a light northerly breeze and a ripple on the water. Sandy and the two old men began to haul their net. He was only a young boy and his arms tired easily He rested for a moment and as he did so, he noticed an object rising out of the water about 50 yd to seaward of them. It was about a yard high when he first saw it, but as he watched, it rose slowly from the surface to a height of 20 or more ft – a tapering column that moved to and fro in the air. Sandy called excitedly to the old men, but at first got only an angry retort to keep hauling the net and not be wasting time. At last Stewart looked up in exasperation, and then sprang to his feet in bewildered astonishment, as he too saw what Sandy was looking at. While this 'tail' was still waving in the air, they could see the water rippling against a dark mass below it which was just breaking the surface, and which they presumed to be the animal's body. The high column descended slowly into the sea as it had risen and as the last of it submerged the boat began to rock on a commotion of water like the wake of a passing steamer.

The three occupants of the boat elected to leave the area as quickly as possible, dropped their nets and rowed for the safety of the shore.

Another encounter occurred at Loch Brittle, off the southeast coast of Skye Sandy Campbell is also the source of this account.

In 1917, Ronald MacDonald, his brother Harry, and their father were in a fishing boat at the mouth of Loch Brittle when a similar kind of phenomenon presented itself to the three astonished fishermen. It was heading north at a speed of about five knots and about a mile away. It appeared as a high column, said to be a great deal higher than the object Sandy had seen in Loch Scavaig and light flashed at the top of the column as though a small head were being turned from side to side. There was a considerable commotion in the water astern of it, but no other portion of the body was visible above the surface. It submerged slowly, until nothing was left showing above the sea, and it seemed to descend vertically and without flexion.

The Kyle of Lochalsh is a narrow channel separating the mainland from the Isle of Skye. Dr Farquhar Matheson, an ear, nose and throat specialist who practised in Soho Square, London, was accompanied by his wife while sailing there. The couple encountered a strange sea creature and their account appeared in the *Strand Magazine* in 1893.

It was a beautiful day, clear as possible, the sun shining brightly and without clouds. The time was between one and two.

Our sail was up and we were going gaily along, when suddenly I saw something rise out of the Loch in front of us – a long, straight neck-like thing as tall as my mast. I could not think what it was at first. I fancied it might be something on land, and directed my wife's attention to it. I said, 'Do you see that?' She said she did, and asked what it could be and was rather scared. It was, at this time, 200 yards away and was moving towards us. Then it began to draw its neck down and I saw clearly that it was a large sea monster – of the saurian type, I should think. It was brown in colour, shining, and with a sort of ruffle at the junction of the head and neck. I can think of nothing with which to compare it so well as the head and neck of a giraffe, that is, it was not so much at right angles to it as a continuation of it in the same line. It moved its head from side to side, and I saw the reflection of the light from its wet skin. I saw no body – only a ripple of water where the line of the body should be. I should judge, however, that there must have been a large base of body to support such a neck. It was not a sea serpent, but a much larger and more substantial beast – something of the nature of a gigantic lizard, I should think. An eel could not lift up its body like that, nor could a snake.

Dr Matheson also claimed that the creature did not have scales, but a smooth skin. Later versions of his account also say that the creature appeared 'three more times at intervals of two or three minutes, lifting its head vertically out of the water each time'. Dr Matheson tried to keep pace with the beast but after a mile or so, it disappeared into the distance.

According to author R.L. Cassie, in his two-volume work, *The Monsters of Achanalt*:

I betook myself to the point of vantage commanding Loch Achanalt. Both sections of the loch always show signs of agitation here and there, and several reptiles – or portions of bodies – can often be seen at a single glance. The colossus of nine hundred feet is often visible, extending over the open loch in a straight line from near the north-eastern end to within fifty or eighty yards from the western bay. About thirty or forty feet of the middle region of the back are often depressed below water. Cavillers will affirm, without an atom of knowledge or experience, that it must be a case of two or more animals in line. But I back my eyesight and knowledge against their armchair conjectures.

Mr Cassie christened the monster of Achanalt, Gabriel.

It should be noted that Loch Achanalt has, in the past, been subject to drainage work, which revealed portions of its bottom. Mr Cassie claims that when this work was carried out, a monster measuring some 50 ft was observed, with a 'long, gently arched hill in the region of its back. This ridge looked as if it was topped with thistles or some kind of rough scrub'. His book, it has to be said, is hardly conclusive in its evidence. He himself admits to being 'handicapped by distance and want of glasses'.

Lewis is the largest and most northerly of the Outer Hebrides. *The Times* of 22 March 1856 reported 'a water creature that looked like a huge peat stack or a six oared boat. It swallowed a blanket left on the shore by a girl herding cattle, then vanished into the loch.'

In 1961 an incident occurred at Loch Urabhal in Lewis. The *Glasgow Herald* of 29 July reported it.

A monster appeared in Loch Urabhal, near the village of Achmore, in Lewis, on Thursday evening (27 July 1961), Mr Ian McArthur, a Forres school teacher who is holidaying in Lewis, said yesterday. Mr McArthur had gone out fishing with Mr Roderick MacIver, a teacher from Stornaway, and his brother Donald, on leave from teaching in Aden.

'Roddy and I were fishing at the shallow end of the Loch, when Roddy jumped to his feet shouting "There's something in the Loch". I then saw it myself. Donald, who was fishing farther up the Loch, did not see it, but he saw we were excited about something. It was about 45 yards away from us in shallow water and it appeared three times. It had a hump and there was either a small head or fin about 6 feet away from the hump. It swam like a dolphin but was much bigger.

'Urabhal is an inland Loch, and no dolphins could get into it. I have been fishing there and so have the MacIver brothers since we were boys and have never seen anything in the Loch. I asked my father if there were any legends about the Loch, but he said there was none. He thought it must have been an otter, but this did not swim like an otter. We saw it distinctly because the sun was shining and the water was calm. I had my camera out ready for a picture when it submerged for the last time.'

According to a local historian, Dr Donald MacDonald, of Gisla, there are no traditions attached to Urabhal. According to him, the only Loch in Lewis with a monster is Suaidabhal, near Uig, where, according to local legend, lambs were thrown into the Loch to feed the monster.

The Stettin Lloyd Steamer *Katie* was returning from New York to Newcastle on 31 May 1882 when, according to one crew member (as reported in *Illustrirte Zeitung*, 1 July 1882):

Shortly after sunset and in that clear light which in this season prevails in fine weather in high northern latitudes, about eight miles west-north-west of the Butt of Lewis (Hebrides), we observed, on the starboard bow at a distance of about two miles, a dark object lying on the surface, which was only slightly moved by the waves. First we took it for a wreck, as the highest end resembled the broken waist of a ship filled with water. As we got nearer, we saw with a glass on the left of the visible object, the water moving in a manner as if the object extended there under the water, and this motion was of the same length as the part of the object visible above the surface. Therefore, we took care not to steer too near, lest the screw should be damaged by some floating pieces of the wreck. But on getting nearer we observed that the object was not a wreck and if we had not known with certainty that on these coasts there are no shallows, we should have taken this dark connected row of bumps for rocks. When, however, we changed our course obliquely from the object, which lay quite still all the time, to our astonishment there arose, about eighty feet from the visible end, a fin about ten feet in height, which moved a few times, while the body gradually sank below the surface. In consequence of this the most elevated end rose, and could distinctly be made out as the tail of a fish of immense dimensions.

The length of the visible part of this animal which had not the least resemblance to the back of a whale, measured, according to our estimation, about 150 feet, the bumps, which were from three to four feet in height, and about six or seven feet distant from each other, were smaller on the tail end than on the head end, which withdrew from our observation. At our arrival in Newcastle, I learned that some days before, some fishermen of Lewis had observed the same or similar animal.

In January 1895, Angus MacDonald of Tobson saw a 60-ft long sea serpent off the small island of Berneray, at the southernmost end of Lewis. The creature displayed two coils, which were about 10 ft apart. MacDonald described the creature as being like 'huge hornless bull'. The following month Mr Berners, a Free Kirk minister, was at the northern tip of the island – The Butt of Lewis – when, 200 yd out to sea, he saw a giraffe-like neck rise 15 ft out of the water. The neck had a ruffle 2 ft behind the ears. 'It had two great staring eyes, like a bull's fixed upon me, and then I saw three joints of its body 120 long fitting into each other like a lobster's tail.' A year after this sighting, Mr Ivan McGregor claimed to have seen a pair of these creatures swimming in the sea between Lewis and Cape Wrath on the mainland.

At Loch Duvat on the smaller island of Eriskay, there was another incident. According to Father Allen MacDonald (a local historian, whose private papers I have read) Ewen MacMillen gave an account of a strange encounter with a creature there. MacMillen, from Bunavullin, Eriskay, of Skye descent and aged about fifty, claimed that at the beginning of June 1893, he had gone to look after a mare and foal that he owned. It was between 9 and 10 p.m., and the animals were by Loch Duvat. As he walked alongside the lake he saw an animal in front of him on the northern side, which he took to be his own mare, and he made his way towards it. He got within 20 yd of it, and although he could not distinguish its colour due to the haze, he saw that it was certainly no bigger than the general Eriskay pony. It then gave out a hideous scream, which frightened not only him but also the horses grazing at the western end of the lake. He ran the whole way home.

According to Celtic myth, the water-kelpie is believed to take the form of a horse-like creature, and this is clearly where this description emanates from.

Loch Maree is more popularly known in lake monster tradition as 'Loch na Beiste'. It is situated on a peninsula between Gruinard Bay and Loch Ewe on Rudha Mor. It is 12½ miles long and 2¼ wide, and mountains surround it. It is renowned for its sea trout fishing. A local legend says that many years ago, local crofters would avoid the loch, as they believed that it contained a fearsome beast or monster. Many local people claimed to have seen the beast's huge back (similar in shape to an upturned boat) rising from the water.

Mr Bankes, a local landlord, heard of the tales of the beast and at once resolved to find out what it was. Having funds at his disposal, he elected to have the loch partially drained. A large pump was brought from Liverpool to aid this operation, along with a gang of workers. It was deemed easiest to pump the water from the loch directly into a nearby burn, which in turn flowed into the sea. To all intents and purposes, this was going to be a straightforward and reasonable operation. However, none of the crew working the machinery had accounted for the fact that another burn running into the loch was adding water to it at a faster rate than they were pumping it out. It took several days for the team to realize this, and when they did so, they stopped.

By now, Bankes, who had spent a considerable sum of money on this operation, was on a crusade to have the loch emptied and the creature it allegedly contained identified. Undeterred by the failure of the pumping operation, he kept the crew on to assist with his next effort. Countless barrels of lime were ordered from Skye and dumped into the areas believed to be deep enough for a large creature to live in.

The lime only filled small areas, however, and Bankes soon realized that it was just too big a task. He was forced to give up any idea of finding the creature. His efforts had become something of a joke, not only amongst the local community, but nationally; his exploits were covered in *Punch* magazine. He therefore decided to fine each of his tenants for their jocular taunts about his 'monster search'.

During a debate in January 1893 (mentioned in the *Daily Graphic*, 17 January 1893) about the existence of the sea serpent, Sir William Flower, Director of the British Museum of Natural History, stated that he did not reject the notion of sea serpents living in the world's oceans. He did however, request, as proof of the existence of this creature, some form of tangible evidence. 'Bring me a scale.' In 1851, Dr W.M. Russell thought he had founds such evidence. Writing to *The Times* (letter published in the edition of 6 January 1893), he said:

I happened to be on a visit to the house of Mrs McIver and I not only heard from her a detailed account of the recent appearance of a great sea serpent in the little bay of Greiss, opposite her residence, but I actually became the possessor of a number of scales about the size and shape of a scallop shell which were found on the reef rock in the bays whereon the monster had comforted itself by scratching its head. Mrs McIver had not merely heard of the strange creature, she had seen it taking a leisurely swim along the beach, to the great alarm of the fish, shoals of which leaped out of the water in front of her.

He continued that local fishermen who had shot and wounded it, had driven the monster to the shore. The creature tried to take refuge upon some rocks, but it was once again pursued by the fishermen and finally sought sanctuary beneath the waves. The fishermen had gone to the rocks upon which the creature had momentarily rested and gathered the scales in. One member of the boat crew had later handed some to Mrs McIver, who passed them to Dr Russell, who in turn lost them!

The North

In 1910 W.J. Hutchinson of Kirkwall, Orkney, his father and his cousin were in their sailing boat heading for the Skerries of Work to shoot duck and plover. They were surprised to see a school of whales leaping clear of the water and moving out of the area at high speed.

> My father was steering, and after the whales had disappeared, looked ahead on the course for the Skerries – and then I heard him say, 'My God, boys, what's that?' whilst pointing ahead. I looked up and saw a creature standing straight up out of the sea – with a snake-like neck and head, like that of a horse or a camel.

The boat was turned, so as to beam on to the strange creature, whilst Hutchinson went for his gun. His father was concerned that they might injure the animal and it would sink the boat. The animal though, eventually sank slowly into the water until, without any bubble or commotion, it disappeared.

On 5 August 1919, Mr J. MacKintosh Bell, a lawyer of Moffat, told Rupert T. Gould of an encounter that day with a strange creature in the Pentland Firth, between the Scottish mainland and the Orkneys. When on holiday on Hoy, he was helping the crew of a local fishing boat pick up lobster pots between Brims Ness on the Mainland and Tor Ness at the southern end of the island early one morning. As the crew, were chatting, they mentioned a curious animal that they had seen several times in the area. The creature then appeared.

> I looked, and sure enough, about 25–30 yards from the boat a long neck as thick as an elephant's fore leg, all rough looking like an elephant's hide, was sticking up. On top of this was the head which was much smaller in proportion, but of the same colour. The head was like that of a dog, coming sharp to the nose. The eyes were

black and small, and the whiskers were black. The neck, I should say, stuck about 5–6 feet, possibly more, out of the water. It disappeared and, as was its custom, swam alongside the boat about ten feet down. We all saw it plainly, my friends remarking that they had seen it many times swimming just the same way after it had shown itself on the surface. My friends told me that they had seen it the year before just about the same place. It was a common occurrence, so they said. That year was the last of several years in which they saw it annually. It did not show itself again for two or three years, and then it was only seen once. Its body, as it was seen below the water, was dark brown, getting slightly lighter as it got the outer edge, then at the edges appeared to be almost grey. It had two paddles or fins on its sides and two at it stern. My friends thought it would weigh two or three tons, some thinking four to six.

Taken from *A Case for the Sea Serpent*

Mackintosh Bell believed that the creature measured about 20 ft in length, and about 10–11 ft around the body. Its neck, he thought, was about 8 ft long. He made a rough sketch of the creature.

In 1937, Mr John R. Brown reported a sighting in the region of the Pentland Skerries in the *Orcadian* newspaper (9 September 1937).

Mr Scot was speaking last night about a monster that had been seen about Fair Isle. To tell the truth, I never believed much in monsters myself, but I saw something today resembling nothing I have ever seen before. It was about noon when we were working down at the East End that on chancing to look out to sea I noticed the sea breaking white as on a submerged rock. As I knew there were no rocks in that particular spot, I watched for a little and presently a great object rose up out of the water – anything from twenty to thirty feet and at an angle of about 45 degrees. It was round shaped and there appeared to be a head on it, but as it was about half a mile from the shore I could not be sure. I called the attention of the other two men but unfortunately before they got their eyes on the spot it had disappeared again, though both of them saw the foam it made. We watched for a considerable time but it never appeared again.

A rather less well substantiated incident, which occurred in Scapa Flow, was reported by Mr W.J. Hutchinson, to author Tim Dinsdale.

Mr Faithful was a diver working with one of the salvage parties who were employed raising sunken German ships from the floor of Scapa Flow in the Orkneys. On one occasion, Mr Faithful was dropped down into the water after depth charges had been ignited in order to loosen the sunken war ships from their position on the seabed. Faithful dropped down into the gloom in order to assess the state of the wreckage after the explosions and to attach cables to the designated points of the wreckage, which would hoist it up.

As he reached the bottom he landed upon something unusual, it was soft; looking down he made out the body of a large animal, and the creature seemed to be eating the fish life, which had been stunned or killed by the explosion. Without further thought, he gave three tugs on his drop line (generally an emergency signal to get the diver up as quickly as possible) and was hauled to the surface where he recounted the incident.

The island of Stronsa or Stronsay lies in the north-east of the Orkneys. It was at one time well known for its so-called natural medicinal springs, which were said to cure leprosy. For cryptozoologists, the name is synonymous with what has become the best-known carcass stranding in history. On 25 September 1808, the carcass of what initially appeared to be a long-necked sea serpent was washed ashore at Rothiesholm Head, on the south-east of the island, where it lay on rocks. A local man noticed seabirds flocking round what appeared to be an animal corpse. Moving his boat towards shore he made his way to the carcass, where he saw what he thought was a creature with a long eel-like neck and three pairs of legs. Its position made closer inspection impossible. However, ten days later a gale blew the decomposing carcass further inland where it could at last be studied in greater detail.

Measurements were taken and the beast was discovered to be exactly 55 ft long, with a neck measuring 10 ft 3 in in length. The head was described as being like that of a sheep with eyes bigger than a seal's. Its skin was grey and rough, yet when stroked from the head down towards the rear, was described as being as smooth as velvet. Six limbs extended from the body and a silvery-coloured bristly mane of long wiry hair grew from the region of its shoulders down towards its tail. The bristles were said to glow eerily in the dark. The *Orcadian* reported, 'its flesh was described as being like 'coarse ill-coloured beef, entirely covered with fat and tallow and without the least resemblance or affinity to fish'. The skin, which was grey-coloured and had an elastic texture was said to be about two inches thick in parts.'

The four men who had originally carried out an examination of the carcass were called to Kirkwall, where they were required to swear on oath the truth of their information before a local magistrate. Soon, news of the Stronsa beast had reached the Natural History Society in Edinburgh and at a meeting in November 1808, the society gave the creature the Latin name *Halsdrus pontoppidani*. Translated, this name means, Pontoppidan's water snake of the sea and was given in honour of the Norwegian bishop who researched such creatures during the eighteenth century.

Naturalist Sir Everard Home viewed what remained of the creature, but was convinced that it was nothing more than a decomposing basking shark, a creature which is commonly seen in the waters around the Orkneys. Comparing vertebrae of the monster and those of a basking shark, he found them virtually identical. Home explained how a basking shark decomposes. First the jaws – which are attached only by a small piece of flesh – drop off, leaving what looks like the remains of a long neck and a small skull. The upper half of the tail carries the spine, so when the lower half rots away it provides a fine serpentine tail. Finally, as the dorsal fin falls away, the remaining rays give the appearance of a hair-like mane. As for the six legs they were seen to be the remains of the lower fins.

This is a perfectly logical piece of scientific detection, and one could therefore dismiss the Stronsa beast as a known phenomenon, the natural decomposition of a living creature – except that the largest known basking shark measures 40 ft, 15 ft less than the Stronsa beast.

The arguments over the Stronsa carcass have raged on ever since. In the 1930s, Professor Ritchie examined three vertebrae of the creature, which had been preserved at the Royal Scottish Museum in Edinburgh. He concluded that Home was correct and as the basking shark is often found in the waters around the Orkneys, this is what the Stronsa carcass was! But the truth of the matter is that no definite conclusion could be reached simply from an examination of the vertebrae; no skin tissue samples were examined, nor any teeth, which could conclusively identify the species.

E. Heath made a study of the sea serpent phenomenon, the results of which were published in a small booklet entitled *An Essay Upon Sea Serpents*. He suggests that the creature seen by Rev M'Clean in June 1808 (see page 140), may well indeed have been the same beast which was washed ashore at Stronsa in September. He compared the details of the living specimen sighted by M'Clean and the dead specimen found at Stronsa as described by witnesses.

Living Animal – Head: When elevated out of the water, broad and oval form.

Stronsa Carcass – Head: Bones of lower jaw like a dog's; the appearance of soft teeth, which could be bent. No teeth in upper jaw. Throat, too narrow to admit a hand said one witness, wide enough to admit a foot said another.

Living Animal – Neck: Smaller, shoulders considerably broader; body tapering towards the tail, which was kept low in the water.

Stronsa Carcass – Neck: Length of neck to shoulder, 10 feet 3 inches, middle of head to mane, 15 feet; ridge of back to belly, 4 feet; circumference, 10 feet, rather oval than round. Extremity of the tail 2 inches thick, and rather rounded, and quite flexible any way.

Living Animal – Fin: None seen.

Stronsa Carcass – Fin: Had six fins or paws, those next to the head 4½ feet long; the toes 8 inches – not webbed except for 1½ inches, but fringed with bristles 10 inches long; the other fins or paddles not so long.

Living Animal – Mane: Head being under water when nearest, no mane was seen.

Stronsa Carcass – Mane: Had a mane from shoulder to near extremity of the tail, bristles from 2 to 10 ins long.

Living Animal – Motion: Undulating up and down, and very rapid when the animal was wholly under water; less so when head above the surface.

Stronsa Carcass – Two canals, one above and another below the back bone, from neck to tail, containing two ligaments, strong enough to raise the animal up or bend its body in a spiral form; bones of a gristly nature, except back bone.

Living Animal – Colour. Not named.

Stronsa Carcass – Colour: Skin grey, without scales.

Living Animal – Length: 70 – 80 feet.

Stronsa Carcass – Length: From junction of head and neck to tail, part of which was wanting, 55 feet.

Witnesses also claimed that the eyes were no larger than a seal's, and there were two spout holes on the sides of the neck, 1¼ ins in diameter, and one on the back of the skull. The flesh was like coarse, ill-coloured beef interlarded with fat or tallow and had no affinity to fish; when put into the fire, neither flamed nor melted, but burned away like gristle. The stomach was 4 ft long, and thick as a firkin, divided right across by a membrane 3/16 in thick, and of the same substance as the stomach itself. It contained a fetid liquid like blood and water, and at either end was the appearance of a gut; a large bone was brought from the carcass, which was thought to be the collarbone.

Like most islands off the Scottish coast, the Shetland Isles can claim some curios sea creature sightings over the years. The *Dundee Advertiser* of Monday, 8 June 1903, carried the following article:

The sea serpent or some terrible imitation thereof has again made its appearance on the coast of Shetland. The monster was encountered last week by Mr P.F. Jamieson, a merchant residing at the West Side, who had been at the village of Scalloway and set sail about 6 o'clock in the morning for his home. He had not proceeded far when, to his amazement and horror, he saw rising out of the water and a short distance from his boat, a sea monster about 30 feet long. In appearance, it was like a boat's sail and on its head or snout there was an enormous flipper-like appendage. Fortunately, it did not venture to come to closer acquaintance with the owner of the boat, who lost no time in turning about and making for Scalloway.

Mr Jamieson's story is collaborated by the crew of a fishing boat *Adelong*, which for successive nights saw the monster on a stretch of water known as Burra Haaf. In their case, so uncomfortably close did it come to the boat, the men were forced to push it away with a boat hook. The animal destroyed ten of their nets. The men state that 'It seemed to be covered by a thick mucous substance which gave off a very bad smell.'

In February 1937, passengers on board the steamship, *Earl of Zetland*, saw something off Shetland. As recounted in *Monsters & Mysteries* (H.T. Wilkins), a strange monster with three large fins, or humps, standing 6 ft erect out of the water, with a body about 30 ft long, appeared and seemed to race the ship. Passengers claimed that it possibly mistook the ship for another monster. It suddenly swung north and one passenger later claimed that as it did so it emitted a blast like that of a ship's siren!

At Fetlar, one of the north-eastern islands of Shetland, another strange encounter with a sea serpent occurred. The *Glasgow Herald* of Friday, 2 June 1882, told the story:

May 1882 – 28 miles south east of Fetlar. 'It was one hundred and fifty feet long. It had a huge head covered with barnacles as large as herring barrels; a prodigious square mouth, with whiskers seven or eight feet long, and of pretty green colour.'

According to the witnesses on board *Bertie*, said to be men of more than average intelligence. When first observed, the creature was only a short distance away and was making straight towards them. On rising to the surface he had blown, but not like any ordinary whale, which these men were used to seeing. Three hillocks, each about the size of a six-oared boat, with water between them, at first they suggested that it might well be three whales in line, it then gradually sank as seals sink and was next seen passing under their craft. The next moment the monster rose and was approaching the craft with a cavernous mouth, so very wide open that it seemed capable of swallowing the boat and all on board in one gulp. The men on board estimated the depth of the upper lip to be four or five feet. The creature followed the crew of the fishing boat *Bertie* for three hours. The crew shouted and screamed at the creature in an attempt to scare it off, but it would not be driven away. Ballast stones were pelted at the creature but 'started off his nose like marbles', a fowling piece was double charged with swan shot and fired into its mouth, this checked the creature and it sank yet again; the fishing lines nearly a mile of which were lost were cut away, every stitch of canvas was set and the boat moved swiftly through the water. The creature surfaced again and followed about one hundred yards astern. They tacked for three hours and travelled about 11 miles out to sea until they lost sight of the creature, and then immediately made for shore. During their flight they observed that the creature had two fins, apparently as large as their mainsail, 'stretched up from his back or sides' and the only resemblance that the creature bore to a whale was its tail, which they were sure would have measured forty feet across. At last, very badly frightened, the fishermen got ashore, and told of their adventure.

The press were more than a little sceptical of the encounter, although they still claimed, 'Of the veracity and trustworthiness of the Shetland we wish to suggest no doubt.' This was because science, and in particular the eminent zoologist Sir Richard Owen, questioned the authenticity of many such accounts. The account also stated that large sperm whale had been seen in or around the waters of the Shetlands, a fact that science had chosen to ignore, since no such creature or specimen had ever been found in British waters, despite the fact that a similar creature had been washed ashore at Le Havre, on the French coast in 1825. This shows that the workings of science can be fickle and particularly stubborn.

The witnesses on board the *Bertie* were later called upon to provide sworn accounts of their adventure to a Justice of the Peace, not to prove the validity of the encounter, but to prove the honesty and integrity of the entire crew. Looked at rationally it would seem that this account may well have been too dramatic to be taken seriously. The dimensions of the creature described and its subsequent actions are more akin to a piece of drama than a real-life encounter. Despite this, the crew of the *Bertie* maintained that the incident occurred as recalled and it has to be regarded as one of the most remarkable encounters with a sea serpent on record, even though its provenance remains in doubt.

The East

Wick is just a few miles south of John O'Groats, on the north-west tip of Scotland. On 21 September 1938, the cargo steamship *Rimsdale*, bound there from the Orkneys, was 3 miles off Rattray Head when members of the crew noted the appearance of a strange fish. The fish, it was said, was about 10 ft long in the body, and had an oval head which sat on top of a 4 ft neck, as thick as a man's thigh. The 'fish', which had surfaced, followed in the track of the steam ship for about half an hour. It then submerged beneath the water. None of those who saw the creature could relate it to anything they had ever seen. One of the crewmen Benjamin Grove, believed it was like an 'over grown eel' (H.T. Wilkins, *Monsters & Mysteries*).

Further down the coast is the scene of a sighting in September 1937, when two experienced long distance yachters, Enno and Sylvia Loo, were bound for Madagascar from Tallin.

Sylvia and I were steering the yacht, when there came a hell of a splash like an airplane bomb falling into the sea. We were then off Berriedale Head, Caithness. Next, believe it or not, we saw a large head peer above the water. It was two feet long. The monster passed us by, and I guess his length was all of 20 feet.'

They could not provide any further information about the creature, which they thought must have leapt up and out of the sea, then landed with a splash. They did believe that it was an 'unknown quantity'. Enno Loo claimed:

> I feel comfortable in the sea, know my limits and set boundaries and safety guidelines for the unexpected, such as damage to the vessel, illness. I am thorough and try to cover every circumstance. When I saw this 'thing' I was genuinely worried, as it was not a usual marine creature. It seemed to want to take a closer look at us, perhaps to see if we were a threat, or a meal, I don't know. But I was relieved when it submerged and never returned.

The hamlet of Dunrobin lies north of Golspie. Letters to *The Times*, beginning with one from James M. Joass on 12 November 1873 discussed a sea serpent off the coast there.

> One latest thing in Natural History has been the sea serpent, an unfortunate name, by the way, as I think the creature when found will turn out to be a saurian, allied to plesiosaurus. About the middle of September last, two ladies from Dunrobin, near Lochbeg, were looking seaward, and one said to the other 'Surely that is the sea serpent?' 'Yes, no doubt,' was the reply, 'or else sea ware.'
>
> Next morning at seven, Doctor Soutar, when dressing, saw a creature apparently forty to fifty feet long, rushing about near the shore, and raising its neck about four feet above the water. He said on meeting his family at breakfast, 'If I believed in sea serpents, I'd say I had seen one this morning,' and you know he is not a man of incredulous turn of mind.
>
> Next day at noon on a calm sea, I saw through a glass about half a mile out a floating subject, which was certainly part of the same sort of beast dead or basking. It drifted along with the tide and suddenly disappeared near the curing shed. At no time did it raise itself higher

than when first seen. Colour brown and light yellow, apparent size of portion seen about eight to ten feet. It was watched for half an hour and two sketches of it were made. The Cestracions of the Australian seas feed with Oalitic type and Terebratula and Treganicle, also Oalitic molluscs. Why may not a saurian of the same age or some nearby allied form still exist in unexplored ocean?

In response Mr Francis Francis of Twickenham wrote on 12 November 1873:

Dr Maynard tells me that Mr Joass is not at all likely to be misled by appearances, being a very scientific man and eminent archaeologist. It would be strange indeed, if the beast after all were to turn out to be some monstrous saurian; though if his food were confined to animals of those types mentioned by Mr Joass, a saurian of this size alluded to would have some time collecting materials enough for a meal. As this, however, seems rather a matter of conjecture, it is evident we must know something more of it before we can construct any reliable theory upon it.

On 20 November, *The Times* published a reply to the Francis letter, from James Joass, confirming that he was an eye-witness and discussing his perception of the creature's head.

The ears seemed to be diaphanous and nearly semi-circular flaps or valves overarching the nostrils, which were in front. The cavity of the eye appeared to be considerably further back, and a peculiar glimmer in it, along with the sudden disappearance of the creature, presented, indeed, the only signs of vitality, so far as I could see, while I watched it for half an hour apparently drifting with the rising tide, but always keeping the same distance off shore.

Then for some reason, having provided such a detailed description of a sea serpent, Joass retracted much of this statement in letters to the *Inverness Courier* of 20 November 1873, claiming that he had 'made a mistake' and that the sea serpent was in fact a sandbank with seaweed being washed over it. This is far removed from his previous description of diaphanous ears and valves or flaps, which overarch the nostrils. Something caused him to change his story, whether because of the possibility of public humiliation or because he had fabricated his earlier descriptive narrative, we cannot be certain. Whatever the reason, his retraction does little to help the case for the existence of sea serpents or lake monsters, nor does it enhance one's opinion of James Joass himself.

Undoubtedly the world's most famous lake monster is the Loch Ness monster, affectionately known as Nessie. The creature which allegedly inhabits this Highland loch, has become one of the greatest enigmas of the modern age. Sporadic reports of a strange creature date back to the nineteenth century, or even before if we include the tale of St Columba, who is said by Adamnan to have encountered the beast in AD 565, though examination of this report clearly indicates that it occurred in the River Ness, as opposed to Loch Ness.

Monster fever hit Britain in 1933 when, on 2 May, the *Inverness Courier* carried the following report:

Loch Ness has for generations been credited with being the home of a fearsome looking monster, but, somehow or other, the 'water kelpie', as this legendary creature is called, has always been regarded as a myth, if not a joke. Now, however, comes the news that the beast has been seen once more, for, on Friday of last week, a well-known businessman, who lives near Inverness, and his wife (a University graduate), when motoring along the north shore of the loch, not far from Abriachan Pier, were startled to see a tremendous upheaval on the loch, which previously, had been as calm as the proverbial

mill-pond. The lady was the first to notice the disturbance, which occurred fully three quarters of a mile
from the shore, and it was her sudden cries to stop that
drew her husband's attention to the water.

There, the creature disported itself, rolling and plunging for fully a minute, its body resembling that of a
whale, and the water cascading and churning like a
simmering cauldron. Soon, however, it disappeared in a
boiling mass of foam. Both onlookers confessed that
there was something uncanny about the whole thing, for
they realized that here was no ordinary denizen of the
depths, because, apart from its enormous size, the beast,
in taking the final plunge, sent out waves that were big
enough to have been caused by a passing steamer. The
watchers waited for almost half-an-hour in the hope
that the monster (if such it was) would come to the
surface again; but they had seen the last of it.
Questioned as to the length of the beast, the lady stated
that, judging by the state of the water in the affected
area, it seemed to be many feet long. It will be remembered that a few years ago, a party of Inverness anglers
reported that when crossing the loch in a rowing boat,
they encountered an unknown creature, whose bulk,
movements, and the amount of water it displaced at
once suggested that ti was either a very large seal, a
porpoise, or, indeed, the monster itself.

This seems to be the first report of a strange creature in
the loch in the twentieth century. The author of the article,
Alex Campbell, used more than a little journalistic license to
elaborate upon the tale; his passage describing water 'cascading' off the beast, and a 'simmering cauldron', do little to
portray the reality of the situation. Was this really how the
witnesses actually described the scene? In fact, they later
described the water disturbance as being something like 'two
ducks fighting'.

Seals, do, of course, enter Loch Ness and have been

photographed, fed, caught and killed, but Alex Campbell can be forgiven for claiming that they do not, as the first report of a seal living in Loch Ness did not occur until November 1984.

The report caused a national sensation as hoards of tourists and casual visitors flocked to the loch, hoping to catch a glimpse of the elusive creature The media quickly seized the opportunity to promote spectacular tales of the monster, and rewards were offered for photographs of it. This led to a number of forgeries and misleading tales.

The mystery continued to attract enthusiastic researchers and 'monster watchers' also known as 'Nessophiles' – during the following decades, and books and pamphlets were produced as Nessie became a tourist industry in its own right. I am not for one moment suggesting that the mystery of Loch Ness is based upon some kind of deliberate misinformation by local entrepreneurs, but it has undoubtedly been inappropriately promoted in some quarters, especially in recent years.

That there is a large and as yet unidentified creature in the loch there is no doubt; the quality and quantity of witness sightings indicate that something does exist. However, this has created a further anomaly. According to some researchers there have, since 1933, been over 10,000 reported sightings. This figure is far from accurate, and less than a thousand is a more realistic figure. Similarly, if we look at the discrepancies in the descriptions provided by alleged eye-witnesses, we can see that Loch Ness must house about thirty different kinds of monsters. We have a horse-like head, a triple-humped body, a seven-humped body, a giraffe neck, a snake-like appearance, a camel-like appearance, a plesiosaur-like appearance, a salamander and an upturned boat appearance. Then we have the colours: black, blue, brown, green, grey, khaki, rust, spotted, white, even yellow! It was as a result of such discrepancies that the Loch Ness Monster Research Society was formed, in an attempt to compile a comprehensive database of information for analysis. Incredibly, no known organization had previously undertaken such a task. Many believe that such attempts are futile and without value. However, as can be seen, the field of Loch Ness information is a veritable minefield of misinformation.

In order to achieve some semblance of order in the information on the Loch Ness phenomenon, it is pertinent to include an incident which occurred to me on the afternoon of 31 March 1999. Along with a number of other witnesses, I saw a strange creature surface and move through Urquhart Bay. It was something which I could easily recognize. I had seen seals, deer, floating logs, bracken, ducks and freak and natural wave and wake formations on the loch during the last decade or so, and I knew that what I saw, along with the other witnesses, was none of these. The creature, and it was very much a living specimen, appeared to be black in colour, and reared its head and neck out of the water to a height I would estimate to be about 3–4 ft. There was a great amount of water disturbance surrounding it. I would estimate that it was about 200 yd off shore. The creature moved through the water for a distance of about 50 yd, before slowly submerging, gradually reducing in height, as opposed to diving. I would describe it as like a submarine submerging, which, of course, it most certainly was not! The whole episode lasted about thirty seconds, and was over before I could appreciate what it was I was looking at. Its entire length I could not estimate, but from the water disturbance I would think it was over 15 ft. If pushed to place it into a definite species category, I would say it was more like a huge eel than anything else. Eels do of course live in Loch Ness, although none of this size have, to the best of my knowledge, been caught, nor do they appear to swim in this manner.

For over sixteen months I have maintained a discreet silence over this sighting. I have desperately searched through hundreds of natural history reference books trying to match it with a known species, but I have not yet been able to categorize it.

Since then, I have received a number of reports from Loch

Ness of a similar creature. In 2000 alone, I have accumulated twelve independent sightings. The honour of the first sighting of the millennium went to Mr George Dawson from Lincolnshire, who, on the morning of 3 January 2000, saw:

> ... a long black object rose to the surface about 300 yards off shore (Lower Foyers). It lay there for about thirty seconds and appeared to be stationary. It began to move and slowly cruised past Foyers. I was above the loch surface, looking down onto the loch and Lower Foyers. I could see through the surface water that it was of great size, about 15–20 feet, its body, the shadow and outline of which was visible just below the surface, was not dinosaur/plesiosaur-like, but much thinner and streamlined. I had no expectation of seeing anything when I visited the loch, but have to express my opinions, that what I saw, was so far removed from what I had read and heard of, that I question if it was in fact a different animal? The creature I witnessed was like an overgrown eel, fatter in body, but nevertheless definitely eel-like. I am no wildlife expert, I saw windrows and natural shadows on the loch, and I can differentiate these from a living creature. From my observation point, the monster, if it was *the* monster, seemed quite tranquil and was calmly floating down the loch (perhaps looking for food), before submerging, when it created a surface wake disturbance. Due to the distance and observation angle, I could see no flipper or paddle action, if it does possess these, they were not evident during this display.

There will, of course, be objections to my inclusion of this sighting by those who claim that I am proposing the 'giant eel' theory. But whichever way one looks at the Loch Ness data, a number of probable explanations can be suggested. I have simply included this account as it is one of the better ones received this year. The argument will continue to rage for many years to come, unless the creature is apprehended and positively identified. Even then, there will no doubt still be those who dismiss the evidence.

Loch Oich, the central loch in the Great Glen chain, is 4 miles long. The *Glasgow Herald* of Friday, 14 August 1936, reported the following sighting:

Story of the appearance in Loch Oich of a creature which closely resembles the Loch Ness Monster, by Alderman A.J. Richards, a member of Camberwell Borough Council and headmaster of Evydale Public School in London and his son, Mr A.J. Richards junior, who lives with his parents at 169 Court Lane, Dulwich, along with a friend, Mr G.M. Wilkinson, of Forest Holme, Queens Road, Forest Hill, London SE23, when boating at the Laggan end of the Loch, early Tuesday afternoon. Mr Richards senior said he saw a 'weird creature' emerge from the waters, which were only a few feet deep.

First two humps like coils of a snake appeared only a few yards from the boat, then the head appeared, and so close were the astonished witnesses they could see it was shaggy like that of a dog. The creature continued to dive and reappear, first one coil being seen then both followed by the head, which was shaken vigorously each time it came up. The coils were 3 feet high by the same length, and were about 3 feet apart with head a seemingly equal distance away, thus the body was over twelve feet overall. The group was in agreement that it was speedy in its movements and that it covered a distance of about fifty yards in just a few seconds.

Mr Richards junior, who is 20 years of age said, 'The creature's nearness made us all feel uneasy, I rowed for shore where we waited for it to reappear, but it didn't do so.'

On Saturday, 19 September 1936, Mr Simon Cameron, a canal bridge keeper of Laggan, Invergarry, told how the creature had risen to the surface in the bay beside his house and with quick powerful strokes of its forelimbs, travelled briskly in an easterly direction, where it was lost to view. Mr Cameron clearly saw 6 ft of furry-like body with a dog-like head. When asked if he thought that the vision he had seen might be nothing more than an otter, he replied, 'There is no otter on earth anything like that size.'

Fraserburgh is a port at the north-eastern point of Aberdeenshire. A sensational incident occurred off its coast on Tuesday 8 September 1903, and was reported in the *Daily Express* on Monday, 14 September 1903.

The sea serpent has at last made its annual appearance in Western waters. This time it was the Scotch steam trawler *Glengrant* commanded by Captain Carter with a crew of 10 men, and the North Sea, which have been honoured with a visit from this ancient scaly monster of the deep. According to their report it is 200 feet long and in fairly good health. The lateness of the serpent's arrival may be accounted for by the fact he was waiting for summer to come, and that he has also had to travel thousands of miles to keep up his reputation.

From the Fiji Islands where it was last seen six weeks ago, to the North Sea is 14,000 miles, so that he has made a record trip, assuming that he came by the Cape of Good Hope. When the monster appeared off the coast of Borneo in 1890, Mr Mustard, a veracious Singapore pilot, stated positively that the reptile was exactly 45 feet long, neither more nor less. On that occasion, he amused himself and the natives present, by gently tossing several fishing canoes up in the air and catching them dextrously on the spiked end of his tail. Since that period the sea serpent has appeared in various parts of the world, and each year he has increased in size and strength.

The terrified Captain and crew of the steamer *Glengrant* who had a brief interview with the serpent on

Tuesday, declare that he is fully 200 feet long. This shows a growth of 155 feet in 13 years.

This statement will cause envy to the Cape Cod fishermen on the other side of the Atlantic, who have, of late years, come to regard the serpent as their own peculiar property. In an interview with an *Express* representative on Saturday at Fraserburgh a member of the crew of the *Glengrant* said: 'About four bells in the early morning watch, last Tuesday, all hands were on deck to try a hand at the draught nets. As far as we could tell the steamer was about eighty to one hundred miles off shore. All of a sudden we heard a roaring sound, like the warning note of a cyclone, which was followed by a tremendous agitation in the water. The cook put his head out of the galley and shouted "Whales boys! Look out for your nets." Then to our horror, an enormous monster with a head like a Chinese dragon rose up from the waves alongside the ship. For a moment or so, the serpent rested his chin reflectively on the truck of the mainmast while the stern of the ship sank down under the enormous strain.

'We stood on the deck forward gazing up at him in a dazed manner unable to move. Suddenly the monster started to slide down again into the sea. As he did so, the open cabin skylight attracted his attention, and he thrust his head down to see what was below. The Captain and the mate were just about to have their morning coffee when the awful looking head swung across the table.

'Both of the men are strict teetotallers and knew this was no vision. They dropped their coffee mugs and fled on deck. The poor steward however, was pinned up in the corner and was unable to move. Slowly the serpent looked round the cabin, scorched the steward's whiskers and the paint work with his fiery breath, and then withdrew back into the water.

'One of my shipmates hit his body with a belaying pin, and it sounded as if an iron tank had been struck.

No sooner had the *Glengrant* righted herself than she began to rise up by the stern high into the air as if lifted by some giant head. The waves foamed like a cauldron. As the vessel went down by the bows, the seas swept her deck and flooded the engine room, forecastle, and gallery. We all thought our passages to Davy Jones' locker were booked.

'The propeller revolved at a fearful pace. This lasted a few seconds, then distinct bumps were felt amidships and the stern gradually sank down again. We saw the serpent away on the port side at the rate of five knots an hour. Then he made a sudden tack and bore down on us again, as if he was resolved to crush the ship to pulp. As he came up alongside, one of our fishermen aimed a gun at his head and fired and the serpent suddenly dived and disappeared.

'He was twice as long as our ship with whiskers that stood out like topsail yards, great green eyes, an immense mane and a huge cavernous mouth, with great tusks.'

This thrilling experience of Captain Carter and his crew in the North Sea was not revealed before, as the Captain was afraid of being ridiculed. It was only through the pleading of the crew that he consented to give the story to the press on the arrival of the *Glengrant* at Fraserburgh on Saturday.

Another report about the adventure of the *Glengrant* appeared in the *Grimsby Observer* on Thursday, 17 September 1903.

The *Glengrant* of Fraserburgh, has returned to port from fishing in the North Sea and the captain and the crew, numbering in all ten men, tell the tale of a terrific encounter with the sea serpent in the North Sea. They were some 80 miles from land on Tuesday and just on the break of dawn the hands turned up to try the draught nets. Suddenly a tremendous commotion across on the weather quarter scarcely forty yards away. One of the crew remarked 'whales' but to their consternation a huge dark body emerged and made for the steamer. The men were almost paralysed at the awful sight of the monster, which came on with a swaying motion. When 20 feet off the vessel, it reared to a great height above and the vessel was lifted at least six feet as the monster worked its way through the water beneath her. The vessel took a great dip by the bows and shipped a huge sea, washing the deck clear and flooding the engine room, forecastle and cabin. The utmost consternation prevailed amongst the bewildered crew as the steamer first looked like capsizing and then swamping.

By the time things were righted the monster was some distance off, but to the horror of the crew it was seen coming on again at a furious pace. Wiseman, one of the fishing hands, appeared the only one not to have lost his head, for he dashed below and got a gun. When the animal was fifteen yards away, he fired at the head. Whether he hit it is not known, but it dived and a long sinuous body followed wriggling like a serpent but travelling at a great speed. Long afterwards, the huge monster's undulations could be seen. He was twice the length of the *Glengrant* or nearly two hundred feet. It had a head like a sea horse with a long mane or fin down the back, great green eyes, and enormous mouth and teeth. The description tallies with a monster seen by Montrose fishermen.

In 1891 Peterhead was a busy port and central to the herring fishing industry of the east coast. The following incident was reported in the *Glasgow Weekly Mail* of 26 September of that year.

A Peterhead fisherman who gives us his name and address, vouched for the truth of the following narrative:

'We were holding in ridicule the story about the
crew of the *Rose and Thistle* having seen the monster
at sea as described by one of her crew, and which was
seen by a fishing boat off Kinnaird Head. We
proceeded to sea on Tuesday, leaving port about 1.30
p.m. and sailed a south-westerly course for four hours,
hoping to fall in with a shoal of herrings some thirty
miles off land. A few more boats were in sight during
the whole time, but were more to the westward than
us. The shades of evening were just closing in upon us,
and the sea bore that leaden hue that indicates a breeze,
a sign in which few mariners are ever mistaken; and
our skipper pleaded caution in shooting out nets,
preferring rather to sail around and look for the
herring, a practice very common during unsettled
weather. A shout from one of the hands drew our
attention to a dark looking object looming up against
the foggy background, and which seemed in motion
and to be swaying backwards and forwards in a strange
manner. The story of the sea serpent at once cropped
up, but was quickly beaten down by the few older
men, who declared the object, which was two or three
miles distant, to be a waterspout. To prove this and to
have a laugh at the Stornaway men who a few days
before declared that they saw a strange monster of
gigantic dimensions, our skipper headed the boat
directly for the object mentioned, and now with the
breeze full astern we were rapidly putting less distance
between ourselves and the supposed waterspout. A few
of the hands, myself among the others, felt no necessity for sailing to decide the cause of our attention,
feeling assured that a waterspout was a quite common
phenomenon at sea, even on our coast: and I, who had
been four years to the Arctic regions and had sailed on
nearly every coast in the known world, had seen many
strange phenomena at sea, but we were about to
witness a sight the like of which I, or any of my mates,

had never dreamt of, nor can we yet well realize the effect the sight had upon us.

On nearing the object mentioned we (although darkness was coming rapidly on) could see that we must at least abandon the waterspout theory, and our hired hand threw out sundry hints to put about, but our old man was determined to dispel the sea serpent story, and held on his course. All at once the extraordinary motions of the object drew the entire attention of all hands, and it was now quite apparent that there was extraordinary life in it and the motion of the water around it showed the presence of some live or mechanical body. Towering in the air a dark looking object, possibly 300 feet in height, and with along projecting head and two fore fins or legs making a steady swimming motion and emitting a hissing sort of sound, was now quite clearly seen, the eyes, the mouth, and even the nostrils were plainly in view: and all the prehistoric monsters I ever read of were mere mites compared with this mammoth. What eyes! The sight of which seemed to make everyone spellbound and powerless, a row of teeth, each one four times the length of a man in appearance, but of so terrifying an aspect that it was a few minutes before we realized our proximity to the monster. The putting the boat up in the wind brought us to our senses, and all hands sprang to put the boat about – the audible prayers of the hired hand being the only words spoken., we all felt so impressed. The face of the old man looked like a sheet of white canvas, and terror seemed depicted on every face. We all huddled together after putting about, and no one said a word, nor dare we look behind; but, still hearing the lashing of the water and the hissing sound, we knew we were yet within a close distance of the monster, if it was not really following us. The mantle of darkness, however, was in our favour, and we felt somewhat relieved when our skipper spoke, assuring us that we were now out of sight and reach of it. Never did any crew reach a port more thankful than we did, and as each winded their way home their thoughts were, ''What could it be? Will anyone believe us?'' Yes it is a verity, and the whole of our crew can prove it, and that this is the exact truth.'

The phenomenon known as a 'waterspout' is a small tornado at sea which sucks water and its contents into the air. According to some, it is responsible for 'fish falls' on land (when it appears to be raining fish) which occur periodically around the world, particularly on coastal towns.

The east coast of Scotland maintained its reputation as a favourite haunt of the sea serpent when The *Glasgow Herald* of 3 February 1898 reported:

A petrifying sailor's yarn was related in Aberdeen yesterday by a seaman named Alick Gavin, of the sloop *Dart*, of Dundee. Gavin stated that the *Dart* left Buckie on Saturday last, calling in at Peterhead over Sunday, from whence they sailed at midnight on their passage to Montrose, but owing to their strange and startling experiences they called in at Aberdeen, and the skipper (named Dawson) had requested Gavin to relate the adventure. The story goes on to the following effect:

'Four hours out from Peterhead, it was then still dark, and we were somewhat off Collieston or Newburgh, when the attention of George Duncan was drawn to some dark object ahead of us and right in our course. He directed the attention of the other three members of the crew to it, and they seemed to think the strange object must be a whale, such as they had often seen before. Its movements were, however, so strange that they, on a more careful survey, and being within almost a hundred yards of it, clearly saw it was not what they thought, but a large dark coloured animal which had by this time come quite close upon us. The shouting of the men awoke the skipper, who came on deck at once and just

192

in time to see the huge monster rear above us some feet of its body between the skyline and us. We were all greatly terror-stricken, and the skipper rushed to the helm, and put the sloop off several points from her course. The monster was then on her weather quarter, and seemed bent on pursuit. We were all so much awe struck as to be unable to act, but the skipper went below for a double barrelled gun, which he at once fired at the monster. Whatever it was, it raised its huge body out of the sea to an extraordinary height, and with a hissing sound it bore down upon us, leaving in its wake a wreath of foam, which we could now plainly see, in the grey light of the morning. Onwards it came till the shadow of its immense body darkened our deck. The men all dashed forward with the exception of one Barclay and the skipper and myself, who was at the helm. I laid the boat round as close to the wind as she would go, and this put the monster directly in our wake. It continued to keep about the same distance and we could plainly see its eyes, which were terrifying, and with a swaying motion it kept steadily on. We were going about nine knots, with a fresh breeze, and we could put no more sail on the sloop, so could not help ourselves in that way.

The huge body of the monster was towering as high as our masthead, and the hissing sound it made struck terror to our hearts, as we feared that every moment it might make a dash forward carrying the sloop over. The skipper ordered a piece of white canvas to be hoisted to the gaff peak. This was done, and it had the desired effect, for the monster then slowed its speed, and taking one last vengeful look, it dived beneath the water and disappeared, leaving the sea a seething mass of foam. It had followed us nearly eight miles. We felt so relieved that words cannot express our feelings. We made all sail, and arriving in Aberdeen we decided to make known the particulars of our singular and fearsome adventure.'

Gavin added that every one of the crew would be prepared to corroborate his statement.

Within four days, Gavin had submitted further correspondence to the *Glasgow Evening News*. Presumably disturbed by the paper's apparent reluctance to make a big deal of his story, he wrote as follows:

Sir,

One of my mates, being a Glasgow man, got your paper, and we find you did not give credit to our assertion, which has been proved beyond doubt. Every one of us (and we here sign our names) saw the monster, and can testify as to its appearance. R. Barclay, one of our crew who can sketch a little, sends a true sketch of the monster which followed us over eight miles and we can all prove at any time the truth of what we say.

The animal was over fifty feet long what we saw of it – and there must have been a great length of body beneath the sea.

In appearance it resembled nothing we can describe, and nearer than the ancient animals of prehistoric existence, that we find described and illustrated by scientific men. Altogether it must have been 180 feet long.

The head was of a long tapering shape. The mouth being open, we saw the full size of it. It must have been large enough to swallow, at least, a cow or horse. The teeth shone in the faint light, and gave the animal a fearful and terrifying appearance. A long flipper-like appendage seemed to dangle from its body about 15 or 20 feet from its head. The eyes shone with a green light, shifting from green to blue and often crimson and drove terror into our hearts. Its body had a mane-like fin running down the full length of the back and breast. It was of a dark colour and unlike any monster, we, in a natural way could ever have dreamt of. We send the sketch and append our names. I have got a writer to give details. George Duncan and Robert Barclay, the strong men of our crew, never left the deck. Neither did I myself, being at the tiller all the time. You can publish the above with all permission, as we can prove every word we say, and have no reason to do otherwise.

Tom Mutch Dawson (Captain)
George Duncan
Robert Barclay
Samuel Brace
A Forbes
Alick Gavin.

Stonehaven, is about 14 miles south of Aberdeen. On 7 October 1898 (as reported in the *Daily Mail*, 10 October 1898), Alexander Taylor, skipper of the fishing boat *Lily* and his crew saw a strange object in the sea about 100 yards from their position off the coast there. It gave the appearance of the hull of a capsized boat. The *Lily* steered a course towards the object and when it was within 50 yd of it, the object moved. It raised its head, which was flatter than a whale's, partly out of the water, then made off, out to sea. Two blue fins were clearly visible upon the creature's back, approximately 20 ft apart and the size and shape of a small boat's sail. Behind the first fin was a hump, similar to a camel's. The creature submerged as it made off.

Further south, at Broughty Ferry, now a residential district of Dundee, there was an incident which was reported in the *Dundee Advertiser* of 5 October 1892.

The crew of the Broughty Ferry fishing boat, *Catherine*, have returned from the haddock fishing, bringing with them the news that they have seen the sea serpent. Thomas Gall, the skipper of the boat, states that on Monday about noon he was running about two miles to the westward of the Bell Rock Lighthouse before a stiff north-easterly gale, when 30 yards ahead of the boat, he saw an object about nine feet long, which he took to be the tail of a serpent, twisting and coiling itself above the

water. It was of a slatey blue colour, lightening towards
the end of the tail, until at the tip it was quite white. It
remained above the water about a minute, when it
suddenly disappeared. Immediately afterwards what
skipper Gall believed to be the head of the monster
appeared – ten yards from the boat. It was large, round,
and of a brownish-black colour. Unfortunately, the
speed of the boat prevented accurate observation, but
the skipper states that he has no doubt the parts he saw
belonged to the same creature, which he thinks could
not be less than 40 feet long. After remaining fully a
minute above water, the head disappeared, and no more
was seen of the strange monster. The statements of the
skipper are corroborated by four of the crew who were
on deck at the time.

The *Glasgpw Weekly Mail* of 8 October 1892, also
featured the story, but provided a little more detail.

A crew of Broughty Ferry fishermen report having had
sight of this notorious monster of the deep in the vicinity of Bell Rock. Thomas Gall, skipper of the boat
Catherine which carries seven hands, reports that on
Tuesday afternoon while the boat was running before a
north-east gale about two miles west of Bell Rock and
while he was at the helm, he saw about 30 yards ahead
of *Catherine*, a long object like the tail of some monster
rise out of the water and wriggle about, the point finally
bending to the surface, and then disappear.
 Skipper Gall called the attention of four hands who
were on deck at the time to what he had seen and while
looking in the same direction the monster rose again but
this time only a dozen yards from the boat. The head
was described as large, round and smooth and of a dark
brown or black colour. The body of the animal was a
blueish tint and seemed to be covered with large scales,
the tip of the tail being white. Gall's idea of its length is

that it was 40 feet if it was an inch. It remained only about a minute above water.

Montrose is an ancient town and popular seaside resort. In August 1903, the fishing boat *Rosa* encountered a six-foot head and neck south-east of the town. The crew, which consisted of eleven men, was about a mile from shore when they saw something rise out of the water. The object, which was tall and slim, made the men curious. As they watched it, they saw that it moved, and gave the impression of being a small head on a long narrow neck. The head was no thicker than the neck, which appeared to expand in girth in its lower extremities at water level. The neck was not rigid, but seemed flexible and curved as the creature moved its head in a side-to-side motion, almost as though it was looking round. After a few moments the entire object dipped forward (head first) and disappeared from view.

A totally different type of creature was seen in 1965 on the A85 road which runs between Oban, on the west coast of Scotland, and Dundee on the east coast. At a point just east of Perth, it passes alongside the River Tay, which gradually opens out into the Firth of Tay and the North Sea. On the night of 30 September, motorists driving along at this point, saw a strange, unidentifiable creature by the side of the road. Mrs Maureen Ford described it as a 'long grey shape' with no legs but pointed ears. A short time later, Robert Swankie saw what may have been the same creature; 'The head was more than two feet long. It seemed to have pointed ears. The body which was about 20 feet long, was humped like a giant caterpillar. It was moving very slowly and made a noise like someone dragging a heavy weight through grass.' It is not known whether the two motorists were known to each other, but the descriptions are similar, especially as they both mention long pointed ears.

As it was night time, both saw the creature illuminated by their vehicle headlights, which may well have caused some distortion in its appearance, especially when one considers that they were moving at speed. It is also unclear how Mr Swankie, whilst driving along, could know that the creature made a noise like someone dragging a heavy weight through the grass. Surely the noise of the engine would prevent him from hearing anything? The sighting, if accurately reported, remains something of an enigma. Reports suggested the creature may have crawled out of the River Tay. Searches of the area carried out the following day provided no further evidence of identity of the creature, and it was concluded that whatever it was had returned to the water. It is worth noting that eels do cross land, as do otters.

West Wemyss is a coastal village to the north east of Kirkcaldy and is named after coastal caves known as weems. In July 1939 fishermen from there saw a large brown creature with a horse's head and large, prominent eyes rise out of the water. The creature was believed to be about 20 ft long, judging from various body parts which appeared above the water, behind the head. It moved through the water for a short distance before lowering its head and disappearing from sight. None of those involved would be shifted from their assertion that it was horse-like, with a mane, although one witness seems to have claimed that the 'mane' could have been the result of surface disturbance caused by it ploughing through the water head first.

Edinburgh is hardly known for sea serpents, but sightings have been reported there. A strange monster is said to have come from the sea and moved across the land near Edinburgh in 1811. The report comes from a manuscript unearthed by archaeologist Guy Dubois, who lived near St Malo, Brittany. No report of this encounter can be located in any British newspaper, magazine or book.

On April 8, 1811, an inhabitant of Edinburgh perceived when he was on his way to Glasgow, and at some miles off the coast, an animal of extraordinary shape and size. It had a head like a bull's. The man fled as fast as his legs would carry him to the nearest village, where he roused the inhabitants. They first jeered and laughed at him, and then they were incited to set forth with guns. They had not gone far before they heard an extraordinary crash. Soon they saw the animal that made the noise. One of them went boldly ahead of his more cautious companions and got near enough to fire at it. He missed, and the monster made for him. He fled back to where his companions were in hiding. They then determined to set fire to the heather, whereupon the monster made back for the sea. The bravest of the pursuers ran after it, discharging their muskets. The first discharge caused it to stagger, the second brought it down. The weight of the monster was such that it was impossible to carry it away whole. So the villagers cut it up into pieces, getting several barrels of oil from the carcass. The forelegs of the animal resembled those of a camel and its hind legs, those of a horse, while it had a bull's head.

In July 1939, a small girl saw an animal less than 400 yd from the shore at Dunbar, 29 miles east of Edinburgh. She told her father and when they both returned to the spot on the beach where the sighting had occurred, both were able to watch the creature for over half an hour.

H.T. Wilkins in *Monsters & Mysteries* tells of a monster which was sighted off the coast of Berwick Bay on the eastern border of Scotland and England in 1934. The creature, which was seen by a lighthouse keeper through binoculars, was estimated at about 40 ft long. It rose from the sea amidst a great swirling and commotion in the water. Several humps which ran along its back and which stood proud of the sea surface were also visible. As the lighthouse keeper continued to monitor its movements, he saw some fishing boats, which had also seen the creature, as they altered course to move in its direction. The creature then moved with great speed, and vanished before the fishing boats could get near it.

It was later reported that, two days earlier, two golfers off Holy Island claimed to have seen a similar creature, which they initially mistook for a motorboat. Watching its movements, however, they realized that it was too large for such a vessel and that the object was flexible with what seemed to be undulations.

3
Ireland

There are tales in Ireland of the horse-eel, and the *phooka*, the Irish term for a lake monster. Thomas Crofton Croker, the nineteenth-century folklorist, described the horse-eel as 'a great conger eel, seven yards long and as thick as a bull in the body with a mane on its back like a horse'. Lough Cleevaun in the Wicklow Hills was said to be home to a strange beast which looked very much like it. This creature was carnivorous and, according to legend, would eat anything that dared enter its watery domain. According to a local man, 'An Englishman who went to swim in it was warned about the beast. He threw his dog in first and it vanished in a swirl.'

Lady Augusta Gregory records in her book, *Visions and Beliefs in the West of Ireland*: 'One day I was coming home with my two brothers from Tirneevan school, and there as we passed Dhulough we heard a great splashing, and we saw some creature put up its head, with a head and mane like a horse. And we didn't stop, but ran.'

The South

Public interest in sea and lake monsters was perhaps at its height in 1933, with tales from Loch Ness occupying much space in the pages of the press. Loch Ness, it seems, provided a platform for eye-witnesses to come forward and tell of their own experiences. The doubters and sceptics, who had so readily shot down all suggestions of the existence of such creatures, maintained an eerie silence when the following article appeared in The *Daily Mail* 23 October 1933:

The fantastic monster, said to be 30 feet long and to have eyes 'like motor car lamps' which many people declare they have seen troubling the calm water of Loch Ness, near Inverness, would seem to be a member of a scattered family of queer marine creatures.

At any rate, a beast as strange as it was once seen by that famous captain of Atlantic liners, Sir Arthur Rostron, who, as the Commodore of the Cunard Fleet, retired in 1931, having been 46 years at sea.

'In 1907 when I was Chief Officer of the *Campania*, and the ship on a Friday was off the coast of Ireland, making for Queenstown [now Cobh, County Cork], I saw an amazing sea monster. I first saw it when it was about two miles ahead, and thought that it was probably a tree trunk. On coming nearer to it, however, and keeping my glasses trained on it, I saw that the thing was alive. Its great head was reared about eight feet out of the water and was darting from side to side with sudden movements such as you see a blackbird make when it's hunting worms on the lawn.

'There were two protuberances where eyes might have been, but I could see no eyes. Its neck was fully 12–14 feet long and although only part of its body was out of the water, it was plain that the complete length of the monster must have been very great. It had very small ears in comparison with its enormous bulk. When it came within the wash of our propellers, it dived rapidly and presently came to the surface again, still moving its head in that queer way. Then it again dived, and again rose. It stayed on the surface for a few minutes longer, and finally submerged and nobody saw it again.

'On the following evening, when I was in Liverpool, I heard of a man who had been found drifting in a rowing boat in the Bristol Channel. This man said that he had lost both his oars and his boat hook while fighting a terrifying monster in the sea. His description of the monster tallied in every detail with that of the strange thing I had seen – and there is the fact that when it had disappeared from my sight it had headed to the eastwards and, presuming that it kept on its course, it would have gone right down the Bristol Channel. While I had my eyes on the monster, I made two sketches of it on the screen before me on the bridge. The third officer of the *Campania* also saw it.

'There are people who laugh and sneer when they hear talk of the "sea serpent" but I tell you, no one in this world knows what strange creatures live in the depths of the ocean.

'If, I, who spent 46 years of my life at sea, saw in that time only one strange monster, people who have made merely occasional journeys over the ocean scarcely have a right to laugh at the "sea serpent" idea because they have never seen anything strange on the sea.'

Few people dared question the authenticity of this report which, perhaps more than any other, promoted a real belief that these creatures existed. This is not at all surprising; after all, it is not very often that a knight of the realm openly admits to seeing a sea serpent. In 1912, Rostron was acclaimed by the survivors of the *Titanic* disaster as 'the kindest man in the world'. When, as Captain of the SS *Carpathia*, he responded to an SOS sent out by the stricken vessel, his actions saved countless lives.

Just three years after Sir Arthur Rostron's sighting, Captain Jorgenson of the Norwegian three-master *Felix* told of seeing a sea serpent off Rathlin Island, north of Ireland, in early July 1910. The creature he saw appeared to be writhing on the surface, where it appeared for only a brief moment.

Captain Jorgenson thought that the part of the body he saw was at least 14 ft long.

A spate of sightings occurred around the south coast of Ireland, and in particular the Cork region, in 1850. These not only made the pages of the local press, but were picked up by the national media.

Sir,

The following particulars, the accuracy of which need not be questioned, will, I doubt not, interest many of your readers. The different fishing establishments on the shore of this extensive bay, [Courtmasherry] extending from the Old Head of Kinsale to the Seven Heads, have been within the last few days abundantly supplied with fish of every description, and the greatest activity prevails to profit by the bounty which has thus sent to us literally in shoals. It has been noticed, too, that some description of fish, haak, for instance, have been captured further within the limits of the inner harbour than was known before. In fact, as I heard it observed, the fish were literally leaping ashore. These novel appearances, however, it was my lot to see fully accounted for yesterday. At about one o'clock a.m. when, sailing my yacht, with a slight breeze offshore, about 2 miles to the south of the beacon erected on the Barrel Rocks, one of the party of four gentlemen on board (Mr B. of Bandon) drew attention towards the structure mentioned, with the interrogatory of 'Do you see anything queer about the Barrels?' In an instant, the attention of all on board was riveted on an object which at first struck me as like the upheaved thick end of a large mast, but which, as it was made out plainer, proved to be the head of some huge fish or monster. On bearing down towards the object, we could distinctly see, with the naked eye, what I can best describe as an enormous serpent without mane, or fur, or any like appendage. The portion of the body above water, and which appeared to be rubbing or scratching itself against the beacon, was fully 30 feet long, and in diameter I should say about a fathom. With the aid of a glass it was observed that the eyes were of immense size, about nine inches across the ball, and the upper part of the back appeared covered with a furrowed shell-like substance. We were now within a rifle shot of the animal, and although some on board exhibited pardonable nervousness at the suggestion, it was resolved to fire a ball at the under portion of the body whenever the creature's unwieldy evolutions would expose its vulnerable part. The instant the piece was discharged the monster rose as if impelled by painful impulse, to a height which may appear incredible, say at least thirty fathoms – and culminating with the most rapid motion, dived or dashed itself underwater with a splash which almost stopped our breaths in amazement. In a few moments all disturbance of the water subsided, and the strange visitor evidently pursued its course to seaward. On coming up to the beacon, we were grateful to find adhering to the supports numerous connected scaly masses, such as one would think would be rubbed from the creature's 'coating' or changing its old skin for a new one. These interesting objects can be seen at the Horse-Rock Coast Guard Station, and will repay a visit. These particulars I have narrated in the clearest manner I am able, and if others, in other boats who had not so good an opportunity of seeing the entire appearance of the animal as those in my boat had, should send you a more readable account of it, I pledge myself none will strictly adhere to the real facts.

I am, sir, your very obedient servant.

Roger W. Travers

Taken from the *Cork Reporter* of 11 September 1850

The *Cork Constitution* reported the following story on 2 September 1850:

On Monday last, a party of gentlemen belonging to this city were enjoying a sailing excursion in the *Antelope* yacht, belonging to Mr Wheeler, along the coast from Glandore to Kinsale. Passing the Old Head of Kinsale, the day unusually fine, they observed an extraordinary commotion in the sea, apparent to everyone on board. The Bay of Kinsale was at the time filled with fish. In a few moments they perceived a large serpent-like fish on the surface, that could not be less than 120 feet in length. The creature was described as being shaped like the long funnel of an immense steamer; however, they were not close enough to provide a detailed description of the creature.

After lying on the surface for a few moments, it was reported that the serpent suddenly dashed ahead, about 60 miles an hour, and, after approximately 2 miles of travel, disappeared. Those on board believed that it acted as though it was actively involved in chasing fish.

The Zoologist magazine published the following communication from a John Good of Kinsale on 9 September 1850:

A few friends accompanied me on a boating excursion this day whose names are William Silk, John Hunt, George Williams, Henry Seymour, and Edward Barry, and, being off the Souverein Islands (off Cork), our attention was directed by one of the party to an extraordinary appearance ahead of the boat; immediately all eyes were turned to see what it was, when, to our astonishment and fright, the monster of the deep was bearing down on us; we were at once thrown into awful fright, and thought it best to retreat for the shore, on our landing, Mr W. Silk, who was armed with a double barrelled gun, discharged both barrels at the monster, but without effect. I need not describe his appearance, as you are aware of it before, but from inquiries from various boatmen I am told he has been off the harbour the last three days.

From all accounts, it does seem that an unknown creature was temporarily resident in the waters of Cork during late August and early September 1850. Its description does not correspond to any known sea creature and is typical of the archetypal sea serpent. All descriptions support the 'serpent-like' appearance.

Mr Travers's judgement of the height the creature rose from the water, seems somewhat excessive (30 fathoms is 180 ft). This rather ridiculous assertion detracts from the veracity of his account. It is understandable that the existence of such creatures was doubted by both the public and the scientific establishment.

In June 1966, Mr W.J. Wood saw a strange creature in Lough Attariff in County Cork. He wrote to author Ted Holiday telling him of his strange encounter, which is described in Holiday's *The Dragon and the Disc*.

I was fishing at Lough Attariff, a 16 acre lake in the hills between Clonakilty and Dunmanway. The sun was strong with a very light south-westerly breeze into which I was fly fishing with an expectant eye open for rising trout. Suddenly and quietly, a long dark brown object surfaced at a distance of about a hundred yards, facing directly towards me. It had the head of a well-grown calf and large glittering eyes almost at water level. The distance appeared to lessen and the creature's approach angle altered until it was parallel to me, about ninety yards distant. It seemed to be abut ten to ten and half feet long and protruded above the surface 5 or 6 inches. After about two minutes the animal submerged.

On 30 July 1915, less than a minute after the German submarine U-28 had sunk the British steamer *Iberian* off Fastnet Rock, a violent explosion occurred beneath the surface, blasting up out of the sea pieces of wreckage, along with a stunned sea serpent. The Captain of the U-28, Georg Gunther Freiherr von Forstner, believed that the creature measured around 60 ft in length and was crocodile-shaped with a long powerful tail, which tapered to a point. It also had four limbs with what appeared to be webbed feet. Referring to it as the 'underwater crocodile' he and the crew gazed in wonder before it fell back into the sea and vanished about ten to fifteen seconds later.

Captain von Forstner recalls (Rupert T. Gould, *The Case for the Sea Serpent*):

On 30 July 1915, our U28 torpedoed the British steamer *Iberian* (5,223 tons) carrying a rich cargo in the North Atlantic. The steamer, which was about 600 feet long, sank quickly, the bow sticking almost vertically into the air, towards the bottom a thousand fathoms or more below. When the steamer had been gone for about 25 seconds, there was a violent explosion at a depth which it was clearly impossible for us to know, but which we can reckon, without risking being far out, at about 500 fathoms. A little later pieces of wreckage, and among them a gigantic sea-animal, writhing and struggling wildly, were shot out of the water to a height of 60 to 100 feet.

At that moment I had with me in the conning tower my officers of the watch, the chief engineer, the navigator, and the helmsman. Simultaneously, we all drew one another's attention to this wonder of the seas. As it was not in Brockhaus nor in Brehm we were, alas, unable to identify it. We did not have time to take a photograph, for the animal sank out of sight after 10 or 15 seconds. It was about 60 feet long, was like a crocodile in shape and had four limbs with powerful webbed feet and a long tail tapering to a point. That the animal should have been driven up from a great depth seemed to me very understandable. After the explosion, however it was caused, the 'underwater crocodile', as we called it, was shot upwards by the terrific pressure until it leapt out of the water gasping and terrified.

There are many inconsistencies in this tale. Captain von Forstner did not actually reveal the sea serpent story for eighteen years, and no mention of the 'underwater crocodile' has been found in any of the newspaper reports on the sinking of the *Iberian*. However, it would be foolish to discount a sighting because an entire crew failed to witness such a thing, the others may have been in a state of shock or had their gaze averted.

The West

In County Galway, about 2 miles from the sea, is Lough Abisdealy, 1 mile long and ¼ mile wide. Translated the name means 'lake of the monster'. In 1914, just before the outbreak of the First World War, a young lady, her groom and her kitchen maid were driving to church one Sunday morning in a dog cart, when they saw a strange creature as they passed close to the lough. It was long and black, with a long neck and a flat head, and three loops of its body buckled in and out of the water as it travelled quickly across the lake,, giving the appearance of a giant snake. The witnesses claimed to have had a clear view of the lough and the creature, and the road down which they travelled actually offered an unobstructed view of the water. The creature eventually submerged.

On another occasion a man at night saw a huge eel-like creature crawling out of the lough, which he reckoned was about 25 ft long. According to Roy Mackel, author of *Searching for Hidden Animals*, an object has also been seen swinging part of its body out of the water in a 2 ft arc; this portion was dark brown in colour, and looked exactly like the tail end of a conger eel.

Mr W.J. Wood, who had an encounter with an unknown creature at Lough Attariff in 1966, (see page 201) had another in 1967, this time at Lackagh Lake, in County Kerry, a 5-acre pool, some 50 miles from Attariff and just a few miles northeast of Killarney. Author Ted Holiday reported his encounter as follows in *The Dragon and the Disc*:

Wood was apparently fishing from a small mound on the lake shore when a light yellowish-brown object, about seven feet long, surfaced directly in front of him. This was only a couple of yards away. The object remained in view for just a few seconds and firmly convinced Wood that he had seen something unusual. He later claimed that he felt it safer to fish from shore as opposed to using his boat.

Holiday also relates another sighting in Lackagh, by an anonymous witness who told him that he had seen something odd in the lake, close to the reeds. Apparently, several feet of a 'snake-like' neck and a small head upon which were two stumpy horns surfaced for a few seconds.

Lough Bran, also known as Lough Brin, is a remote lough in County Kerry measuring just 1 mile by ½ a mile and is believed to be 190 feet deep in places. It is only approachable by a rough track, and according to ancient legend it is named after Finn's hunting dog, called Bran, who entered its waters and drowned. The dog's spirit is said to haunt the water. Various 'monster' sightings have occurred here according to the Irish folk historians. In the 1920s, a local man is said to have seen a combined 'horse and fish-like' creature some 14 ft long, and in 1940, a 14-year-old boy claimed to see a strange creature lying on the bank, basking in the sun.

Timothy O'Sullivan, a farmer, was out checking on his cattle on Christmas Eve 1954, when he saw a commotion in the water which he thought was two ducks. As he watched, the 'ducks' rose out of the water revealing two fins or humps. These objects were thought to be 2 ft long and 2 ft high, with a distance between them of about 12 ft. O'Sullivan ran home to get his shotgun, but the creature had gone and failed to show itself again when he returned.

In the summer of 1979 two farming brothers saw a reptilian creature something like a cross between a giant seal and the mythical dragon. It was as black as soot and about 10 ft long, and they watched it swim the length of the lough,

which is just over 500 yd, before submerging. Upon returning home, they spoke of their sighting to other members of
the family, only to be told that their father had also seen the
creature, and he too believed it to be a cross between 'a giant
seal and a dragon out of the pictures'.

An incident which occurred at Lough Leane, also in
County Kerry, is of a more dubious nature, and involved one
Pat Kelly, who, claimed to possess psychic powers. Kelly is
said to have sent Tony 'Doc' Shiels a photograph showing a
large two-humped creature in the lough which he claimed to
have taken himself in August 1981. The provenance of this
photograph is at the very least debatable, since it is virtually
identical to those which were supposedly taken of Morgawr,
the Cornish sea serpent (see page 104) in 1976 by the anonymous Mary F.

Kelly apparently further claimed that his father, Laurence
O'Talbot Kelly, knew the infamous satanist Aleister
Crowley, and believed that Crowley successfully raised the
Loch Ness monster from the loch in the early part of the
twentieth century. No evidence to support this claim has
been provided, and there is certainly no mention of it in
Crowley's own writing.

To my mind, there is no credibility in the claim that a large
unidentifiable creature lives in Lough Leane.

Lady Augusta Gregory mentions a creature in Lough
Graney, in County Clare, in *Visions and Beliefs of the West of
Ireland*, she says:

The lake down there is an enchanted place, and the old
people told me that one time they were swimming there
and a man had gone out into the middle, when they saw
something like a great big eel making for him. They
called out 'If ever you were a great swimmer, show us
now how you can swim to the shore.' For they would-
n't frighten him by saying what was behind him. So, he
swam to the shore and he only got there when the thing
behind was in the place where he was.

Loch Auna, County Limerick, had long had a tradition of being the home of a curious water creature, reports of which date back to the early years of the twentieth century. This particular account was given to a journalist in 1974 by Tommy Joyce, who told a similar tale to author F.W. Holiday (*The Dragon and the Disc*):

> This story was told to me by my parents, so I cannot vouch for the facts, although my parents would never have told untruths about such matters. There was a local woman who, late one evening, was working at her bog, which ran down to the lake shore; she was looking after her turf and was close to the lake. A splashing and commotion in the water caused her to look up, she saw what she believed to be a 'Horse-Eel' coming out of the water, it came up the bank and very close to her. As I would have done, she ran off. The woman told people that the creature had a horse's head and its body tapered off like that of an eel.

Another sighting occurred a few years later, when two people (a mother and son) saw a creature, 35–40 ft long, with three or four humps, disporting itself, rolling and plunging in the water about 200 yd offshore, the waves this disturbance created crashing against the shore. It was claimed that the creature remained in view for about fifteen minutes before diving.

A more recent sighting (14 May 1980), was by Air Commander Kort, a retired officer of the Netherlands Royal Air Force, who had held a barbecue by his cottage, which stands about 120 yd from the water. The barbecue party had moved inside when Kort looked out towards the lough and saw something odd moving through the water. One of his guests, Adrian O'Connell, stood and watched the object for a short time. It moved at a speed described as 'no more than walking pace', towards the western end. Another guest thought he caught a glimpse of the creature as it disappeared into the reeds. Initially, one of the witnesses thought it was a fish, or an otter with young on its back, but Kort dismissed these ideas, as he felt that neither of them explained the calmness of the water. Any other creature would have created a V-shaped wake, but what they saw caused no surface agitation. He later said (Graham J. McEwan, *Mystery Animals of Britain and Ireland*): 'The uncanny thing about it was the gliding movement without any disturbance of the water surface.' The more he watched the creature, the more convinced he became that this was something extraordinary. Because of the way it moved, he could not truly assess the size of the creature, but he felt it was about 5 ft long, rising to a height of about 1 ft above the water.

Lough na Corra in County Limerick, would seem to house several creatures, if Mrs A.V. Hunt of Tipperary is to be believed. One afternoon in 1911, she was looking out over the waters of the lough with a friend.

Suddenly, the surface of the water was disturbed by a huge black shape that rose and swam the length of the lake in what appeared to be a few moments. Other similar shapes appeared and these weird things kept playing about, diving and swimming like a lot of seals. The lake is between two and three miles long and from the height on which we were, in comparison with the cattle, the creatures looked bigger than any house we could see; even with the aid of binoculars, we could not distinguish any detail at that distance. We called the men at work at the chapel to come and watch. After a short time the creatures disappeared, one by one, and the lake resumed its normal tranquil appearance.

The memoirs of Captain Hugh Shaw are housed at the National Maritime Museum, Greenwich, and tell of a sea serpent sighting at Limerick. Shaw was the owner-master of a number of ships in the Irish coastal trade. One afternoon in July 1922, one vessel was tied up at Limerick, being prepared to set sail, when the mate shouted to him to come on deck (Graham J. McEwan, *Mystery Animals of Britain and Ireland*).

When I reached the deck I saw the quays on both sides of the river [Shannon] crowded with people and then I saw the reason for this. They were watching the most amazing creature they or I had ever seen or read about. The object was close alongside my vessel, in fact it was only a few feet way.

My first impression on seeing it was of its resemblance in the size and shape to a small submarine. It was large and black and shining, and had a very long neck, at least twelve feet long, held proudly erect and shaped like a swan's. It waved its smallish head from side to side, and its bright shining eyes seemed to express alarm.

Behind its long neck for a distance of about ten to twelve feet was a massive black cone-shaped hump, which rose a few feet out of the water, but no part of the creature's body could be seen between the hump and the neck, this part being submerged.

It was heading upstream at a very slow speed. All the sea birds resting on the buoys flew away as the creature came near to them. After it passed my ship, it saw the bridge close to and straight ahead of it, and with movements like a stately ship, it made left-handed turn. It did not hurry. It now began to head downstream gathering speed as it cleared the narrows.

One hour later, we left on our way to sea. After we had passed Foynes, about twenty miles below Limerick, it was nearly dark when I and my crew heard a blowing sound, like a porpoise makes when it surfaces for air, and we saw the long neck of the creature shoot out of the water. Then it disappeared. It returned within a few seconds, surfacing to blow and take in air again. It then dropped astern as it was not travelling as fast as our vessel. That was the last we saw of it.

Several people on the quayside at Limerick confirmed the account, including a Mr MacMahon, whose son, Mr D. MacMahon, confirmed the details of the incident many years later to Daniel Doyle, a Limerick librarian, who reported his tale as follows (Elizabeth Montgomery Campbell, *The Search for Morag*):

> My information is second-hand, coming from my father, who was a sober man, not given to over imagination, and on quite a number of occasions he told me that he was down the quays one day when he saw this 'monster' in the river. He described it as having a long neck sticking up out of the water with a small head, the sort of effect you would get if you had a giraffe immersed in the water with his body covered and only his head showing. He stated that the 'monster' turned its head several times to survey its surroundings before disappearing; he made no reference to any hump showing. It seems to have been dated some time during the civil war because he suggested that a soldier fired a shot at it.

On 18 May 1960, three Dublin priests were fishing in Lough Ree, County Galway, off Holly Point. Friar Matthew Burke, Friar Daniel Murray and Friar Richard Quigley, who had all visited the lough the year before and knew it reasonably, saw a long necked, flat-headed animal swimming in the water only 100 yd away. It was a warm calm evening and the creature was in clear view. The priests submitted a full report to the Inland Fisheries Trust.

> There were two sections above the water; a forward section of uniform girth, stretching quite straight out of the water and inclined at the plane of the surface at about thirty degrees, in length about 18–24 inches. The diameter of this long leading section we would estimate to be about four inches. At its extremity, which we took

215

to be a serpent like head, it tapered rather abruptly to a point. Between the leading and the following sections of this creature, there intervened about two feet of water. The second section seemed to us to be a tight, roughly semi-circular loop. This portion could have been a hump or a large knob on the back of a large body under the surface, that was being propelled by flippers. As to the dimensions of this section, if a loop, we should say the girth of a large fifteen pound salmon; if however, a round hump ... we should put its base at around eighteen inches ... we would estimate the overall visible length to the two visible sections measured along the surface from tip of snout to end of hump, at about six feet. The movement along the water was steady. There was no apparent disturbance of the surface, so that propulsion seemed to come from a well-submerged portion of the creature. There was no undulation of its body above the water. It was cruising at a very leisurely speed, and was apparently unconcerned about our presence. We watched it moving along the surface for a period of two or three minutes in a north-easterly direction. It was going towards shore; then it submerged gradually rather than dived, and disappeared from view completely. Another couple of minutes later it reappeared still following the same course ... It reached a point thirty yards off shore, when it submerged and we saw it no more.

The priests later visited Colonel Harry Rice, an expert on the River Shannon. Rice interviewed and cross-examined the three young men, noting down everything they said over a period of two hours. He described the witnesses as expert fishermen and thoroughly qualified to observe such a matter. Rice also contacted the local press and asked for further witnesses of such incidents to get in touch with him. Later, a local postman, Paddy Hanley, came forward and told how he believed he had once almost caught the creature. With his family, Hanley had been fishing north of Yew Point, at the mouth of Bally Bay, when he hooked something. The fishing line he used (which was the strongest on the market) stretched out, as the boat was towed across the loch by something very powerful beneath the water. Eventually, he was forced to cut the line at a point the other side of Adelaide Buoy.

Mr F.J. Waters also recalled a similar experience close to the same location, at Beam Island, again with a heavy line. Suddenly he hooked something, which dived sharply to the bottom, causing the line to snap after about seventy feet had run off. Mr Waters had no idea what he had hooked, but was adamant that no known fish in that environment could dive so quickly.

In 1958, two English tourists also had an unexpected journey while fishing on the lough. Something large, and clearly very strong, took their line whilst they were fishing and towed the boat in which they were sat a short distance. No doubt in a state of panic they, too, were forced to cut the line to free themselves.

The next four accounts appear in Graham J. McEwan's *Mystery Animals of Britain and Ireland*.

In February 1960, two net fishermen, Patrick Ganley and Joseph Quigley of Inch Turk, were out netting pike. The men claimed to have caught something large in their net and tried to pull it on board. However, whatever it was broke the net and escaped. One of the men later said: 'It must have been the size of a horse.' The incident occurred in 60 ft of water, not too far from where the three priests had their encounter.

In early March 1960, two men were out walking on the shore of St Mark's Bay one summer evening, when they saw an animal swimming parallel to the shore. The creature held its neck erect, out of the water, about 1 ft above the surface. Behind this was a gap of water, followed by what appeared to be a black hump. Both men thought it was a swimming calf. They put out in a boat and rowed to the place where they had

217

seen the object, but whatever it was had submerged by the time they reached the spot.

Some time around 1955, Patrick Canning went to fetch his donkey, which had been left out in the rain at Lough Shanakeever, County Galway. From a distance of about 200 yd, he saw a black animal the size of a foal apparently circling his donkey (as though stalking it). The creature had a long neck and a head without ears. As he approached the scene, the creature saw him, returned to the lough and sank from view. Canning described the beast as a 'lovely black foal'.

In 1963 or 1964, a local farmer was walking by the lough, when he saw what appeared to be a dark grey object swimming at the surface of the water. He looked across but could not define just what it was, other than that the visible part of it was about 7 ft 6 in long. He said it was not like anything he had previously seen.

Lough Dubh, also in County Galway, has a record of sightings of unusual creatures dating back to 1956, when three men saw something 'strange' swimming in the water, but were too far away to identify the creature. In 1960, Con Mahon, a local man, saw three monsters swimming in the lough, one large one and two smaller. But it was a sighting in March 1962, which captured the media's attention. Schoolteacher Alphonsus Mullaney, told of the following encounter.

We were working on the bog after school and I had promised to take young Alphonsus fishing. We carried a twelve-foot rod with strong line and spoon bait, for perch or pike, of which there are plenty in Lough Dubh. For a while, I let the boy fish with the rod and used a shorter rod with worm bait. After five minutes, I decided that the fish were not there that evening, but I took the long rod and walked up and down the bank. Suddenly, there was a tugging on the line. I thought it might be a root, so I took it gently. It did not give. I hauled it slowly ashore, and the line snapped. I was examining the line, when the lad screamed. Then I saw the animal. It was not a seal or anything I had ever seen. It had for instance short thick legs, and a hippo face. It was as big as cow or an ass, square faced, with small ears and a white pointed horn on its snout. It was dark grey in colour, and covered with bristles or short hair, like a pig. The creature had, in fact, attempted to get out of the lough and attack young Alphonsus, which had been the reason for him crying out.

Alphonsus senior and his son, ran from the lake. They then told their tale to some local men, who were clearly concerned about the actions of the beast in the lough. The men at once went to the lake, taking guns with them to shoot the creature. By the time they got there, however, it was gone, and no trace of it could be found.

At Ballynahinch Lake in County Galway, according to local legend, there was a giant eel-like creature, which became jammed beneath Ballynahinch Bridge, close to Ballynahinch Castle. This creature was believed to be about 30 ft long and as thick as a horse. The incident is believed to have occurred in the late 1800s. A local blacksmith was called to spear the creature. which had been stuck for some days. However, by the time he got to the scene, a big flood had freed the creature, which was never seen again.

In about 1903, a strange creature took to disporting itself in Camus Bay, Connemara. Mr Howard St George, who was fishing at Screbe, recalled the incident for a local newspaper.

I saw a sea serpent calmly floating in Kilkierian Bay into which Camus Bay opens. It looked about the size of a large farm cart. The serpent had a large hairy body which I took to be about twenty feet long, with serpent's neck held erect, with head and neck about six feet long.

This report which is given in *Monsters & Mysteries* by H.T. Wlkins is somewhat sketchy, but nevertheless important, as it as it reveals a similarity to other sightings.

Miss Georgina Carberry, a librarian from Clifden, County Galway, had a strange encounter in 1954, whilst she was fishing with three friends at Lough Fadda, the story of which she first told to author Ted Holiday (*The Dragon and the Disc*). The group had been out fishing on the lough in a small boat for several hours. They decided to take a short break from the fishing and pulled their boat ashore for a break. As they stood by the waterside, one of the group pointed out something, which initially appeared to be a man, swimming towards them. As the shape neared them, they realized that it was not a swimmer but a creature which they could not recognize. Miss Carberry claimed, 'It was like nothing we had ever seen before.' When it was about 20 yd from them, they retreated from the edge of the lough. Miss Carberry recalled that the creature possessed a 'huge great mouth', which she described as being 'white on the inside.' She described the creature's body as 'wormy-creepy'. It seemed to move all the time. The head stood high above the water on a long neck, and it dived round a rock and showed a forked tail. After a while it surfaced further up the lough, when they were able to see definite humps behind the head and above the water level. Miss Carberry stated that after the event, she had 'nightmares' about the creature for several weeks.

On 16 October 1965, as a result of Miss Carberry's report, Captain Lionel Leslie, a cousin of Sir Winston Churchill, gained permission to detonate 5 lb of gelignite in the lough, in an attempt to create a shock wave, which in turn might cause the creature to surface (F.W. Holiday, *The Dragon and the Disc*). This episode was witnessed by the Reverend E.C. Alston and Mr Edmund Foyle. At 4.30 p.m. the charge was detonated, and some ten seconds after the explosion, Leslie claimed to see a large black coloured object break the surface amid much splashing about 50 yd from their position on the shore. Very little detail could be discerned during the brief sighting due to the amount of splashing and commotion in the water.

Captain Leslie returned in the autumn of 1967, for further

efforts to locate and identify the creature. On 7 October, he placed a polystyrene net, with a breaking strain of 350 lb, measuring 50 ft by 15 ft with a 1-in mesh across the entire width of the water. Various attempts were made to create noise and water disturbance in the hope that the creature might be flushed from its lair and swim into the net. But after two weeks, the attempt was called off, all efforts failed and the net remained empty.

Not to be outwitted by the creature, Leslie then produced a plan to drag the lough. However, heavy storms prevented the attempt from taking place, and the mystery of the creature remains to this day.

Crolan Lough, County Galway, is connected to Derrylea Lough, which in turn is linked to the sea. Some time around 1890, it was claimed that an enormous, repulsive eel was trapped in a culvert between the two. None of the local people would go near it and it was left to decompose.

In April 1961, Tom Connelly, 65, from Maam Cross, a few miles from Clifden, was looking through a window at his home, which overlooked Lough Crolan when he saw what he thought was otters moving through the water. Hs curiosity was aroused when the objects seemed to remain in one place for a long time, so he went outside to get a closer look. Standing at the water's edge, he looked out and at a distance of around 40 yd, saw an object which he thought was about 12–14 ft long and dark velvety in colour with the sun shining on it. He thought the head, which he could only partially see, was round on top and sloped to the front and back. He said he saw a tail, which he described as being 'eel-shaped', about 18 in long, and wriggling. It was visible at the same time as the middle part of the object and the head.

The creature submerged and rose in the same place for over half an hour. Indeed, Connelly actually left the waterside and went to get a pair of binoculars in order to see better. He was away for several minutes and upon his return the creature was still there. He recalled that when he was younger, his parents advised him to stay away from the lake!

He believed that his sighting was not unique, but one of the creatures known locally as horse-eels (Graham J. McEwan, *Mystery Animals of Britain & Ireland*).

On 22 February 1968, Stephen Coyne, a local farmer, was out gathering peat at the side of Lough Nahooin, a small stretch of water 100 yd long by 80 yd wide near Claddaghduff, early in the evening. With him were his 8-year-old son and the family dog. Coyne saw a black object in the water and believing it to be his dog, whistled at it to return to him. To his surprise, the dog came running from behind him; it was not the object he had seen in the water. The dog suddenly stopped in its tracks when it too saw the object in the water, and began to bark. The creature, which was clearly a living animal, then swam towards shore, its mouth open, seemingly responding to the dog's barking. When Coyne went to his dog, the creature changed direction and swam round the lake. Coyne sent his young son to fetch the rest of the family, and they joined him at the lough side. They all watched the creature until light failed and darkness fell.

They described it in some detail, as at one point it had been just 5–10 yd from them. It was about 12 ft long, black and hairless, with an eel-like texture to the skin, and tail. When it submerged its head, two humps appeared on the surface. The neck was pole-like and about 12 in. in diameter. The inside of the mouth was a pale colour and the creature had two horns on top of its head. They saw no eyes.

On 8 September 1968, sheep farmer Thomas Connelly saw a black coloured creature, bigger than a young donkey, on the lough shore a few yards from the water's edge. It appeared to have four stumpy legs and was slithering towards the water. He watched it move into the water and sink. (F.W. Holiday, *The Dragon & The Disc*).

Captain Lionel Leslie, who tried to capture the creature of Lough Fadela (see page 220), carried out a netting operation at Lough Nahooin on 15 July 1968. By 17 July 1968, a line of nets had been strung out cross the entire width. At its deepest point, Nahooin is just 23 ft deep. Empty petrol tins containing pebbles were then distributed in the water and pulled along in an attempt to raise the monster. David James was also on site and used an electronic fish-attracting device. Despite their efforts, no trace of the monster was found and the nets stretching across the water remained empty. Leslie and his team later tried to drag the lough with chains, but this failed because the chains continually became entrapped in the thick water lilies. (*The Dragon and the Disc.*)

Glengarry Lake in County Mayo is approximately 1,200 ft in circumference and covers about 4 acres (including woodland on two sides). The *Dublin Evening Herald* of 5 June 1968, reported a curious sighting there.

The beast of Glengarry Lake has been seen many times. A local fisherman, Mr Jim O'Gorman, of Station House, Kell, saw a fish about two feet long with what appeared to be four legs, in a stream leading from the lake. A Thomas Cooney, of Straheens, Achill, claimed that his cousin had seen it about 35 years prior to the 1968 sighting. Mrs Annie Cattigan of Saile was also reported to have seen it around the same time as Cooney's cousin.

On the night of 1 May 1968 two local men, John Cooney, a local part time contractor, and Michael McNulty, a sheep farmer of Belsfearsad, were driving home, passing the lough at around 10.00 p.m. Suddenly, a strange creature ran across the road in front of the car in which they were travelling and disappeared into thick undergrowth beside the Lough. In the light from the car headlights, they clearly saw the creature. Cooney described what he saw.

'It was between eight to twelve feet long, with a long neck like a swan, only much bigger. The tail was very thick. It was moving at an angle to us and we couldn't see exactly how long it really was. And it was weaving and curving. We could see it clearly. It was dark brown in colour and was shiny and scaly. The eyes were glittering. I don't know whether it actually looked at us, but it disappeared in an instant, into thick undergrowth – and we didn't stop to make further enquiries.'

One possible explanation for this creature may well be an otter, since its description is not dissimilar. Otters are not frequently seen and do tend to be more active during the hours of darkness. They also possess a similar coloration, and would run in a manner similar to that described by Mr Cooney and Mr McNulty. Although they both thought that the creature was 8–12 ft long, they admit that they saw it at an angle, and were unable to make an accurate assessment; it could have been larger or smaller. The artificial light thrown from a moving car headlight would also be likely to give an impression of the presence of scales, which would be very difficult to spot on any creature from a moving vehicle at night.

Just a week later, a 16-year-old trainee carpenter, Gay Dever, had a sighting of a strange creature, this time in daylight. He was cycling by the lough on his way home to Mass. He had alighted from the cycle and was pushing it up a hill when he heard a curious splashing noise near the shore. He stopped to seek out the source of the noise, and saw a creature 'humping itself along' and climbing up a turf bank about 50 yd from the lough by a clump of trees. It was moving with a 'kangaroo-like jump'. It had a head like a sheep (which was small by comparison to the rest of the body) and a long neck and tail. The hind legs were bigger than the front ones. It was, he estimated, about 12 ft long, much bigger than a horse, and dark in colour, and it had a humped, bumpy back. Dever said nothing about his encounter, as he felt no one would believe him. It was only when he heard of other sightings that he spoke out. (*Dublin Evening Herald*, 5 June 1968).

Two days after the Dever sighting, the creature was seen again, this time by two women, 23-year-old Mary Callaghan and 21-year-old Bernie Sweeney, who were trying to hitchhike home to Achill Sound. A car pulled up to give them a lift. One of the girls turned back to the lough as she was about to get into the car and both she and the driver saw, by the light of a full moon, a creature which they described as a monster.

On the first Sunday in June 1968, a Dundalk businessman stopped to give a lift to two young girls, Mary O'Neill of Mullingar and Florence Connaire from Galway. As they passed the lake at one o'clock, one of the girls pointed out a huge animal on the shore 100 yd away. The man got out of his car and photographed the creature with a Polaroid camera. The object seemed to be about 40 ft long, with a head like a greyhound and a long tail. Mary O'Neill claimed that it looked like a dinosaur.

Joseph Gallagher from County Donegal, told Dom Cyril Dieckhoff (see page 142) the following story in a letter.

About 1885, a young woman waded out as far as she could off the shore of Lough Muck to pull bog bean, and when she stopped, heard a splash no distance from her. She made for the shore as fast as she could. Then for a year or two afterwards it was seen occasionally. It would raise two humps above the water. This Lough is less than three quarters of a mile long by half a mile across. Salmon might come into it in November when spawning. Only now for the last 40 years nothing was seen in the Lough. It's 40 miles from the sea, it could not get food there, only brown trout. No one there could tell what kind of animal it was. The young woman that seen it first always declared that its eyes was in or about three inches each way.

Captain Brown, who was on a voyage from America to St Petersburg reported an incident to Constantin Samuel Rafinesque-Schmaltz which occurred in July 1818 off the north coast of Ireland. The French-American naturalist later wrote of the incident:

In swimming the head, neck and forepart of the body stood upright like a mast: it was surrounded by porpoises and fishes. It was smooth, without scales, and had eight gills under the neck, which decidedly evinces that it is not a snake, but a new genus of fish! Dark brown above, muddy white beneath: head obtuse. Captain Brown adds that the head was two feet long, the mouth fifteen inches, and the eyes over the jaws, similar to the horse's, the whole length might be 58 feet.

The East

The following is a report of an incident at Lough Mask which was allegedly made to Captain Lionel Leslie by Mr A.R. Lawrence of Tullamore, County Offaly.

16 June 1963. Calm, sunny day. 9.15 a.m. Visibility clear. Object seen from shore of Inishdura Island. Range of 250 yards. As I stood on the boat slip looking north-west across the bay, I suddenly saw what appeared to be the head and tail of a large fish close to the rocks. A second or so later, the movement was repeated in about the same place. Then there occurred another head and tail rise ahead (north-east) of the first two, followed by the same movement some yards further north-east.

I then realized I was watching two humps, one behind the other, moving forward slowly and regularly across the mouth of the bay. It seemed to me like the back of a very large eel-like fish. I never saw the head or tail, but I would guess the humps were about five or six feet in length and the distance between them about eight or ten feet. The water through which the object travelled was only about three or four feet deep. It disappeared from my sight when a point on the island blocked my view.

Mr Lawrence watched the object for about one and a half minutes, in which time it travelled about 250 yd. He estimated its height above the water surface to be between 12 and 15 inches. It was black and the skin texture seemed to be smooth. Behind the humps was a wash.

Lough Major is in County Monaghan. In the last week of July 1911, three youths, G. Kelly, Talbot Duffy and Paul Pentland, claimed that when they were on the way back from a fishing trip, they saw a monster splashing up and down in the lake like a sea lion (as recorded by historian, James Dougal). Although frightened, they watched it for a few minutes and threw a few stones at it. It made towards them and they fled. Talbot Duffy claimed to have shot plenty of otters and was confident that the creature they had seen was no otter. They described the creatures as having a 'hairy head with two protruding horns'.

In their rush to leave the scene, the group dropped a dozen or so bream on the bank of the lough. Returning to the same spot the following day they found that the fish had all been consumed, with just a few bones remaining. After the event another witness, Paddy Brady, came forward. He too claimed to have seen a horned monster in the vicinity of the lough.

In mid-August 1999, a mystery creature was sighted in a 50-mile stretch of water known as Lough Erne, near Killykeen, County Cavan. The creature was said to be over 8 ft long and looked to weigh about 300 lb. (*Sunday People* 22 August 1999). Claudia Westrich, a member of a local Cavan Icebreakers Swimming Club, was swimming in the lough followed closely by colleagues in a boat. She suddenly felt something pushing her down. At first, she thought it was an oar from the accompanying boat, but when she looked up, she saw that the vessel was about 5 yd from her. She tried to get a glimpse of the object, which was now causing her some distress, but, whatever it was dived under the water. A local man, Sean Walsh, was on the nearby boat and inadvertently took a photograph of the creature.

I was photographing calves on the foreshore. When I developed the film, I realized what I had taken. I took the film and my camera equipment to a local professional photographer Ray Reilly to check for faults. Ray confirmed the film had not been tampered with. I don't know what it is, but there is something in the water. It has been there for years. There have been several sightings. People say it is up to eight feet long with a spikey head. It's bizarre.

He further revealed he has had two body contacts with what he believed to be the same creature. 'The first was 25 years ago in almost the same place that Claudia had her eerie encounter. I could feel it between my legs and swimming around me. It was a strange feeling. I have never been afraid of it. It only seems to appear when there are swimmers in the water. A similar, but totally separate, sighting occurred later that day when a group of sea scouts from Dalkey, in Dublin, reported seeing a large strange looking creature make a huge splash in the water.

Other sightings of the creature have been made along this huge stretch of water, which runs through Eniskillen, County Fermanagh, and Belturbet, County Cavan, including a peculiarly shaped beast seen swimming at the surface by Alex Moran, Chairman of the Cavan Icebreakers. But the local community remains somewhat sceptical of 'monster' reports. Many believe the creature is a huge catfish or a wels, which can grow to a size exceeding 15 ft and weigh up to 600 lb.

Sean Walsh has his own opinion as to how the creature managed to get into the waterway. He says: 'Many years ago, hundreds of English anglers used to use the Erne Waterway. They brought all sorts of baits with them to catch large pike. I think the creature is some form of bait from a foreign country, which has thrived in the area. That's the only explanation I can think of.'

Walsh was so concerned about the reported sightings of

this creature that he asked a detective friend to investigate them and to examine the evidence. The policeman was later reported to be in Cavan making enquiries in the hope of building a profile of the creature, but no sightings have been reported since the incident of August 1999. Whether the police investigation revealed any data is unknown. I do not know why Walsh sought the services of the police as opposed to someone qualified to assess the information, such as a zoologist. Moreover, much of the anecdotal evidence for the existence of this creature seems to emanate from Mr Walsh himself. He claims that he has had a number of encounters with the beast. In my research into such phenomena, I have found many people who claim to have had many sightings, but I cannot understand why they should be susceptible to sightings when many people who have lived by the particular stretch of water all their lives see nothing. One researcher believes that it is the psychic powers of the open mind which allow such individuals to witness these incidents, while others claim that local people regularly see such creatures but prefer to stay silent, especially to outsiders. However, I am of the opinion that reports from witnesses who claim to have seen the same creature several times are less credible than single sightings. To see such a creature once in a lifetime is possible; to see it several times in a relatively brief period is close to fantasy. It may well be that after one sighting, there is a desire to see something again and again, at which point, anything can be misconstrued as a sighting.

On 17 June 1963 a correspondent signing himself 'L.R.' wrote to the *Dublin Evening Press* about a sighting in Lough Bray, County Wicklow, on Whit Monday, 3 June 1963.

Soberly and without exaggeration, we are convinced that we saw a creature which could only be described as a monster. Looking down into the lake, which was perfectly clear (i.e. calm) in the evening light, we saw a large hump like the back of a rhinoceros emerge from the water. Ripples spread out to each side of it and then a head, something like a tortoise only many times bigger, broke the surface of the water, moved slowly around and swam forward for a few yards. As it did so, the body was clearly revealed, circular and not less than ten or twelve feet in circumference. It was dark greyish in colour. Suddenly and silently, the creature seemed to dive and smoothly vanished leaving an agitated swirl of water. We saw it for not less than three minutes. Comparing our stories, we found them to be identical to a surprising degree, although my friend thought the head was more like that of a swan. It may have been a trick of the light or shadow, but to be honest nothing will ever convince us that such was the case.

4
Wales

The South

Fall Bay is part of the Gower Peninsula, 15 miles of undulating limestone which points down into the Bristol Channel. A.G. Thompson, walker and author, recalls seeing a sea serpent in his book, *Gower Journey*. As he stood on the high cliffs overlooking the bay, he saw what he thought was a floating log, 30 ft long.

> Suddenly one end moved and it became plain that a head, like that of a horse with a mane, was standing out of the water and watching something on the rocks at the foot of the cliff. What a thrill! After staring for what seemed minutes, the monster appeared to be satisfied and dived with what looked like two distinct undulations of the hind portion. What an uncanny feeling.

He continued to watch the area for over half an hour, but the creature did not resurface. He spoke with local people about the incident, including a local expert (what kind of expert is unknown), who was of the opinion that the creature may have been a real sea horse. With a touch of irony, Thompson concludes: 'So Loch Ness cannot boast that they have a monopoly of monsters.'

The competence of the so-called 'expert' has to be questioned, as there is no known species of 'sea horse' which grows to a size of 30 ft. It would appear that he was more concerned with legend and folklore, as a 'sea horse' of a similar description is commonplace in such stories.

One cannot dismiss Thompson's account, however. Indeed if his description is accurate it is a creature which has been reported for many decades in the waters of the British Isles. Could we really have an undiscovered species of giant sea horse in our waters? Or is it a case of a misconception of the horse-like head caused by the creature's movements through the water? A head and neck appearing on the surface and cutting through the water would cause spray and a white wake. This could, in itself, give a mane-like appearance to a head which is angled like that of horse but could equally be attributed to any number of known creatures with an extended muzzle. The fact that this creature has been credited with 'horse-like' features could be attributed to the fact that a horse is commonly known, and therefore easy to use for purposes of comparison.

In March 1907, a group of fishermen from Tenby, Dyfed, who had been trawling in an area just outside the Bristol Channel, returned to shore and claimed to have had an encounter with a sea serpent. The crew of ten were adamant that what they had seen was not a whale or other such creature. They spoke of seeing a monster fish, which they estimated, from the parts they saw, to be about 200 ft in length. There were four separate fins on the creature's back, each as big as a sail. It was black or very dark in colour and created a great commotion in the water. When asked to describe what type of fish they thought it was, the men stated that it gave the general appearance of a 'sea serpent.' Further reports of such a creature were reported by other fishing crews, one of whom stated:

I heard of the 200 feet serpent seen off this shore last week. I was not surprised as we have seen these beasts for many years now, they are plentiful in these waters. The creature I saw just two days ago was not as great in size as the 200-foot beast, nor had any great fins obvious to the naked eye. The beast I have always seen is the sea serpent, long and snake-like in body and head, it writhes in the water and sinks below when approached. I have not been any close distance to it; when it is approached it does not stay in view for long. This serpent is 30–40 feet long, with a body girth as thick as a large sailor's body; it has serpent features. We have named it the Tenby Sea Snake.

The West

The monster of Brynberian is said to have roamed the countryside destroying villages and decimating crops. Eventually it was captured and slaughtered near a bridge in the village and was taken up a nearby mountain for burial. The tomb, it is said, is still out there on the moorland.

At Llycynwch, just north of Dolgellau, a terrible water monster lived. Large and fearsome, it does not seem to have bothered with human prey, but preferred livestock and wild animals. The local people became distressed at the loss of revenue this creature was causing and decided to hunt it down and destroy it. But few people were keen to confront the beast; the task was left to the farmers in outlying districts. A local shepherd met with the monster on one of its forays on nearby land and followed it. Knowing that he stood little chance in combat, he waited until the creature was resting and then attacked it, beheading it with his axe.

In late August 1963, Mr P. Sharman was on holiday in New Quay, Dyfed, when he saw a strange animal while he was walking along the cliffs. Looking down a rocky cove, about 100 ft below, he saw a plesiosaur-like animal in the water. It was 30–40 ft long, black with a short tail, four flippers and a long neck surmounted by a small head, and was surrounded by a number of seals swimming away from it as though escaping from it. He said of the encounter (as recorded in *Mystery Animals of Britain & Ireland* by Graham J. McEwan): 'After I had watched the thing for a few minutes, I realized there was a remote possibility that I was looking down on a floundering basking shark. This seemed more and more possible, so I left the area.'

But thinking later about what he had seen, he began to doubt this conclusion. The impression he had was more of a plesiosaur than basking shark. He could not understand why, if it was a dead basking shark, the seals should be swimming away from it. He also thought about the long neck and small head, which was at the time of the sighting outstretched, the four flippers which he saw, one on each quarter of the body, and the short tail. These did not match the image of a dead shark. And when he returned to the place, he found no remains or carcass, which was also unusual, as it would have been washed ashore. For these reasons, Mr Sharman was uncertain what it was he *did* see.

Barmouth, in Gwynedd, has been a favourite resort for the people from the Midlands region of England since Victorian times. In 1971, two people from Colwyn Bay were out walking on the beach near the village of Llanaber, close by. They came across some large footprints in the sand at the water's edge 12–18 in., in diameter. Believing that someone had been playing a practical joke, they thought no more of the matter. But on 2 March 1975 six Barmouth schoolgirls, all twelve years old, were walking along the beach at dusk. The girls disturbed a large creature about 200 yd away, about 10 ft long, with a long tail, a long neck and huge green eyes. They also saw the feet, which were like huge saucers with three pointed, protruding nails. They described the skin as 'black, patchy and baggy – unlike anything they had ever seen before'. The girls ran away and looked back towards the creature in the sea and they could still see its eyes above the surface. The following day they told their art teacher of the sighting, and from the description provided, he drew a sketch.

In the summer of 1975, another sighting was made from a fishing vessel, not far from Bardsey Island, at the end of the Lleyn Peninsula. The experienced fishermen saw a creature with a huge body and a long neck surface next to the boat. It appeared three more times during the following hour, so they were able to get a good look at it and, when they were shown the schoolteacher's sketch of the Barmouth monster, they at once recognized it.

Some 10 miles north of Barmouth lies Harlech, also in Gwynedd. In the summer of 1975, a 30 ft sloop was sailing about 5 miles from Shell Island off the coast there. It was a sunny day, with the sea dead calm, when a husband and wife believed they saw a seal playing with a couple of tyres. They approached the creature and realized that it was not a seal.

As we drew closer we thought it was a huge turtle, but it turned out to be unlike anything we'd ever seen. It had a free moving neck, fairly short, rather like a turtle's, and an egg shaped head about the size of a seal's. Its back had two spines, which were sharply ridged, and it was about eight feet across and eleven feet long, although the ripples on the water when it dived indicated that it was probably twice that length.

The husband went below to get his camera but on his return the creature was submerging. The couple were shaken and did not sleep for a couple of nights afterwards.

In December 1975, a man found large footprints in the sand near Dolgellau, close to Penmaenpool toll bridge. He said that they were 'a little larger than a good sized dinner plate'. He also saw signs, which indicated they were webbed. He also recalled that the tide had swept over the prints several times, yet had not erased them from the sand.

It is interesting to note that in 1988, the largest leatherback turtle in the world was caught at Harlech. Could this same creature have been responsible for the Harlech and perhaps the Barmouth sightings?

The North

Lake Bala, in Gwynedd, is 4 miles long and about 150 ft deep. Wales's largest natural lake, it is also known as Llyn Tegid. It lies on the Bala geological fault, which runs about 30 miles north-east, from the coast up to the Tallyllyn Valley. The first recorded sighting of 'Teggie' the monster of the lake was made in 1975 by Mr Dafydd Bowen, a former lake warden. 'I looked out of my office window and saw this thing moving through the water, 200 yards away. It was grey, about eight feet long and looked like a crocodile with a small hump in the middle.'

Mrs Anne Jones caught a glimpse of an odd-looking creature in October 1979. It had the appearance of a 'humped back' surfacing amidst much foam and water disturbance. And John Melville Rowlands, a local businessman from Bala, was fishing on the lake in 1979 with his cousin. The pair saw a creature, which they described as follows:

It had a large head, like a football and rather big eyes. We could see the body, which was nearly 8 feet long. It wasn't aggressive at all. It swam towards us to within a few yards and then turned and disappeared. I wouldn't say I had seen a monster. It was just a large being. But I have caught some rather big pike in the lake before now and it was bigger than any of those.

In March 1995, brothers Paul and Andrew Delaney from London were fishing on Lake Bala.

It was calm and we were about to finish when we noticed something coming up to the surface about 80 yd from the boat. At first we thought it was a tree trunk. Then it straightened up and towered 10 feet in the air. It had a small head and long neck, like the pictures of the Loch Ness Monster.

The January 1883 edition of *Nature* magazine carried a report of an incident in Llandudno from Mr F.T. Mott of Leicester.

Believing it to be desirable that every well-authenticated observation indicating the existence of large sea serpents should be permanently registered, I send you the following particulars:

About three p.m., on Sunday 3 September, 1882, a party of gentlemen and ladies were standing at the northern extremity of Llandudno Pier, looking towards the open sea, when an unusual object was observed in the water near to the Little Orme's Head, travelling rapidly westwards towards the Great Orme. It appeared to be just outside the mouth of the bay, and would therefore be about a mile distant from the observers. It was watched for about two minutes and in that interval, it traversed about half the width of the bay, and then suddenly disappeared. The bay is two miles wide, and therefore the object, whatever it was, must have travelled at the rate of thirty miles an hour. It is estimated to have been fully as long as a large steamer, say two hundred feet; the rapidity of its motion was particularly remarked as being greater than that of any ordinary vessel. The colour appeared to be black, and the motion either corkscrew-like or snake-like, with vertical undulations. Three of the observers have since made sketches from memory, quite independently, of the impression left on their minds, and on comparing these sketches, which slightly varied, they have agreed to sanction the accompanying outline as representing as nearly as possible the object which they saw. The party consisted of W. Barfoot, JP., of Leicester. F.J. Marlow, solicitor, of Manchester, Mrs Marlow, and several others. They discard the theories of birds or porpoises as not accounting for this particular phenomenon.

In the same magazine on 1 February 1883, Joseph Sidebottom of Erlesdene, Bowdon, recalled how he too had seen the Llandudno phenomenon four or five times before and said that he was in no doubt that it was a shoal of porpoises.'

I never, however, saw the head your correspondent gives, but in other respects what I have seen was exactly the same; the motions of porpoises might easily be taken for those of a serpent; once I saw them from the top of the Little Orme. They came very near the base of the rock, and kept the line nearly half across the bay.

William Barfoot, JP, of Leicester responded in the 8 February 1883 issue:

Like your correspondent, Mr Sidebottom, I have frequently seen a shoal of porpoises in Llandudno Bay, as well as in other places, and on the occasion referred to by Mr Mott ... the idea of porpoises was at first started, but immediately abandoned. I will venture to suggest that no one has seen a shoal of these creatures travel at a rate of from twenty-five to thirty-five miles an hour. I have seen a whale in the ocean, and large flocks of sea birds, such as those of the eider duck, swimming its surface, but the strange appearance seen at Llandudno on September 3 was not to be accounted for by porpoises, whales, birds, or breakers, an opinion which was shared by all those present.

In October 1805, a small ship, the *Robert Ellis*, was sailing slowly between Anglesey and the mainland near Caernarfon. The weather was good and the sea calm. The crew on board suddenly saw what appeared to be 'an immense worm' swimming after the ship and closing in on it at a rapid rate. The creature eventually overtook the ship and climbed aboard

238

through the tiller-hole, coiling itself on deck under the mast. The crew were terrified, some contemplated plunging overboard. One member then approached the creature and attacked it with an oar. The rest of the men followed suit and somehow forced the creature from the ship, back into the sea. The creature continued to follow the ship until a good breeze allowed the vessel to pull away from its pursuer and leave it behind (*Wild Wales*, 1862).

In February 1875, staff of the Minydon Hotel, close to Red Wharf Bay, Anglesey, on several occasions saw a strange creature entering the main channel at the western end of the bay. At one time, five people watched a black object about 12 ft long and protruding about 1 ft above the surface, swim into the channel. About 30 ft behind it, a large tail could be seen (*Western Mail*, 8 March 1875).

Conclusion

There ends our fascinating tour of the British Isles. I am certain you will feel some scepticism about some of the events related. Many people will, no doubt, dismiss them as products of over-fertile imaginations, perhaps caused by the boredom of long voyages at sea, or even a desire to see something they have previously heard of, and become part of the select group who claim such sightings. But what if these creatures did surface and were a reality? How would that make us feel – insecure, frightened, worried? Not too many people would go swimming in shark- or piranha-infested water, yet not every species of shark or piranha is dangerous to mankind; it is the impression gained from minimal information that makes them appear so fearsome and unfriendly.

The sea serpent or lake monster is generally regarded as impossible, because we are told that these creatures do not exist. Yet, to date, no one has provided definitive proof that they do not; it is all assumption and opinion. The Cryptozoologists and Dracontologists are brave enough (some may say foolish enough) to say that they might. Not many scientists state positively that these creatures do not exist, they simply provide reasons why they could not exist. This creates a grey area – a no man's land between 'do they' and 'don't they'. Until a specimen is located and identified, this grey area will remain, filled with uncertainty, and eventually it will develop into a chasm. It could provide a danger to professional careers; the 'what if' area is a remarkably dangerous place to tread. The coealocanth has already reminded science that they cannot make too many assumptions, which is why we find that so few are prepared to state categorically that sea serpents and lake monsters do not exist. These creatures should not, in any case, be described as serpents or monsters; such titles are media inventions. It may well be that, if cryptozoologists were to formulate a more socially acceptable way of identifying these creatures, the subject would become more acceptable; again, it is a matter of conforming to society's rules.

Whilst I am a confirmed believer in the existence of hitherto undiscovered large marine creatures, I find it frustrating that some people, without much knowledge of the subject, continue to put forward one view, that the plesiosaur is responsible for all such sightings, when, for example, a known zoological species, which has adapted to new surroundings and altered its physical form as it has evolved, such as large or giant eel, might prove a more realistic explanation. I confess to being a proponent of the 'eel theory' in relation to many sightings, but, as can be seen from the descriptions in this book, this hypothesis does not always conform to what is being described.

The large creatures which have been seen in the sea cause me greater doubts, simply because we know so little about the inhabitants of the ocean's depths. I believe that large, hitherto undiscovered species do exist there, and that they should be regarded as totally separate to sightings of creatures seen in lakes, lochs or loughs. As I have said, in all walks of life one should keep an open mind; to be singled-minded can only detract from our understanding and our ability to expand our knowledge.

Bibliography

AA Secret Britain (Automobile Association, 1986)

Adamoli, Vida, *Amazing Animals* (Robson Books, 1989)

Alexander, Marc, *To Anger the Devil* (Neville Spearman, 1978)

Alexander, Marc, *Enchanted Britain* (Arthur Barker Ltd, 1980)

Anderson, Iain F., *Scottish Quest* (Herbert Jenkins, 1935)

Ashman, Malcolm, *Fabulous Beasts* (Collins & Brown, 1997)

Attenborough, David, *Zoo Quest for a Dragon* (Lutterworth, 1959)

Attenborough, David, *Life on Earth* (Collins, 1986)

Bailey, Patrick, *Orkney* (David & Charles, 1971)

Banks, F.R., *The North West Highlands and Skye* (Letts, 1969)

Baring-Gould, Sabine, *Myths of the Middle Ages* (Blandford, 1996)

BB, *September Road to Caithness* (Nicholas Kaye, 1962)

Blue Guide to Ireland (Benn, 1979)

Blundell, Nigel, *The Unexplained* (Sunburst, 1995)

Bord, Janet and Colin, *Alien Animals* (Granada, 1985)

Bord, Janet and Colin, *Modern Mysteries of Britain* (Grafton, 1987)

Bradley, Michael, *More Than a Myth* (Anthony Hawke, 1989)

Briggs, Katherine M., *A Dictionary of British Folk-Tales* (Routledge & Kegan Paul, 1971)

243

Bright, Charles, *Sea Serpents* (Popular Press, 1991)

Bright, Michael, *There Are Giants in the Sea* (Robson Books, 1989)

Buehr, Walter, *Sea Monsters* (Archway, 1970)

Burton, Maurice, *Animal Legends* (Coward McCann, 1957)

Busson, Bernard, and Gerard Leroy, *The Last Secrets of the Earth* (Werner Laurie, 1956)

Candlin, Lillian, *Tales of Old Sussex* (Countryside Books, 1992)

Cassie, R.L., *The Monsters of Achanalt* (Privately published in Aberdeen, 1935–6)

Chase, Owen, *Narratives of the Wreck of the Whale Ship Essex* (Dover, 1989)

Clarke, Jerome, *Unexplained* (Visible Ink, 1999)

Cleave, Andrew, *Giants of the Sea* (Parkgate, 1997)

Cohen, Daniel, *A Modern Look at Monsters* (Tower, 1970)

Cohen, Daniel, *Encyclopedia of Monsters* (Fraser Stewart, 1991)

Cornell, James C, *Nature at its Strangest* (Sterlin, 1979)

Costello, Peter, *In Search of Lake Monsters* (Berkley Medallion, 1974)

Cotterell, Arthur, *Celtic Mythology* (Sebastian Kelly, 1998)

Darwin, Charles, *The Origin of Species* (Watts, 1929)

Dash, Mike, *Borderlands* (Heinemann, 1997)

Deane, Tony, and Tony Shaw, *The Folklore of Cornwall* (Batsford, 1975)

Desmond, Adrian, *Huxley – The Devil's Disciple* (Michael Joseph, 1994)

Dictionary of Prehistoric Life (Claremont, 1995)

Dinsdale, Tim, *Loch Ness Monster* (Routledge & Kegan Paul, 1961)

Dinsdale, Tim, *The Leviathans* (Routledge & Kegan Paul, 1966)

Dixon, J.H., *Gairloch and Guide to Loch Maree* (Gairloch Parish Branch & Ross & Cromarty Heritage Society, 1974)

Douglas, Ronald Macdonald, *The Scots Book* (Chambers, 1949)

244

Edwards, Frank, *Stranger Than Science* (Bantam, 1973)

Eggleton, Bob, and Nigel Suckling, *The Book of Sea Monsters* (Overlook, 1998)

Ellis, Richard, *Monsters of the Sea* (Robert Hale, 1995)

Ellis, Richard, *The Search for the Giant Squid* (Penguin, 1998)

Evershed, Samuel, 'Legend of the Dragon-Slayer of Lyminster' (vol. 18, 1866, pp.180–3)

Eysenck, Hans J. and Carl Sargent, *Explaining the Unexplained* (Weidenfeld & Nicolson, 1982)

Fascinating Secrets of Oceans and Islands (Reader's Digest, 1972)

Fawcett, Col P.H., *Exploration Fawcett* (Hutchinson, 1954)

Fenton, Caroll Lane, and Mildred Adams Fenton, *In Prehistoric Seas* (Harrap, 1964)

Firth of Clyde and Isle of Arran (Photo Precision, 1960s)

Folkore Myths and Legends of Britain (Reader's Digest, 1973)

Froude, James Anthony, *English Seamen in the Sixteenth Century* (Longmans, Green & Co, 1895)

Furneaux, Rupert, *The World's Strangest Mysteries* (Ace Star, 1961)

Glover, Judith, *Sussex Place Names* (Countryside Books, 1997)

Gould, Charles, *Mythical Monsters* (Senate, 1995)

Gould, Rupert T., *Oddities: A Book of Unexplained Facts* (P. Allen, 1928)

Gould, Rupert T., *The Case for the Sea Serpent* (P. Allen, 1930)

Gould, Rupert T., *The Stargazer Talks* (Geofrey Bles, 1946)

Gray, Adrian, *Tales of Old Essex* (Countryside Books, 1995)

Gregory, Lady Augusta, *Visions and Beliefs in the West of Ireland* (Smythe, 1992)

Hadfield, John, *Shell Guide to England* (Michael Joseph, 1970)

Haining, Peter, *Ancient Mysteries* (Sidgwick & Jackson, 1977)

Hall, A., *Lakeland Legends and Folklore* (James Pike, 1977)

Halliwell, J.O., 'The Serpent of St Leonard's Forest' (vol. 19, 1867, pp90)

Hamilton, A., 'Legendary Lyminster' (vol. 22, no. 4, 1948, pp.110)

Harrison, Paul, *The Encyclopaedia of the Loch Ness Monster* (Robert Hale, 1999)

Heath, E., *An Essay Upon Sea Serpents* (Privately published, 1823)

Helm, Thomas, *Monsters of the Deep* (Dodd, Mead & Co, 1962)

Hendrickson, Robert, *Ocean Almanac* (Hutchinson, 1992)

Hervey, J.P., 'St Leonard's Forest and its Legends' (vol. 15, no. 5, 1941, pp.50)

Heuvelmans, Bernard, *In The Wake of the Sea Serpent* (Rupert Hart Davis, 1968)

Heuvelmans, Bernard, *On the Track of Unknown Animals* (Rupert Hart Davis, 1958)

Hidden Places of Ireland (Feature Press, 1996)

Hidden Places of Scotland (Feature Press, 1996)

Hidden Places of Wales (Feature Press, 1996)

Hitching, Francis, *The World Atlas of Mysteries* (William Collins Ltd, 1978)

Hoare, Bob, *More True Mysteries* (Carousel, 1974)

Hogarth, Peter, *Dragons* (Penguin, 1979)

Holiday, F.W., *The Great Orm of Loch Ness* (Faber & Faber, 1968)

Holiday, F.W., *The Dragon and the Disc* (Norton, 1973)

Hoult, Janet, *Dragons* (Gothic Image, 1987)

Hunt, Robert, *Cornish Legends* (Tor Mark Press, 1990)

Illustrated Dictionary of Oceanography (Bloomsbury, 1995)

Ingersoll, Ernest, *Dragons and Dragon Lore* (Payson & Clarke, 1928)

Joiner, Charles G., 'The Knucker of Lyminster' (vol. 3, no. 12, 1929, pp.28)

Keel, John, *Strange Creatures from Time and Space* (Greenwich, 1970)

Kingsland, Rosemary, *Savage Seas* (Boxtree, 1999)

Kirk, John, *In the Domain of the Lake Monster* (Keyporter, 1998)

Lambert, David, *Book of Dinosaurs* (Wordsworth, 1998)

Laycock, George, *Mysteries, Monsters and Untold Secrets* (Scholastic Books, 1978)

Lee, Henry, *Sea Monsters Unmasked* (London, 1883)

Lee, Henry, *Sea Fables Explained* (London, 1884)

Levy, Joel, *A Natural History of the Unnatural World* (St Martin's Press, 1999)

Lover, Samuel, and Thomas C. Croker, *Legends and Tales of Ireland* (Bracken, 1987)

Lythgoe, John and Gillian, *Fishes of the Sea* (Blandford, 1971)

MacGregor, Alasdair Alpin: *Strange Stories and Folk Tales of the Highlands and Islands* (Lang Syne, 1995)

Mackenzie, Osgood, *A Hundred Years in the Highlands* (Edward Arnold, 1921)

McEwan, Graham J., *Mystery Animals of Britain and Ireland* (Robert Hale, 1986)

McEwan, Graham J., *Sea Serpents, Sailors and Sceptics* (Routledge & Kegan Paul, 1978)

McCulloch, John Herries, *The Charm of Scotland* (Bourne, 1960)

McHardy, Stuart, *Scotland: Myth, Legend and Folklore* (Luath, 1999)

McLaren, Moray, *The Highland Jaunt* (Jarrolds, 1954)

Magnus, Olaus, *A Compendium History of Goths, Svvedes, and Vandals, and Other Northern Nations* (London, 1658)

Mackal, Roy, *Searching for Hidden Animals* (Cadogan, 1980)

Main, Laurence, *Walks in Mysterious Wales* (Sigma, 1995)

Mallinson, Jeremy, *Endangered Species* (David & Charles, 1989)

Malmesbury, Lord, *Memoirs of an Ex-Minster* (Longman, Green & Co, 1857)

Masson, Rosaline, *Scotland the Nation* (Nelson, 1940s)

Maxwell, Gavin, *Harpoon at Venture* (Viking, 1952)

Melville, Herman, *Moby Dick* (Penguin, 1994)

Meurger, Michael, *Lake Monster Traditions* (Fortean Times, 1988)

Michell, John, and J.M. Rickard, *Phenomena – A Book of Wonders* (Thames & Hudson, 1977)

Miller, Carey, *A Dictionary of Monsters and Mysterious Beasts* (Piccolo, 1974)

Montgomery Campbell, Elizabeth, *The Search for Morag* (Tom Stacey, 1972)

Moriarty, Christopher, *Eels – A Natural and Unnatural History* (David & Charles, 1978)

Morvan, F., *Legends of the Sea* (Minerva, 1980)

Mysteries of the Unexplained (Reader's Digest, 1982)

Norman, Dr David, *Illustrated Encyclopedia of Dinosaurs* (Salamanda, 1998)

Ortelius, Antoon, *Theatrum Orbis Terrarum* (1570)

Oudemans, A.C., *The Great Sea Serpent: An Historical and Critical Treatise* (privately published – London, 1892)

Out of This World (Orbis, 1989)

Palmer, Douglas, *The Extinction of the Dinosaurs* (Weidenfeld & Nicolson, 1997)

Parker, Derek and Julia, *Atlas of the Supernatural* (Guild, 1990)

Parker, Steve, *Ocean Life* (Parragon, 1994)

Peattie, Noel, *Hydra and Kraken, or the Lore and Lure of Lake Monsters and Sea Serpents* (Regent Press, 1996)

Peele, Cecily, *The Encyclopaedia of British Bogies* (Hoklan, 1978)

Pennick, Nigel, *Dragons of the West* (Capall Bann, 1997)

Perry, Janet and Victor Gentle, *Monsters of the Deep* (Gareth Stevens, 1999)

Piehler, H.A., *Scotland for Everyman* (Dent, 1934)

Pontoppidan, Erik, *The Natural History of Norway* (1752–3)

Proujan, Carl, *Secrets of the Sea* (Aldus Books, 1971)

Randles, Jenny, *Truly Weird* (Collins & Brown, 1998)

Randles, Jenny, and Peter Hough, *Encyclopedia of the Unexplained* (Brockhampton Press, 1998)

Rappoport, Angelo. S., *The Sea – Myths and Legends* (Senate, 1995)

Rickard, Bob, and John Michell, *Unexplained Phenomena* (Rough Guides, 2000)

Rolleston, T.W., *Myths and Legends of the Celtic Race* (Harrap, 1912)

Rostron, Arthur, *Home from the Sea* (Cassell & Co, 1931)

Russell, Eric Frank, *Great World Mysteries* (Mayflower, 1962)

Sawyer, Amy, 'Sussex Witches and Other Superstitions' (vol. 9, no. 4, 1935, pp.134)

Shell Guide to Ireland (Ebury Press, 1967)

Shuker, Karl P.N., *In Search of Prehistoric Survivors* (Blandford, 1995)

Shuker, Karl. P.N., *Dragons; A Natural History* (Aurum, 1995)

Shuker, Karl. P.N., *Mysteries of the Planet Earth* (Carlton, 1999)

Simpson, Jacqueline, *The Folklore of Sussex* (Batsford, 1973)

Smith, J.L.B., *Old Four Legs – The Coelacanth* (Longmans Green & Co Ltd, 1956)

Somerville, Edith, *The Smile and the Tear* (Methuen & Co, 1933)

Speath, Frank, *Mysteries of the Deep* (Llewellyn, 1998)

Squire, Charles, *Celtic Myths and Legends* (Siena, 1998)

Strange Tales of Scotland (Lang Syne, 1980)

Sutherland, Halliday, *Hebridean Journey* (Geofrey Bles, 1939)

Sutherly, Curt, *Strange Encounters* (Fate, 1996)

Sweeney, James B., *Sea Monsters, A Collection of Eyewitness Accounts* (David McKay, 1977)

Sweeney, James B., *A Pictorial History of Sea Monsters and Other Dangerous Marine Life* (Crown, 1972)

Swire, Otto F., *The Highlands and Their Legends* (Oliver & Boyd, 1963)

Sykes, Egerton, *Dictionary of Non-Classical Mythology* (Dent, 1961)

Taylor, Michael, and John G. Martin, *Big Mouths and Long Necks* (Leicestershire Museums, 1990)

Tayside in Colour (Jarrold, 1975)

The Trossachs and Loch Lomond (Photo Precision, 1960s)

The Unexplained Files (Orbis, 1996)

Thompson, A.G., *Gower Journey* (Privately published, 1950)

Thompson, C.J.S., *The Mystery and Lore of Monsters* (Bell Publishing, 1978)

Underwood, Peter, *Mysterious Places* (Bossiney, 1988)

Waghenaer, L.J., *Mariners Mirrour* (1588)

Watson, Jane Werner, *The Giant Golden Book of Dinosaurs and Other Prehistoric Reptiles* (Western Publishing, 1972)

Wayre, Philip, *The Private Life of the Otter* (BT Batsford, 1979)

Welfare, Simon, and John Fairley, *Arthur C Clarke's Mysterious World* (William Collins Ltd, 1980)

Whyte, Constance E., *More Than a Legend* (Hamish Hamilton, 1957)

Wilkins, H.T., *Mysteries – Solved and Unsolved* (Odhams, 1959)

Wilkins, H.T., *Monsters and Mysteries* (James Pike, 1973)

Williams, Jerome, *Oceanography* (Franklin Watts, 1974)

Wilson, Colin, and John Grant, *Mysteries* (Chancellor, 1994)

Archives, newspapers and journals consulted

British Museum of Natural History: Official files and private papers held in library section, relating to Professor Richard Owen, Meade Waldo and sea serpents.

National Maritime Museum, Greenwich: Memoirs of Captain Hugh Shaw and other documentation relating to sea serpent sightings.

Transactions of the Wernerian Society, vol. 1, p. 442.

Camborne/Red Packet, 27 July 1985

Cork Constitution, 2 and 7 September 1850

Cork Reporter, 11 September 1850

Cornish Life, January 1977; November 1990

Daily Chronicle, 30 April and 30 December 1907

Daily Express, 14 September 1903; 22 October 1938

Daily Mail, 10 October 1898; 22, 23 and 25 October 1933; February 1934; 23 October 1937; 22 and 24 October 1938; April 1967; June 1974, June 1975

Scottish Daily Mail, 3 February 1962
Daily Mirror, 8 August 1938; 22 and 24 October 1938
Daily News, 8 October 1959
Daily Sketch, 30 August 1911; 29 September 1913
Daily Telegraph, 1 March 1934
Dublin Evening Herald, 4, 5 and 6 June 1968
Dublin Evening Press, 17 June 1963
Dundee Advertiser, 5 October 1892; 8 June 1903
East Anglian Daily Times, 22, 26 and 28 October 1938
East Anglian Magazine, June and July 1978
Eastern Daily Press, 24, 25 and 26 July 1912
Eastern Evening News, 7, 8 and 11 August 1936
Edinburgh Evening Dispatch, 6 November 1934
Evening News And Star (Oban), 28 April 1877
Falmouth Packet, 5 March, April and 4 May 1976; 9 May 1996
Fate Magazine, December 1950
Fate & Fortune, no. 14, 1975
Fishing News, 30 January 1934
Flying Saucer Review, November/December 1964
Fortean Times, Issue numbers 2, 4, 10, 11, 14, 15, 18, 21, 22,
    23, 24, 25, 27, 29, 30, 31, 32, 33, 34, 35, 36, 37, 39, 41, 42,
    43, 44, 46, 47, 48, 49, 51, 52, 53, 54, 57, 58, 59, 60, 61, 62,
    64, 65, 66, 67, 68, 70, 71, 72, 76, 77, 78, 81, 82, 84, 85, 86,
    88, 91, 92, 95, 96, 98, 100, 101, 102, 104, 105
Galway Observer, May 1935
Gentleman's Magazine, December Edition 1750
Glasgow Evening News, 28 April 1877; 3 and 9 February 1898
Glasgow Herald, April 1877; 2 June 1882; 1 January and 25
    September 1934; 14 August and 22 September 1936; 29,
    and 31 July 1948; 29 July 1961
Glasgow Weekly Mail, 26 September 1891; 8 October 1892
Graphic, The, 20 October 1883
Grimsby Observer, 17 September 1903
Helford Packet, 14 September 1995
Illustrated London News, 7 September 1850; 4 June 1960; 14
    October 1961
Inverness Courier, 2 May 1933

Journal, The, 29 October 1938
Liverpool Echo, 30 April 1907; 7 April 1995
Lowestoft Journal, 29 October 1938
Nature, 1 and 8 February 1883
News of the World, 23 October 1938
Northern Chronicle, 11 October 1933
Observer, 27 December 1964
Scotsman, 18, 19, 20, 24 November and 3 December 1873; July 1939
Shetland Times, 21 July 1961
Skegness Standard, June–December 1937; June–December 1938; 10 August 1960; 19, 26 October and 6 November 1966
Sketch, 30 August 1911
Stornaway Gazette, 2 February 1895
Strand Magazine 10 August 1895
Sun, 22 September 1997
Sunday Chronicle, 1 February 1942
Sunday People, 22 August 1999
Sunday Post, 31 May 1964; 15 September 1996
Sunday Referee, 23 October 1938
Sunday Telegraph, 26 March 1995
Times, 1851; 6 and 22 March 1856; 22 September 1859; 11 June 1863; 2 and 5 September 1872; 12, 13 and 20 November 1873; 4 July 1874; 8 November and 28 December 1876; 16 January, 3 and 7 September, 22 December 1877; 24 September 1879; 12, 17 and 20 October 1883; 7 January 1893; 9 and 15 December 1933; July 1934; 22 March 1956; 30 May 1962
Unexplained, The, No. 7, 38 and 81 1980
Weekly Dispatch, 8 September 1850; September 1903; 22 March 1956; September 1903
Weekly Journal, October 1933
Western Mail, 3, 5 and 8 March 1975; 10 March 1995
Western Morning News, March 1907; 14, 16 and 18 September 1907; June 1928; June 1933; February 1980; 6 October 1990; 4 April 1995

Westmeath Independent, May–June 1960
Wide World Magazine, 1924
Zoologist, The, 26 March 1849; May and December 1873